THE BOOK OF HOMELESSNESS

THE BOOK OF HOMELESSNESS

THE STORY OF ACCUMULATE & THE BOOK OF HOMELESSNESS
Marice Cumber, Founder and Director, Accumulate

The Accumulate Art School for the Homeless uses creative education and creativity to help improve the lives, confidence, skills and wellbeing of people who are homeless or with experience of homelessness. All of the Accumulate creative activities are delivered by professional art, design and digital media tutors who provide university level tuition and structured learning activities that challenge and educate the Accumulate students and enable them to stretch their talents and potential beyond their own expectations.

The Accumulate Art School for the Homeless also fundraises for scholarships so that the Accumulate students can progress their creative learning, become university students and study on the one year Access to HE Diploma Course in Design and Digital Media at Ravensbourne University London.

This unique Accumulate scholarship scheme was set up in 2016 and is funded by business and individuals. So far, 20 Accumulate students have received scholarships and 8 have progressed onto degree courses. This transition is life changing and forever, and shows just how much arts education and the Accumulate Art School for the Homeless is a tool for social change, empowerment and impact.

The story for the Accumulate Book of Homelessness started when graphic novelist Henny Beaumont and I met in May 2019 and, over a coffee and a camomile tea, bashed around lots of random ideas about graphic novels and homelessness and whether we could connect the two through an Accumulate project.

The outcome of that initial conversation, between two very animated women, was to produce a graphic novel that would be created by people affected by homelessness and in which they could tell their own story in, whatever that story may be. This issue of authorship became the central aim of the project, with the mission to reverse the norm of the 'non homeless' writing about 'the homeless' and to give creative control and agency, ownership and identity to the people whose story it was — a group who are so often defined as a faceless, homogeneous commodity and are continued to be wrongly stereotyped and marginalised by society.

A further decision was for Accumulate to take ownership of the project itself and to crowdfund for the resources needed to run The Book of Homelessness project. Accumulate set itself the task, and succeeded, in crowdfunding a mammoth £18,000 to cover the costs of all the workshops, materials, tutors, participant travel and lunches, art direction, production and book launch for The Book of Homelessness.

Once the funding was secured, we started planning the creative workshops for the Accumulate students and which would build their skills and creative confidence for the graphic novel project. The first Book of Homelessness workshop took place at the beginning of January 2020 at the education space at Autograph Gallery in Shoreditch and the Accumulate students continued to attend the Accumulate workshops every week right through to the middle of March 2020. During this time the Accumulate students learnt about and produced their own creative writing, visual art, illustrations and typography for The Book of Homelessness. They discussed complex subjects and emotions, shared stories and learnt from each other. They began to trust and open-up, build new friendships and feel a connection to each other based on the project and its purpose. They returned every week to learn, sit with their friends, chat together and work on their own stories. A visible, industrious energy emerged within the group, with everyone really committed to delivering their best work, not wanting to let anyone else down and, most importantly, wanting to do themselves and the project proud.

But the most visible shift that was witnessed was the positive change and increase in confidence amongst the Accumulate students — confidence in themselves, how they communicated and connected with others, confidence to tell their hidden story, confidence in their work and their skills, a self confidence that said they valued themselves and would be missed if they didn't turn up, that they were part of something fantastic and that they were central to its success. The feel good factor was growing and invasive and the Accumulate students felt that they belonged to something purposeful, worthwhile and meaningful that pushed away feelings of isolation, vulnerability and loneliness, and gave a rewarding and warm community in its place. The Book of Homelessness project became the critical well-being and empowerment pivot in the Accumulate students', sometimes chaotic and difficult lives.

The stories that the Accumulate students drew, wrote and produced for The Book of Homelessness are personal, emotional, raw and honest. The stories are of pain, of abuse, of dysfunction, of families, of war and of rejection and of misplaced love, of overcoming difficulties and of fighting and succeeding. The greatest respect, admiration and appreciation needs to be given to each of the authors for having the courage and bravery to share their stories and give us access to their private world. The biggest thank you to each of these and to all of them: Amalia Walrond, Chris Fox, Dave Sohanpal, Eyitayo Babatola, Farahnaaz Roshan, Hamahoullah Diallo, Jade Amoli-Jackson, Lida Mansourian, Luke Smith, Mitchell Ceney, Nikolett Eszes, Phil Olunniyi, Prosper Kouayep, Ria Wallace, Sally Coker, Sean Gonçalves-Berriero, Shianne Wright, Ulika Valentim.

The Book of Homelessness commences with three pieces from external contributors and is followed by the stories that the Accumulate students have created.

SPARE CHANGE

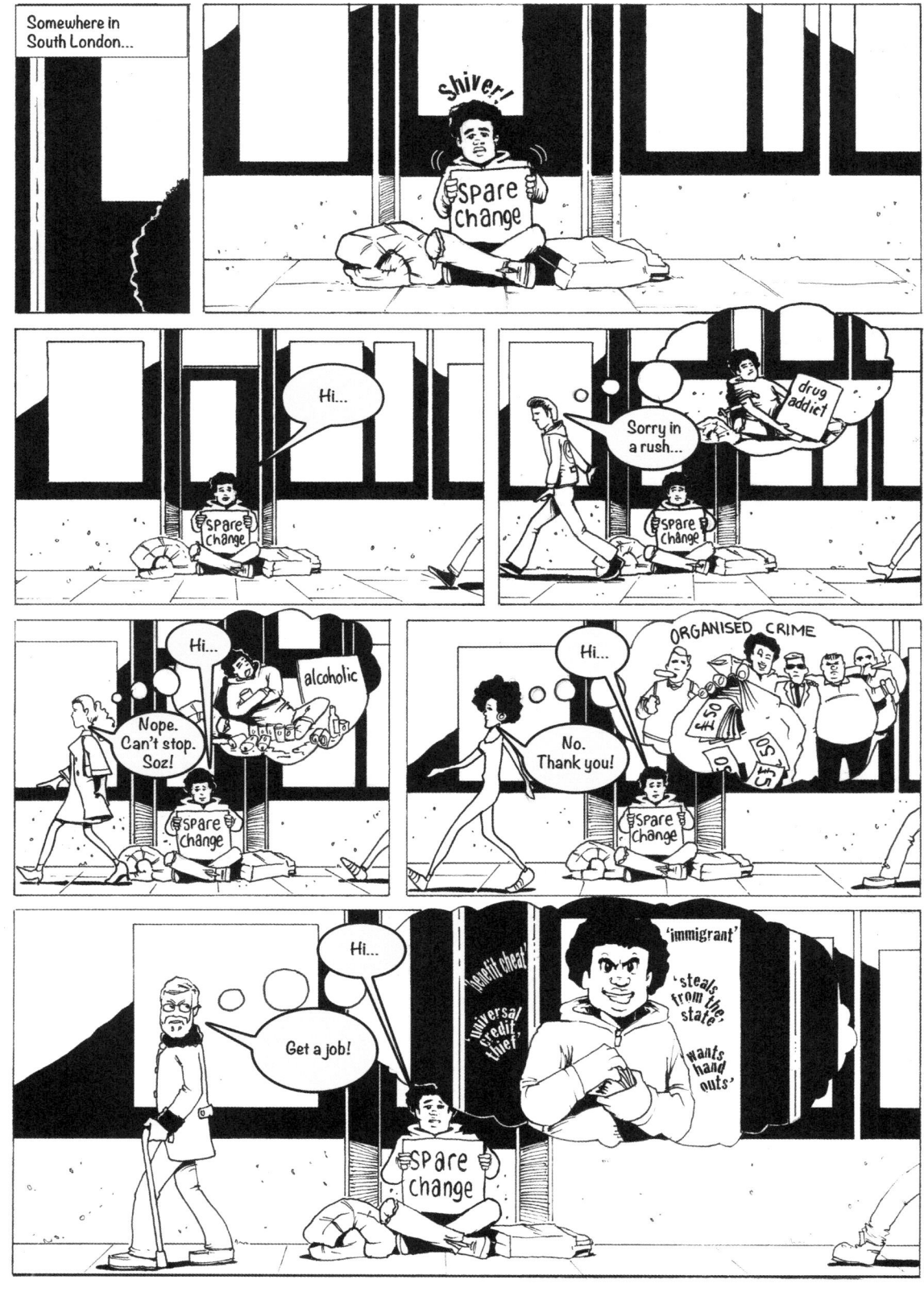

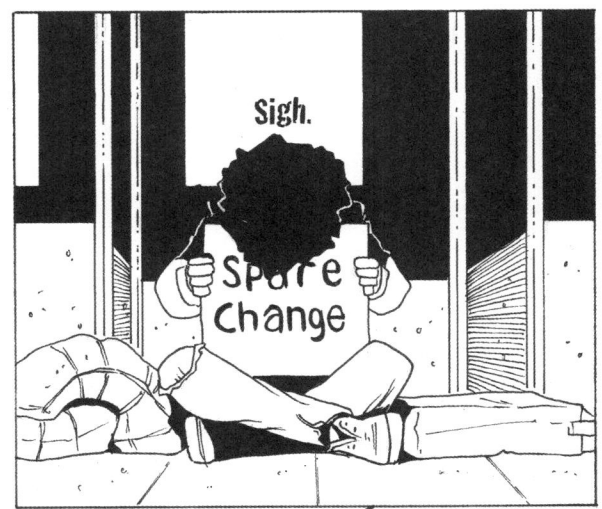
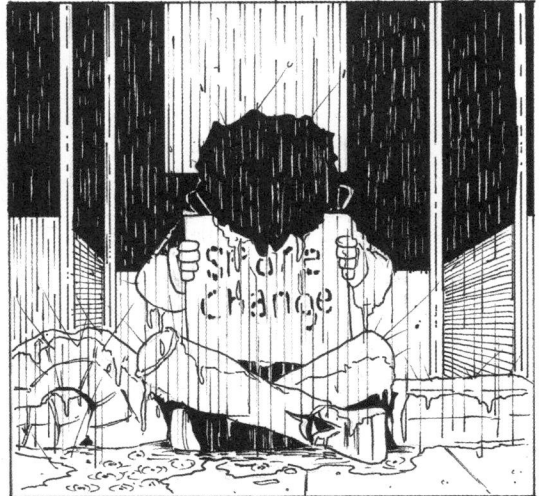
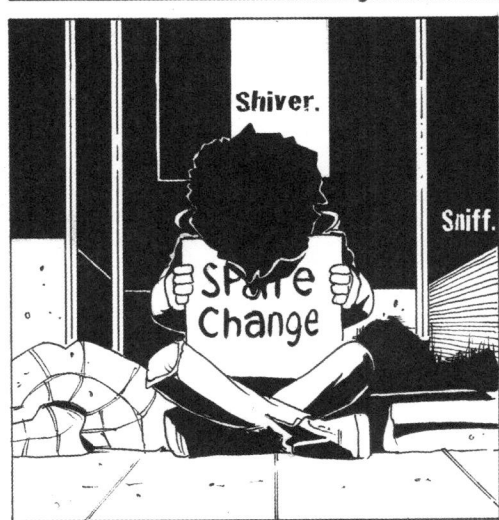
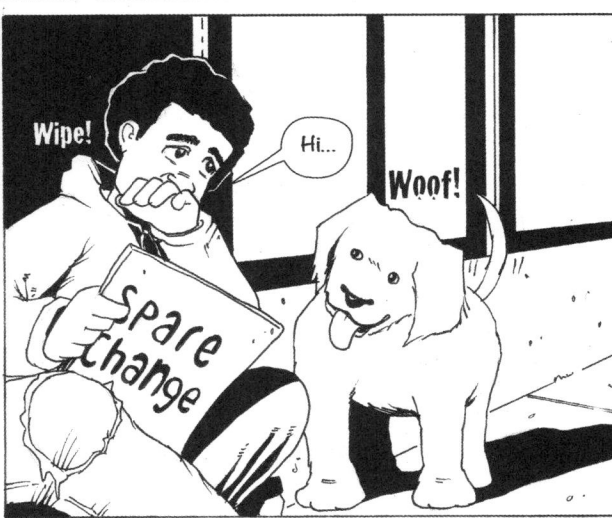
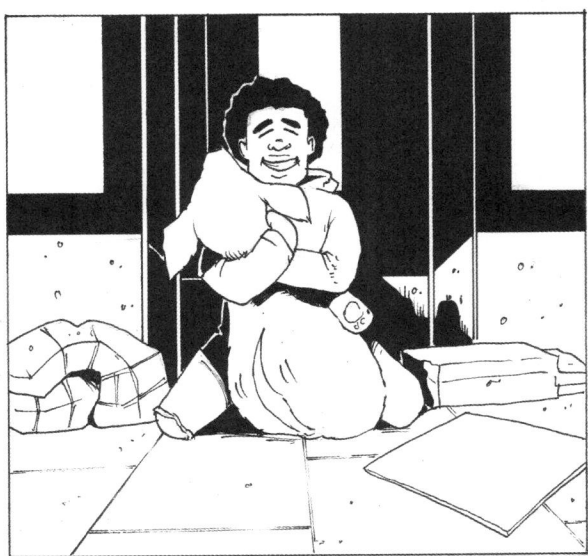
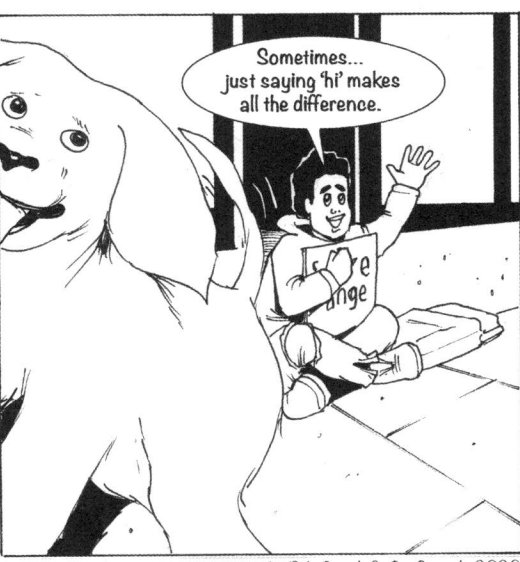

by Bob Joseph & Joe Samuels 2020

BURNING AMBITIONS
Sue Pickford Cheung, Author

Relocating to London from the Midlands in the 80's when I was seventeen was a bold move, but I'd won a scholarship to The London College of Fashion through a competition in Mizz magazine and couldn't turn it down. It was an exciting opportunity and meant I could be free at last!

Up until then I'd been working in my parents' Chinese takeaway since the age of eleven. I'd come home from school, prep food, clean up and serve customers, effectively missing out on a whole chunk of my youth. I wouldn't have minded so much if that's all I had to endure but I also put up with racism from customers, bullying at school and an abusive dad who regularly beat me and my siblings.

I was glad to leave home but I was also very naive. My parents never talked to us due to the language barrier as they never taught us how to speak Chinese and Mum's English was poor (Dad's English was good but he just didn't like talking). All I knew was that I wanted a better life, so at college I studied hard and partied hard. During my last year I met a fella while out clubbing (let's call him Jez) and we started seeing each other. Then one day something happened, which would be the start of a future that was way off my game plan.

A fire started in the shared house I was staying in. It damaged most of my belongings and caused the building to be a write-off, so the tenants had to vacate. I had nowhere else to go so I moved in with Jez who was living in a squat at King's Cross at the time. It wasn't exactly The Ritz but it was free and there weren't as many unidentified stains as I'd anticipated!

I finished my college course and started looking for work. Everything was back on track, or so I thought. I didn't have a clue about contraception so it wasn't long before I accidentally fell pregnant. When I told Mum about her unexpected grandchild she told me to get rid of it or get out of her life — I chose the latter.

So there I was up the duff, in a squat with a bunch of rough-arse builders. The open door policy meant that all sorts of people invited themselves in whenever they liked: drug dealers, drug users, criminals on the run, the mentally ill. Once a fight broke out and I had to negotiate squeezing my expanded gut through a tiny second floor window in a bid to escape. I knew I couldn't stay in that madhouse, so I waddled off to the housing office to see if they could help me find somewhere safer.

Meanwhile, Jez ran out of work so we signed on for benefits. We were pretty destitute by then and while waiting for our cheque to arrive, I was reduced to scrabbling around in gutters for pennies (admittedly to fund my prenatal craving for doughnuts!).

After a few weeks of paperwork and gnawing of fingernails we were offered a room in a homeless bed and breakfast in Acton, while they sorted out something more permanent for us — hurray, salvation! The B&B was full of alcoholics and refugees, which would have sent some running straight back to the squat, but they were sound people, plus the mattress was clean and on a bed frame, not the floor, so it had my approval.

At seven months pregnant we were transferred to housing association accommodation up the road. It was a ground floor flat with a living room and garden, a veritable palace compared to our previous places. What a relief to bring my newborn back to somewhere resembling a home, even though he still had to sleep in a cardboard box (because a bag of nappies was a luxury at that point never mind a cot!).

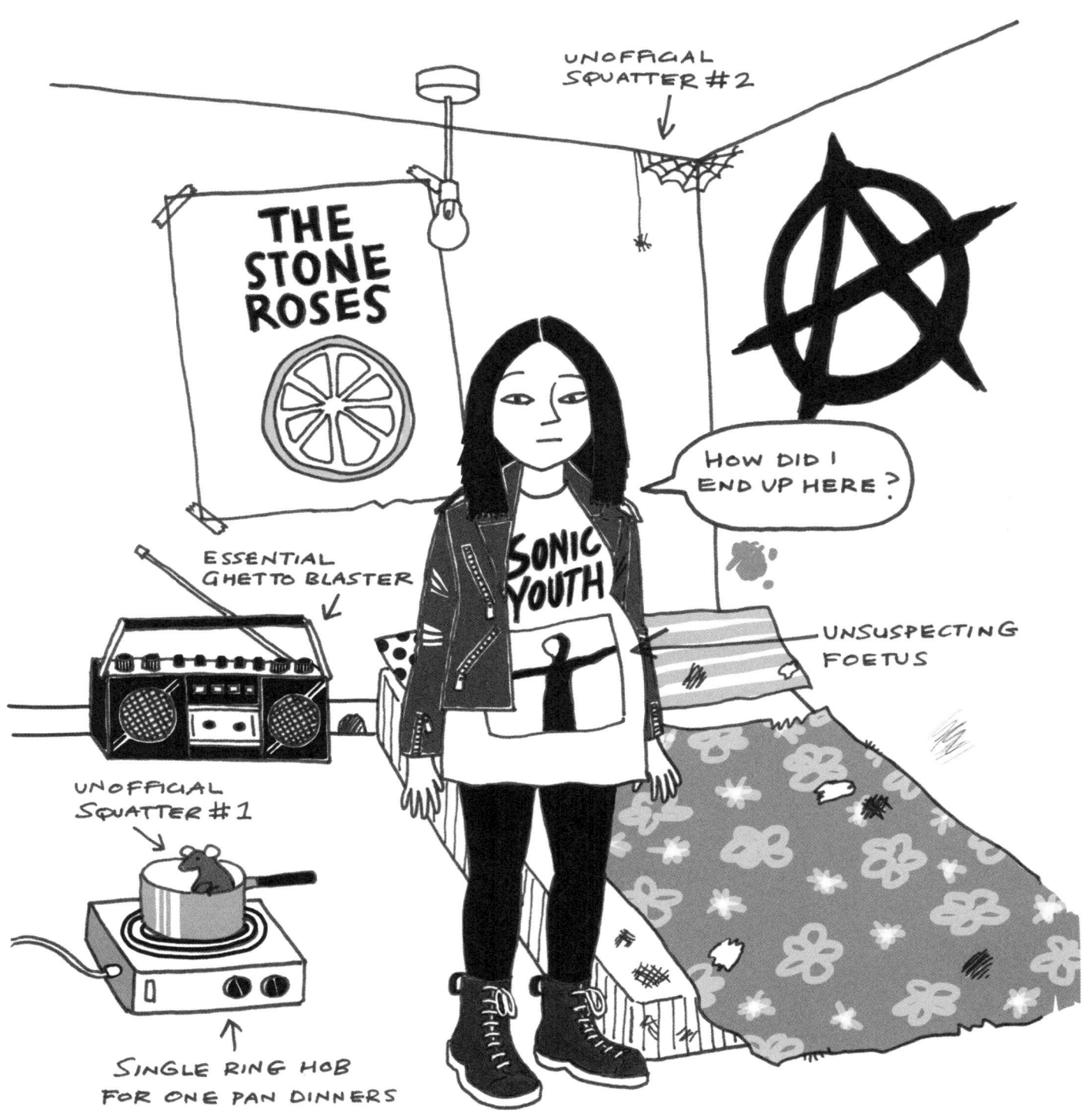

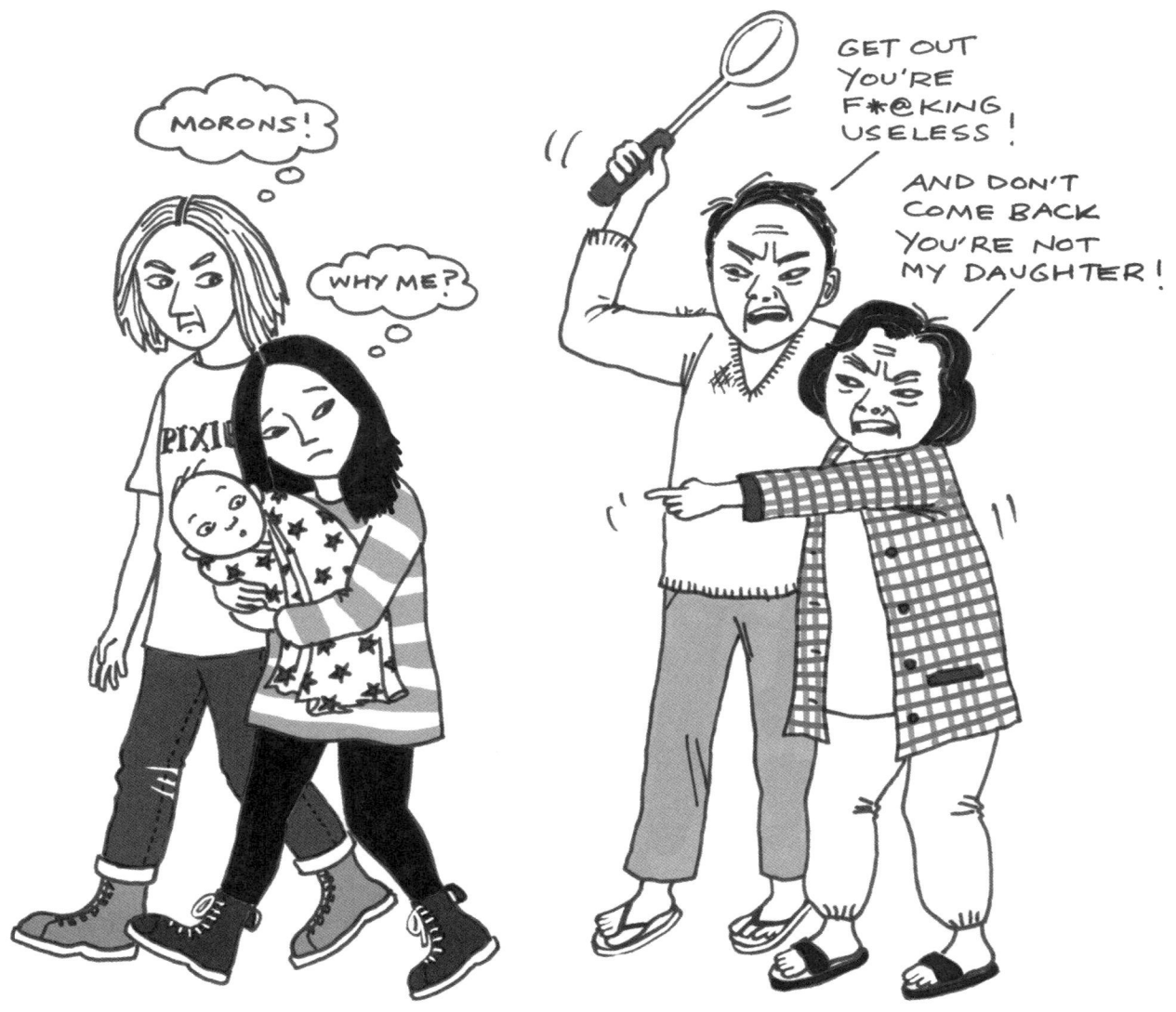

Mum insisted on visiting, so I agreed and she talked me into moving back in with her. I was blinded by promises of secure, paid work in the takeaway and forgot all about the past traumas of living with her and Dad, so I said yes — what a mistake! Not long after Jez caught my dad beating up my little sister and intervened. This culminated in us being kicked out onto the streets yet again.

After that I was determined to turn my life around, I was fed up of falling down holes wherever I turned. If anything, at least the work ethic my parents instilled in me paid off. A kind family member took us in while I knuckled down and completed a Higher National Diploma at art college, found a good job with prospects and got my own council house. That was almost thirty years ago. Now I'm footloose and mortgage free!

It was a long and winding road, with loads of other potholes along the way, but with sheer hard work, focus and belief I managed to get my life together and find peace and happiness in the end. It would have been amazing to have had a charity like Accumulate back then to help me find hope in my dark days. What they do for creative, homeless young people is a huge lift, not just in a practical sense but also the empathy and compassion shown goes a long way. I am honoured to be part of this incredible organisation.

HOW HOMELESSNESS SHAPED MY LIFE
Samantha Morton, Actress

My experience of homelessness began, I think, when I was seven, and my family were moved into a place called Highwood House in Nottingham. Then we got moved into bedsits run by unscrupulous landlords charging the council a fortune. They were unbelievable shit holes beyond filthy, piss-stained mattresses that had never been cleaned. They were dangerous places, too. We'd all sleep on the cleanest bed we could find in our clothes because a) we were freezing and b) we didn't want to get too close to the mattress. It was like a Bill Brandt photo from the 1940s.

I was in and out of care from pretty much birth due to family circumstances. Around the age of nine I started to live in children's homes. I hated them. I didn't feel safe there. The very people who were there to look after us were abusing us – physically and sexually.

From the age of 12, I would regularly run away from the homes and often I slept rough. I felt safer on the streets, where I met some amazing people, than I did in my home. I would go to raves when I was far too young – still 12 – and I'd end up meeting people and staying with them for a couple of weeks, just floating around, till I knew they couldn't look after me any more.

Then I was placed in an 'independence unit' in a children's home. Another girl and I were given our own annex, with a bedroom and kitchen and we'd make garlic rice and feel grownup and independent. But there were terrible things going on at that home too, and ultimately we were still part of the home. So again I'd run away to the streets. The streets gave me the opportunity to meet people who understood me, who had been through what I'd been through, who wouldn't hurt me.

I went to the streets for safety – I know it sounds mad, but it's true. I felt more in control of my life on the streets. I could go into a shop, steal some food, have a wash in market square toilets, shoplift toiletries from Body Shop, and get by.

When I was 16 I was placed in a homeless hostel – another 'independence' unit. I was officially an adult. But there were so many rules and regulations that it didn't feel independent. Looking back now, I can understand why, but back then I just thought 'why can't I have visitors in my room? why can't I come and go as I please?' It felt like prison.

So I experienced homelessness as a child, as a teenager on the streets and then in a homelessness hostel. And all three had a lifelong impact on me. It has made me more resilient, but it has also left me with mental health problems. I suffer with PTSD and have major panic attacks. My anxiety can be debilitating, and I have suffered with it for years. For a long time I couldn't talk about it, but now I can. I think it's important to do so, to show other people they are not alone.

When I was young and homeless I had survival techniques. There were the obvious ones – stealing, finding somewhere to stay. But there were also things I did that I didn't have a clue were survival techniques at the time. For example, getting hold of a pen and a piece of paper. I'd do whatever I could to get pen and paper, whether hanging around bookies or writing on the back of a receipt. It's such a basic thing, but to me it was special. Part of my survival. I'd write my feelings down, or write a poem, doodle and draw. Back then I didn't realise what I was doing was to calm me and help my mind process the trauma it was going through.

When I was asked to write an introduction to The Book of Homelessness, I was thrilled. First because homelessness has been so important to my life and sense of self. Second, because I know how crucial it is for people's stories to be heard or seen — and this book allows for both. And finally because this is a graphic novel. Being cast in The Walking Dead, the TV series based on the great graphic novel written by writer Robert Kirkman and artist Tony Moore, has opened my eyes up to the wonders of the graphic novel. As a kid I'd grab a Beano or whatever comics my foster brother had, but they weren't really written for girls. And I definitely wasn't into girly mags, like Jackie. I think if I'd found graphic novels back then they would have definitely been my thing.

Asking people to share their stories about homelessness is such a beautiful concept, and to then go on to illustrate them graphically makes it even better — and more accessible. There's something so much more moving and profound when stories are unmediated; when they come direct from the horse's mouth, as here. And of course, telling stories is cathartic

By writing down your story, you're facing up to what has happened to you. Sometimes it can be traumatising (but, I believe, it's a trauma worth going through) and sometimes it's simply liberating. Writing it down is like purging yourself. Something so powerful happens to you. You make your memory solid. It's yours, it belongs to you, it's there in front of you, and nobody can fuck with that memory. And it's not just important for us as individuals that we write down our experiences, it's important for society and history — we're bearing witness to all that has happened to us, that has been done to us in our name. If we want society to learn from its failings, if we want to eradicate homelessness, we have to document how it happened in the first place.

The austerity of the past decade has led to a horrifying increase in the number of homeless people — and the number of people who have died homeless. According to the last Shelter report in November 2018, at least 320,000 people are homeless in Britain (a 4% year on year rise), almost 5,000 are rough sleeping (likely to be a huge underestimate) and 726 people died homeless in England and Wales in 2018 (a 22% rise from 2017). When I was a kid at least I could go into a library and get some spiritual sustenance, some inspiration, from reading. This is harder and harder for today's homeless kids as more libraries are shut down.

I directed a film about my time in care called The Unloved. Tony Grissoni wrote the script based on conversations we had about my childhood. It was the first time I'd told my story to anyone. It was really tough because it brought so much back, but in the end turned out to be a form of therapy in itself. At times, it was like forcing yourself to vomit up your past. Doubtless the experience for many of the people telling their stories in The Book of Homelessness was similar. You think you're cool with your past, you've done enough therapy, you can cope with what happened to the younger you because you're in a different space and time. But you're still you. On a molecular level, I will always be little Sam, 15-year-old Sam, 20-year-old Sam. And the same with everyone else. Because that's part of our shadow, our history, part of the mark we've made. Dredging up those memories was the toughest. The creative aspect — getting on set and turning it into art if you like — was the liberating bit. That's when you regain control because you are telling your story. In shaping the story of my past, I felt that I was finally in control of it.

Have I paid for being outspoken? Probably. Let's just say I'm never first in line when the establishment hands out honours. But again that's hardly surprising. My film doesn't show the council and social services in an impressive light. If you're constantly shining light on something wrong , there will always be people who are hostile to you. But if that's the price you have to pay, it's one well worth paying.

In the end the most important thing is to make sure we have a voice. Because nobody will give us one if we don't exercise our own. We have to shout louder, we have to demand to be heard, to shout out 'Hello! This is wrong, and I'm not going to just lie down and take it.'

And you never know who might hear you. Perhaps the future prime minister could pick up The Book of Homelessness and start to think radically different about how to treat people without a roof on their head. Perhaps the future prime minister will discover that homeless people are just ordinary people who have hit on bad times and need a helping hand to recover their lives.

Amalia Walrond

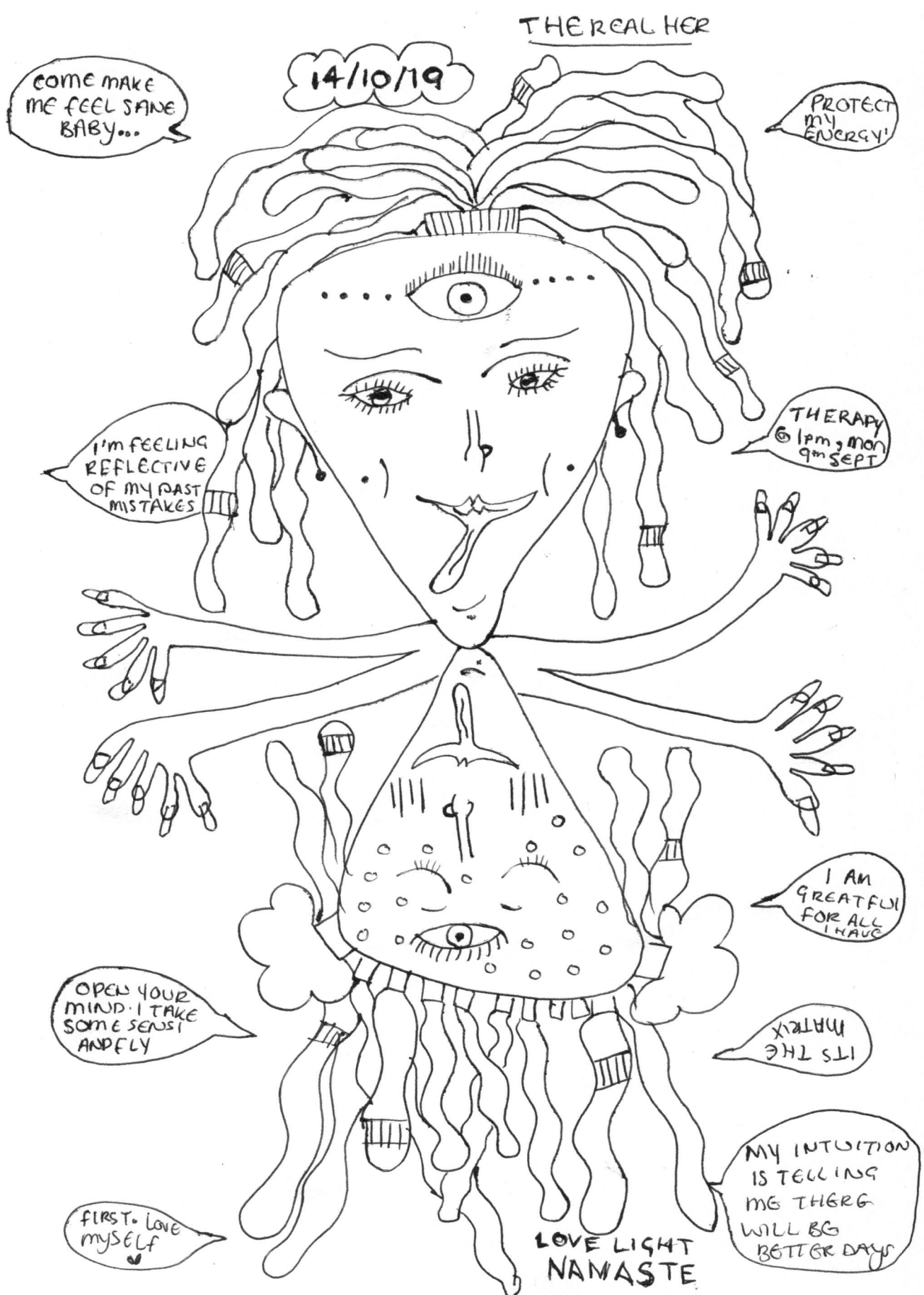

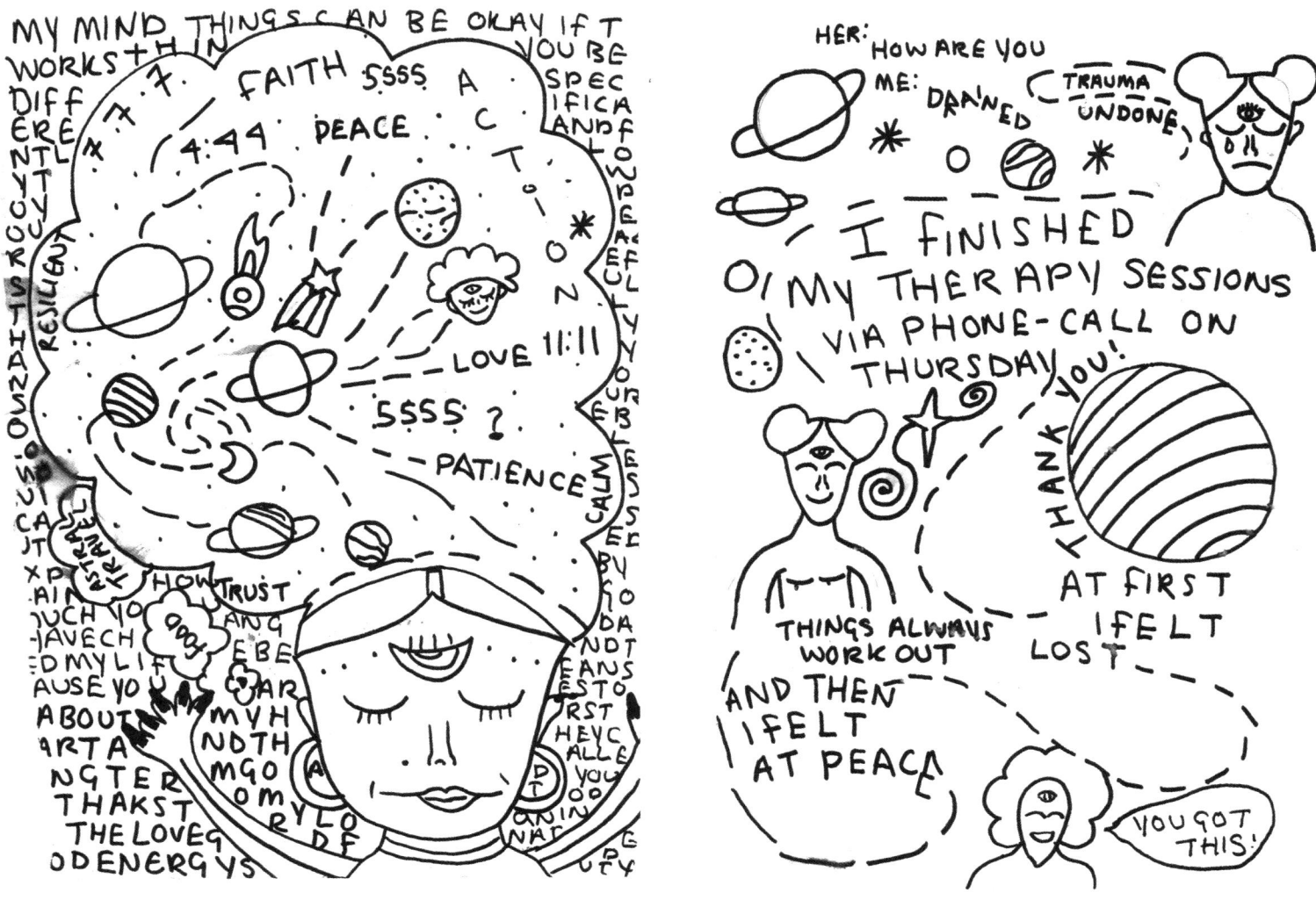

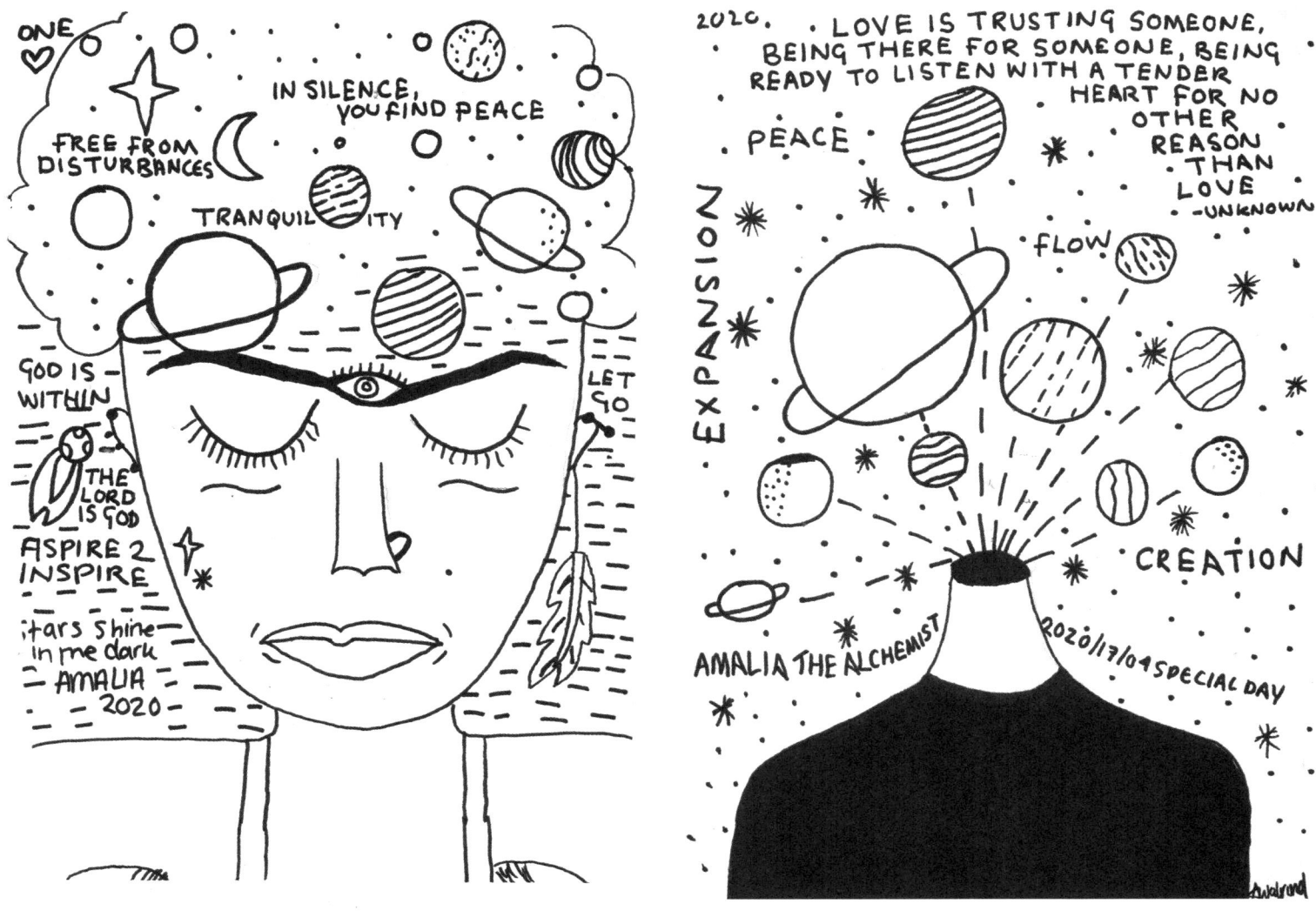

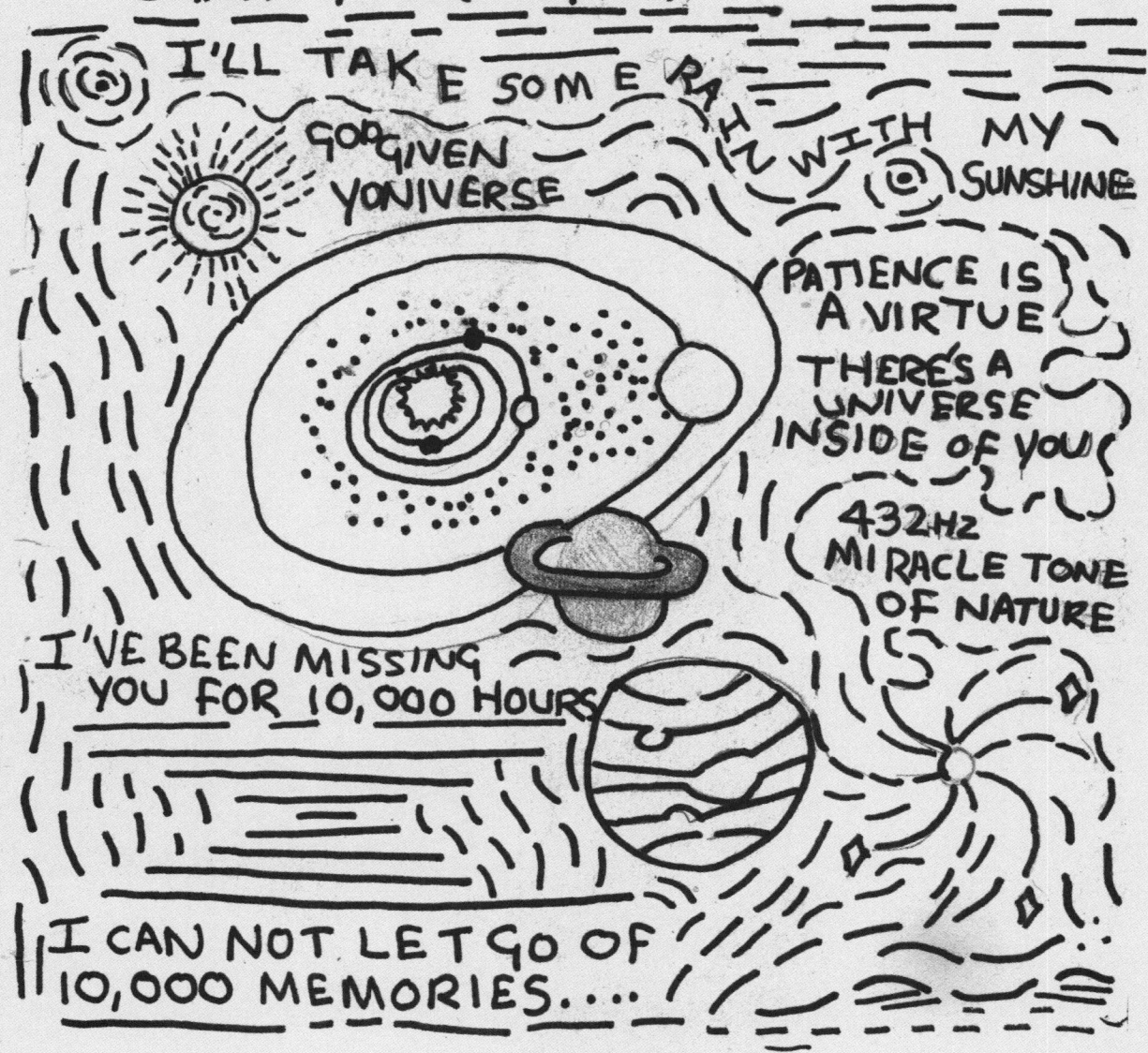

YOU'RE JUST WAITING TO TALK

Wading through this energy
I see delicate daises to the left of me
Sunflowers growing in the soil
My brain recovered from turmoil
I wonder to ask your name
Not the one you use for fame
But the one in your brain
When you remember yourself again
I realised
I just want to be loved in a way
That calms my soul
And R.H.Sin says it better than most
I know its within that creates the space
Justice, love, character and faith
The love free falls floats and dives
I jump I saw your eyes and I saw that
It was inside we said hello
The eyes the window to our souls
Saw our souls
See saw we saw self
On both sides
From the most high
To the low tides
We saved each others souls
We have not spoke in a long time
Soul stayed afloat

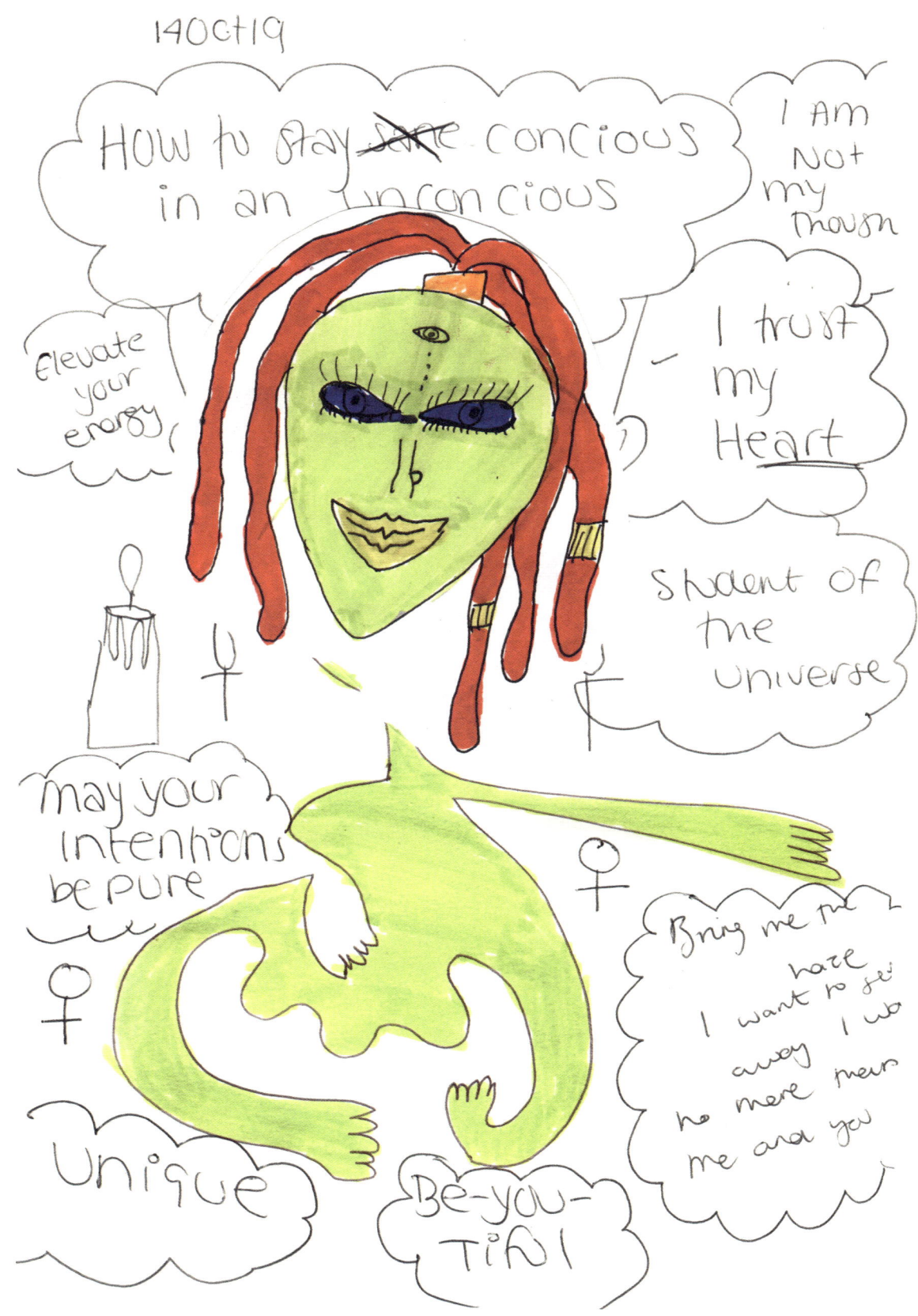

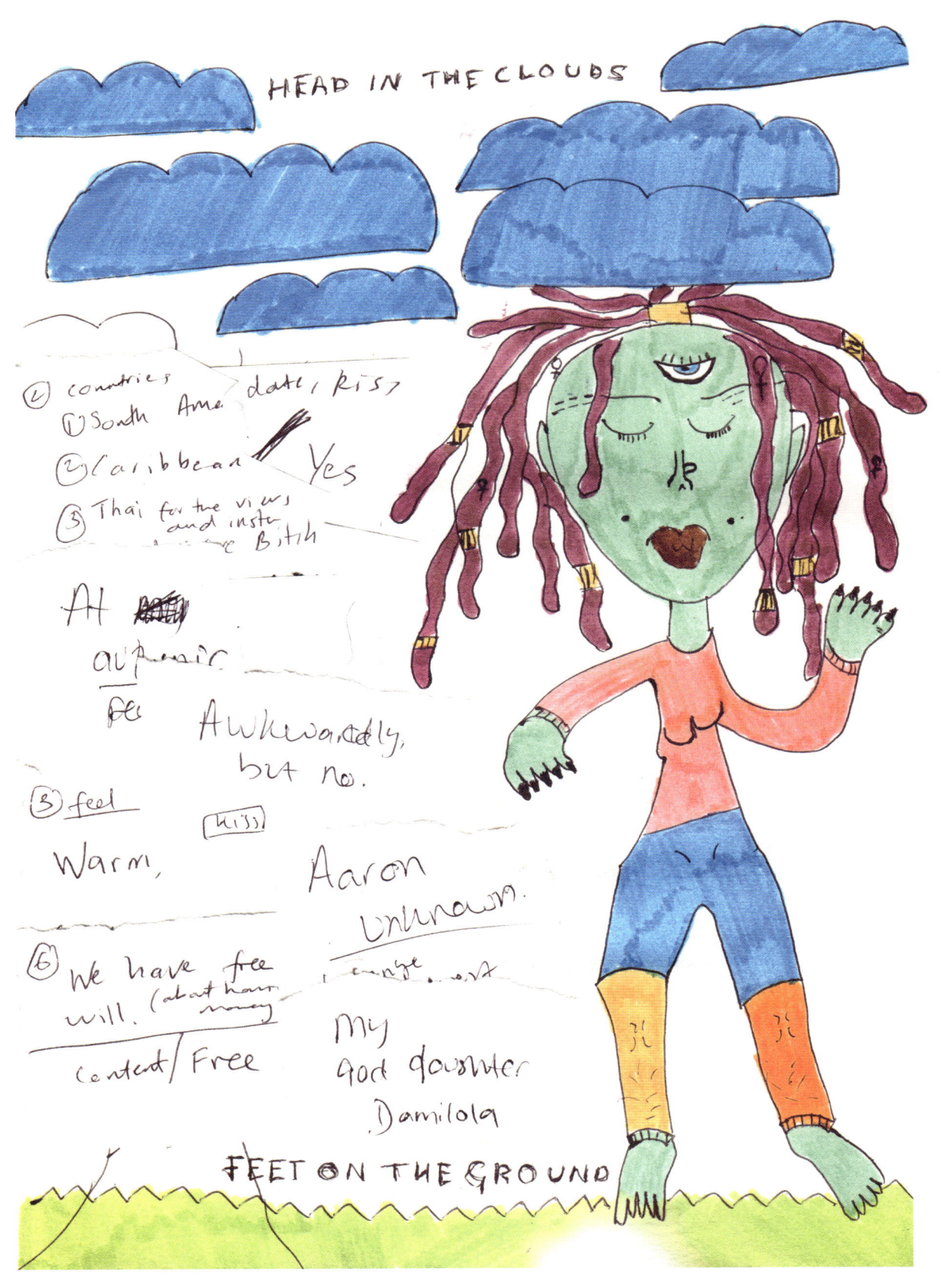

MEMORIES OF GRANDMA

Through the darkness, there is only light
Both the sun and the moon give that same light
So I looked up to find you in the stars Grandmama
Instead I saw myself, so in that — I wrote this:

Your dementia took away your smile
and replaced it with a love that I felt so deep in my soul for you
You aged like the moon the same way Mount Gay Bajan Rum in my Bajan blood does too
But on topic my sweet grandmother, you rose up like the sun
Your life was a candle flame of wonder
Bare faced with honesty, nothing to fear
Even though you're not here in the physical
You still vibrate here
You still love here
You see me here
I'm stripping my pain
I'm replacing the game of fame they call 'What's your artist name?'
Well you call me Amalia, the homeless poet with purpose, Marls
Whatever on Earth makes you feel good and makes you smile
A flame of wonder I am so bright
So bright
That I aim to cross the seven seas
Just like you my grandmother, I know you're making your way back to me
We're going to say, 'This planet, oh how it was fun to play here, to be here'.
Now I'm dreaming and I just saw you in my profile
I'm on Neptune I wrote a next tune
Took me to the last place that I saw your face
Space
Sentiment sentient being
Giving me feeling
Relieving all the actions
We took flight
There I saw your sight
I said I do and so did you
So I wrote a next tune whilst being on Neptune
I feel it a sweet muse
To see you on this earth with me
Why on earth would we spend so much time away?
Floating through thought in distant galaxies
But this time round we are sharing our brains
I am you and you are I
I am creating happiness where we can reside
Relax and open your third eye
Bring it back
Retract the fear so we can recline
Let's open our eyes and

Play a game with our minds
It's called 'Dare'
Should we dare
To love instead?
Should we choose us
and love instead?
Yes
I saw you near Egypt's Pyramid
And like the Alchemist
I searched for you
I found you whilst finding my treasure
I see you
In everything
In the birds and the trees,
The spring flowers and the leaves
Sunlit days and the winter breeze
I count the clouds with ease
Knowing your light is piercing through them
I am of your same light my Gran, you are light my light prism, creeping through and through like the intensity of the Jupiter moon
For you I remove taking off insecurities leaving them at the door like shoes
I choose to respect, believe and reflect the youth
Because in my space 10 years from now
This little black lady will look somewhat like you
5ft something, dress size 8 plus 2

I've consciously come a long way from smoking skunky zoots
I am confident now but I was not calm seeing my grandma embalmed
I will remember you
You will remember me, purpose
I thank God that she paved a way
So that I can come away
From the drugs that smoked the pain away

I explored my Grandmother's final thoughts
For those I'd have to find
Deeper stored metaphors
As those thoughts are reachable in dreams in astral realms
Somewhere between Galaxy 9 and a light Prism
my grandmother can be felt

Grandma
You are my owl totem
In the dark night sky
I see your eyes bright and wise
You once heard I was coming to earth and made your way to protect me
Non romantically I was your King in Egypt with lots of flowers on the throne
I just landed back on this planet so I could make my way back to you
And I will have all these stories to tell my little girl

Chris Fox

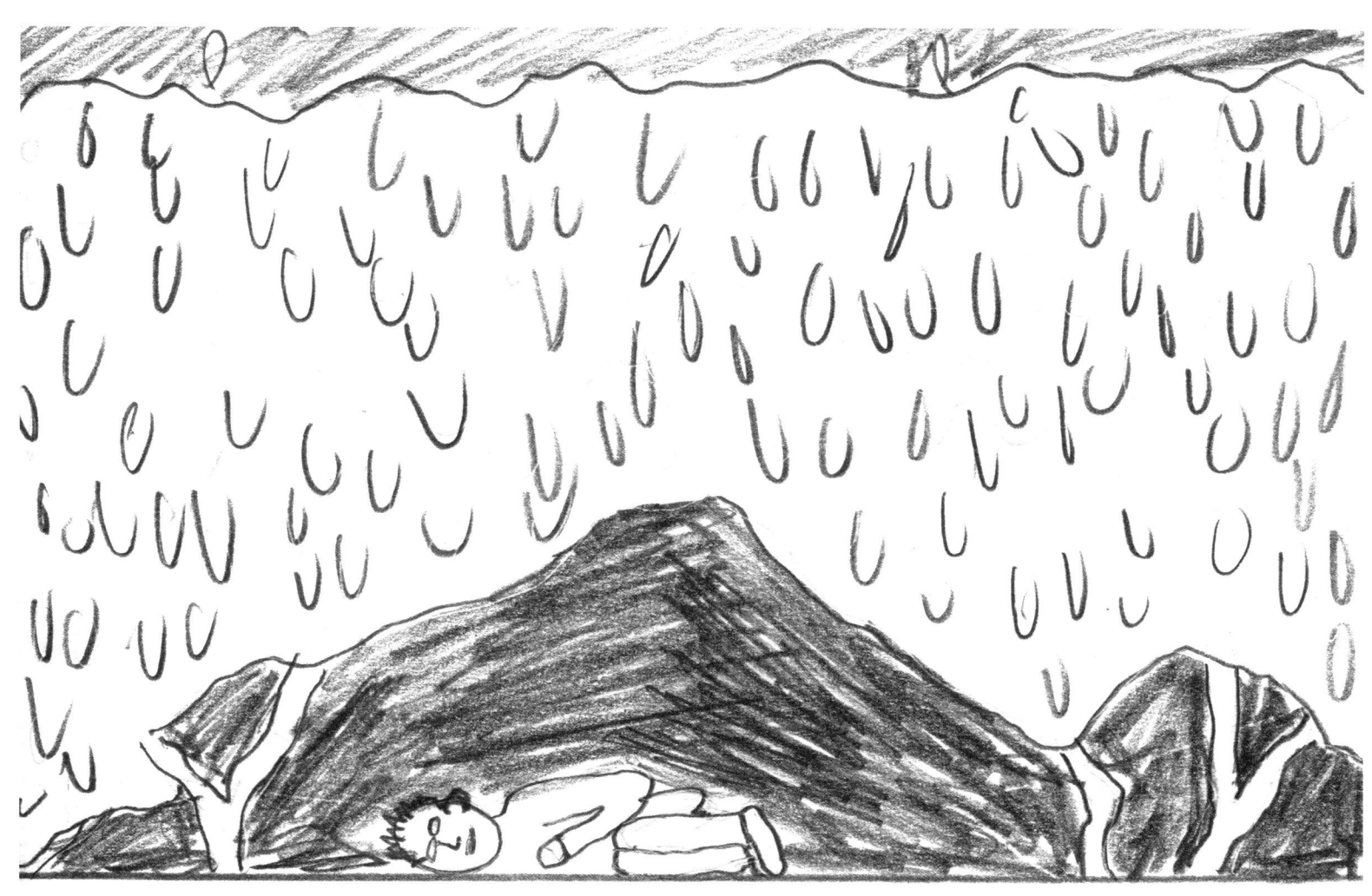

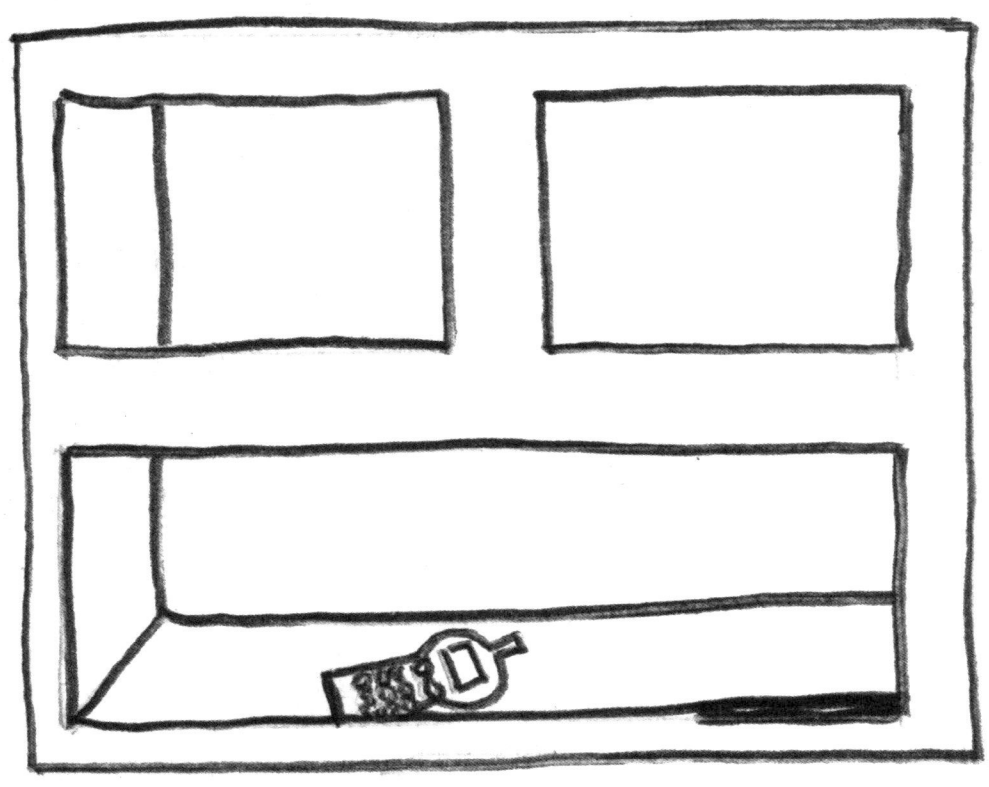

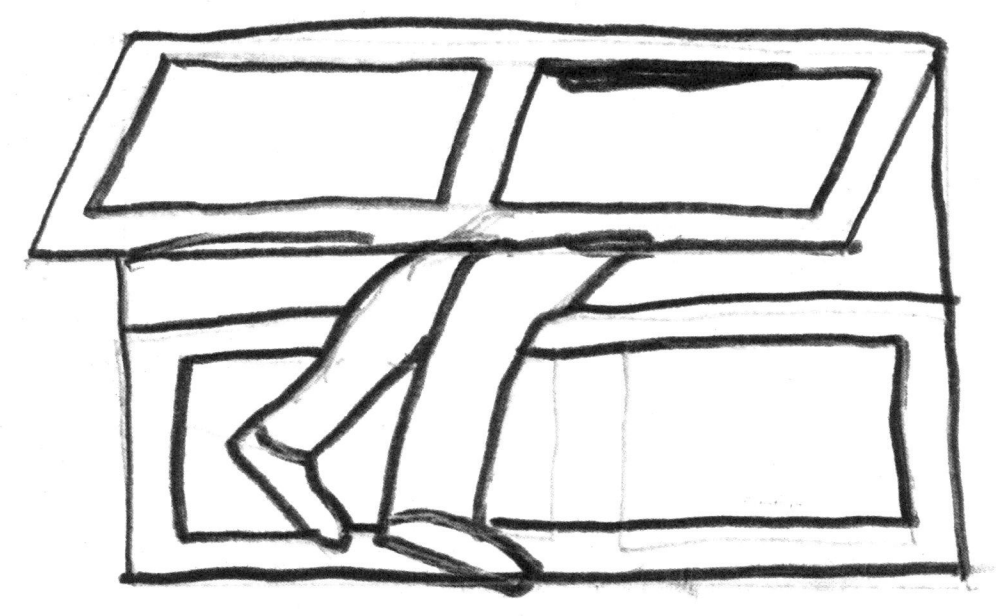

YOU LITTLE BASTARD I'M GONNA FUCKING KILL YOU.

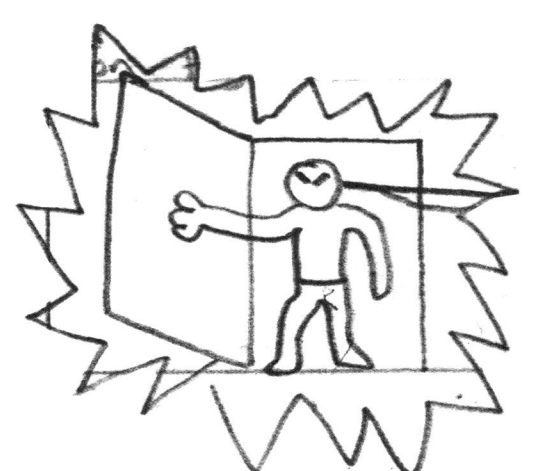

HE KICKED THE LIVING SHIT OUT OF ME AND THREW ME OUT THE DOOR LIKE A RAG DOLL.

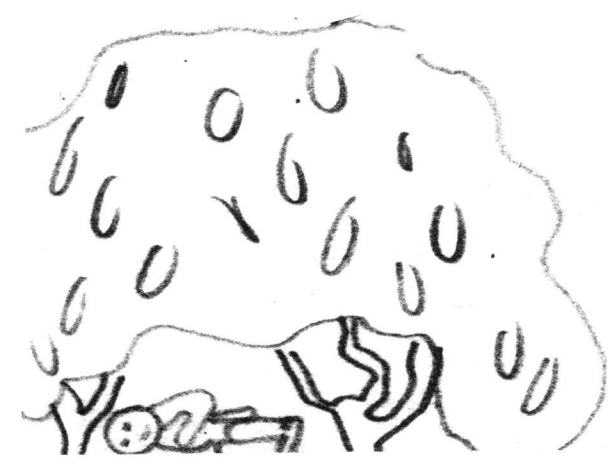

I DECIDED THEN AND THERE I DIDN'T WANT TO GO BACK. I SPENT THE NEXT MONTH HOMELESS FREEZING MY BALLS OFF. IT'S NOVEMBER.

WE SAT DOWN TOGETHER AT 2:30AM. NOW I'M USED TO WAKING UP 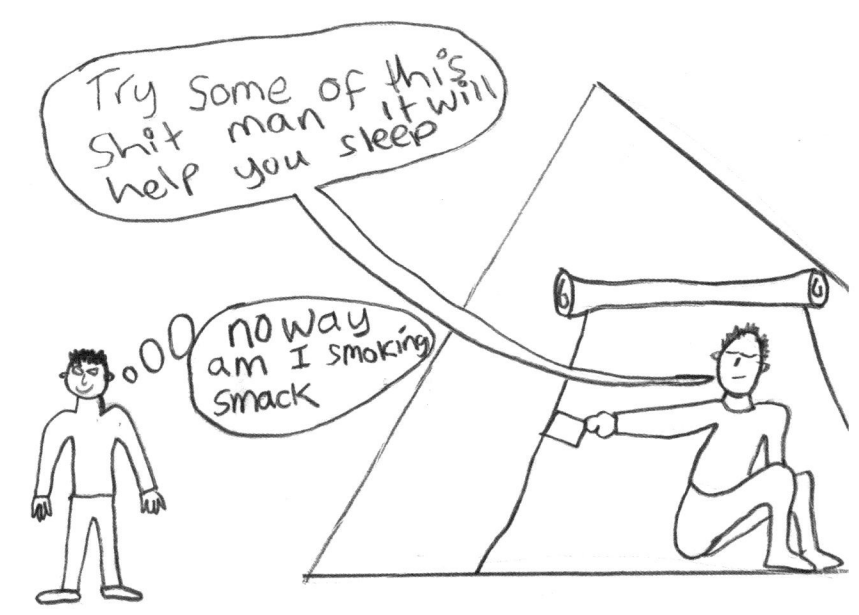 AT LEAST 6-8 TIMES A NIGHT YET AFTER SMOKING JUST A FEW LINES OF SMACK I WOKE UP AT 3PM THE NEXT DAY. BOOM!

I WAS IMMEDIATELY HOOKED: DUE TO FEAR OF MY FATHER I HADN'T SLEPT A FULL NIGHT THAT I COULD REMEMBER, NOT EVER. I HAD FOUND A WAY TO SLEEP AND I LOVED IT.

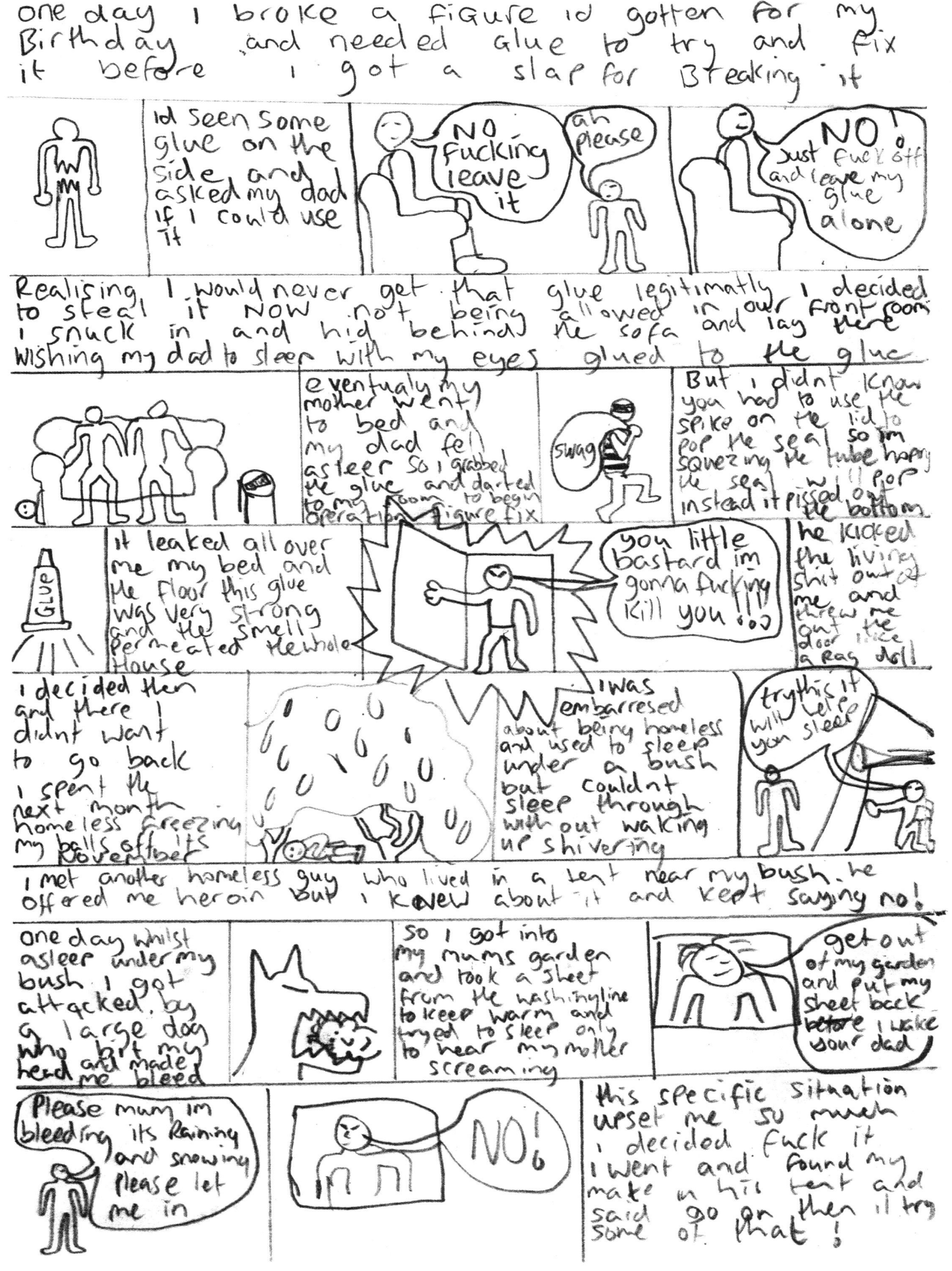

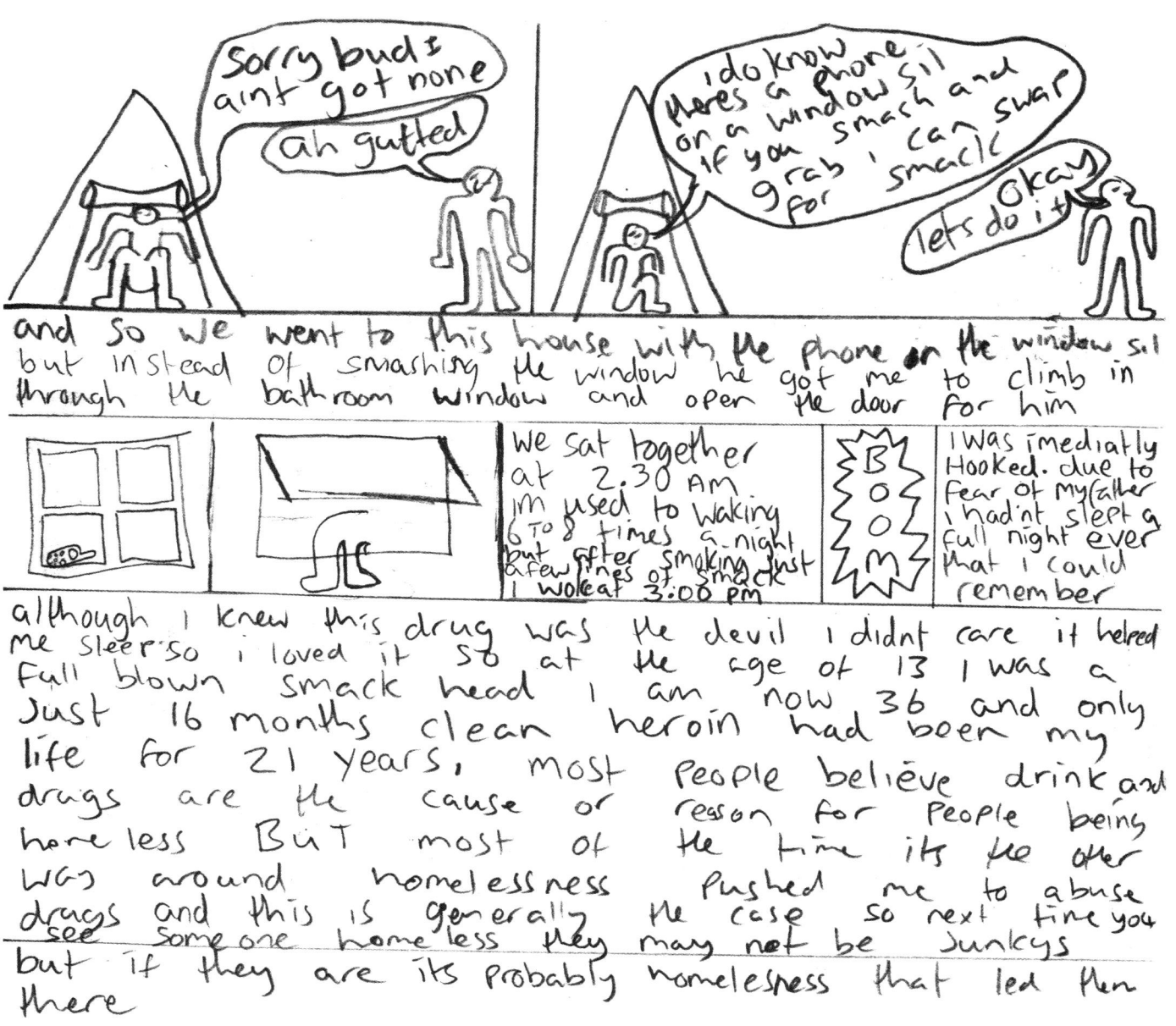

and so we went to this house with the phone on the window sil but instead of smashing the window he got me to climb in through the bathroom window and open the door for him

although I knew this drug was the devil I didnt care it helped me sleep so i loved it so at the age of 13 I was a full blown smack head I am now 36 and only just 16 months clean heroin had been my life for 21 years, most people believe drink and drugs are the cause or reason for people being homeless But most of the time its the other way around homelessness pushed me to abuse drugs and this is generally the case so next time you see someone homeless they may not be junkys but if they are its probably homelessness that led them there one day whilst asleep under my bush I got attacked by a large dog who bit my head and made me bleed

So I got into my mums garden and took a sheet from the washingline to keep warm and tryed to sleep only to hear my mother screaming

Dave Sohanpal

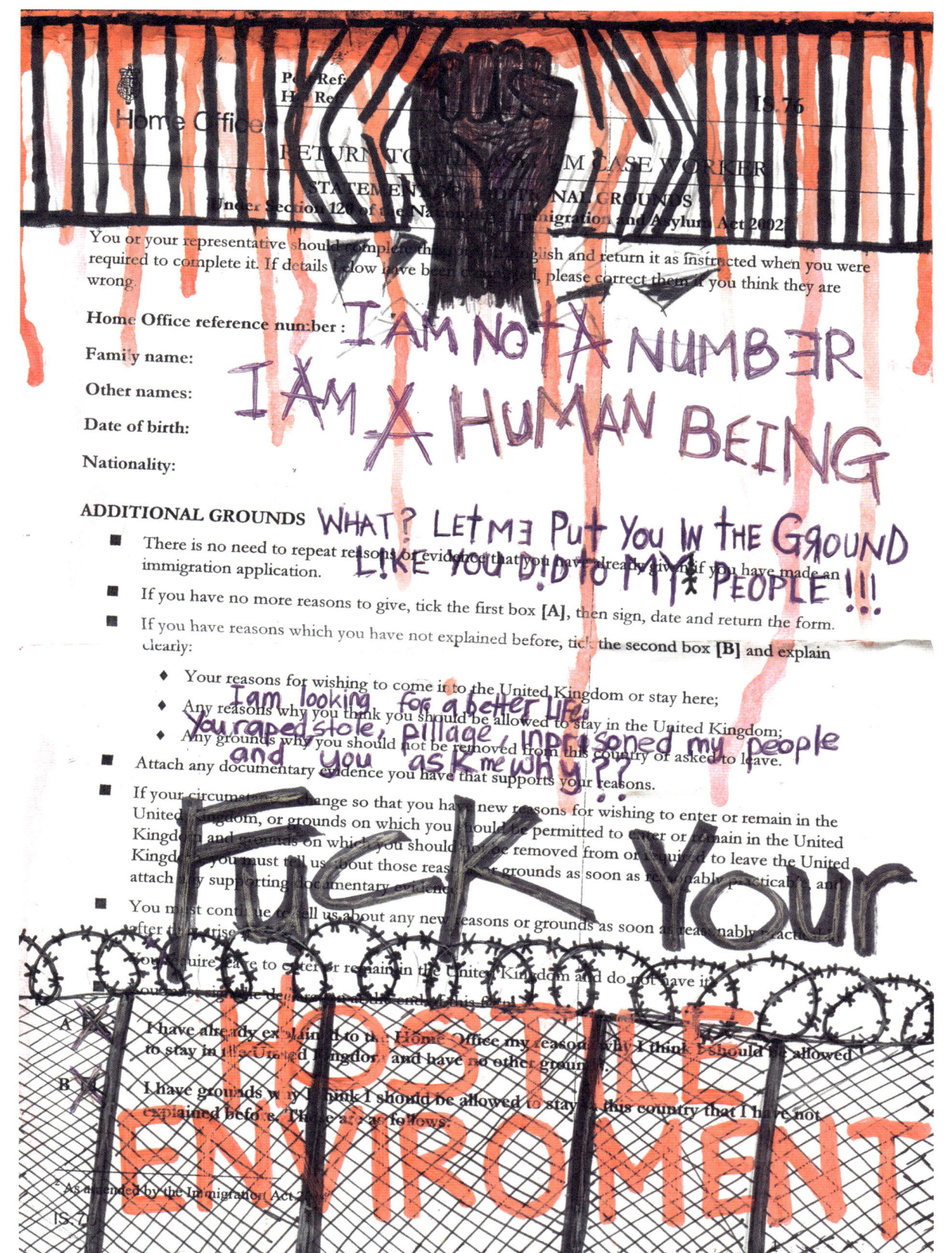

ANGEL IN MY WINDOW

My story begins with an angel coming into my room. I believe it was an angel: a guardian angel sent by my Nana to watch over me when I was going through a very tough time. I was dealing with the death of my partner, trying to manage my asylum claim with the Home Office and I was having a mental breakdown.

Back in 2018, during the holiday season, a good friend asked me to spend some time with him over Christmas. We used to watch a lot of films and series on Netflix: mainly horror stories. We binge-watched the entire series of The Haunting of Hill House. I was terrified of a character called the Bent Neck Lady. My friend and I would do silly things to frighten each other: send texts, bang on the doors, make scary noises.

After the holidays I returned to my place in London. It was a stormy night. I was trying to get to sleep when suddenly there was a loud noise in my room — bang! I didn't think much of it but then I heard a second bang. Now I was worried. What if it was a ghost, or the Bent Neck Lady coming after me? Yet another bang! This time I pulled my duvet up over my head. I was shitting myself! I started to pray: 'Please, please don't be her!' If it was the Bent Neck Lady I knew that I needed to comfort her. Slowly, I pulled up the duvet and peeked through a tiny crack: there was no terrifying lady looking down at me from above.

I finally gathered the courage to get up and find out who or what was making that noise in my room. I crept out of bed and as I turned the light on I saw… a little angel looking at me, stunned. We were both shocked and scared as we stared at each other from opposite corners of the room. I was looking into the green eyes of a cat. She had climbed in through an open window and was creeping about knocking things over in my room. Our eyes were locked for a brief moment and then we both ran in opposite directions as if we had seen a ghost.

Once the dust had settled and we were both calmer, I made a makeshift bed for her. Lying in bed that night I decided to call her 'Guardian Angel'. That was a wee bit too long so I called her 'Kitty.'

I am a chicken when it comes to cats. All my life I had only ever had dogs, even when I was studying in the US. This was the first cat to come into my life. I didn't know what cats ate or what they liked doing. I got her a ball and some toys but she wasn't impressed. She didn't want to play fetch. Or go for walkies. I thought Kitty might be broken and I was worried that she was sick. For two days I fed her on what I was eating, which was vegetables, but on the third day she didn't even look at the food that I had given her. So I rang my friend who had a cat to get some advice: when I told her that Kitty did not want to play fetch or go for walkies, she said, 'Dave, you've never had a cat before, have you? They are not like dogs!' I went to the pet store and got some cat snacks and cat food. My friend asked me if I had bought a kitty litter. What was that?! I was lucky that Kitty went out on the balcony to the neighbour's flower beds to do her business. She was very clever and I was very lucky: no training needed in that department.

I made her a lovely bed so she had her own space to chill and to sleep. She really liked her new bed and was settling in beautifully. I left the window open so that she could come in and go out as and when she pleased. When her back legs were close together, they made the shape of a heart: it was a sign. Love at first sight. We found and comforted each other in our own way.

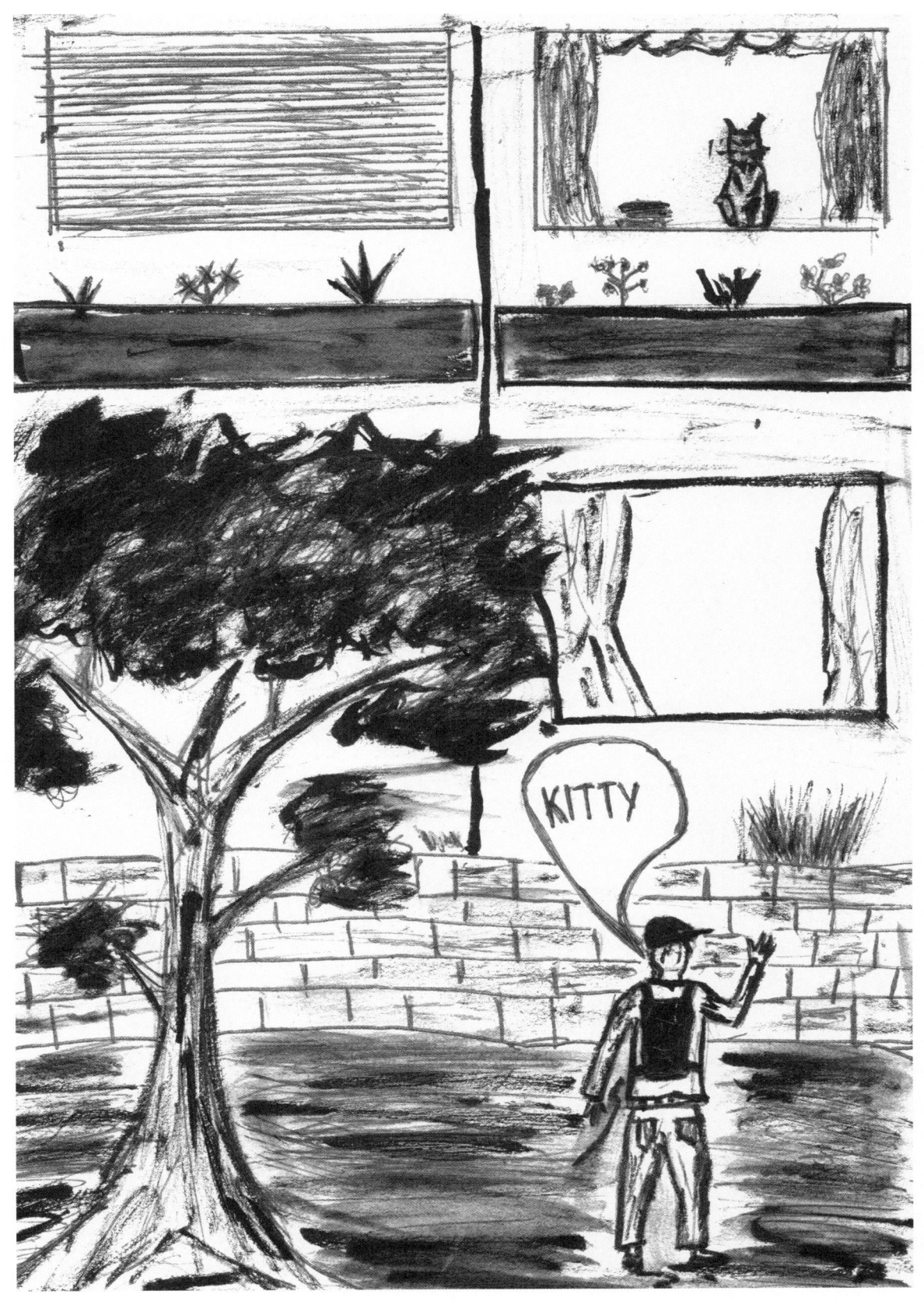

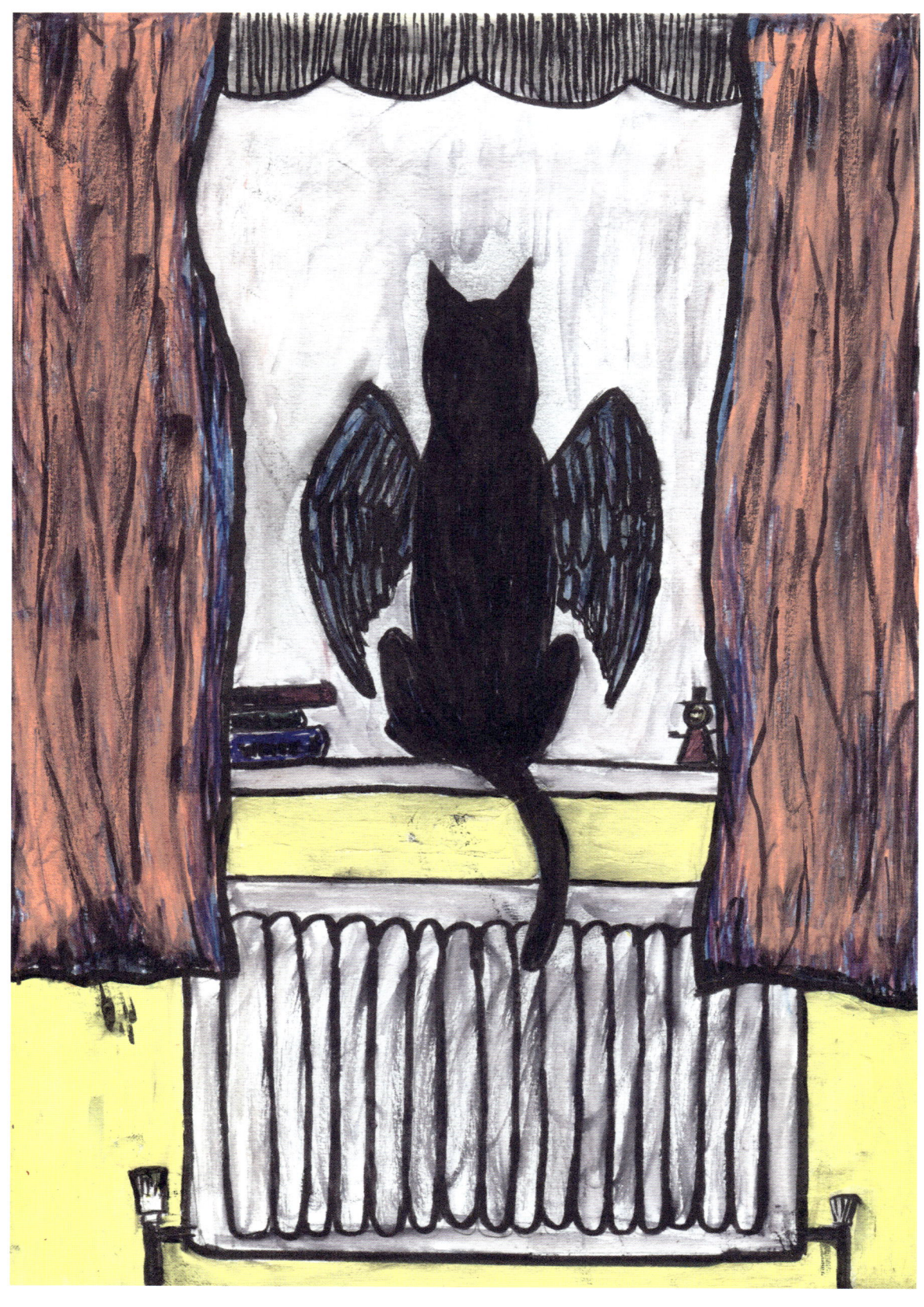

I believe she was an angel sent by my Nana to look after me during the traumatic time I was going through. She was the gentlest cat I ever met. I took her out to my community centre: everyone loved her and said how calm she was for a feral cat. My mood changed: I was much happier and more lively. It felt like destiny: we were meant to meet and be together.

Whenever I was on my laptop or resting she would slowly approach and curl up on my pillow. In the morning she would wait next to my head and gently tap me with her little paw, as if to say, 'Hello! Time to wake up: I'm hungry, please feed me.' She was so patient and would wait until I was up before meowing at me. When I went out she would sleep on my pillow rather than in her own bed. Sometimes she would sleep on my feet: she'd get in under the duvet, snuggle up next to me and start to purr. Sometimes I would tease her when she was sleeping by opening the packet of her favourite treat and she would come running from her deep sleep: just so I could hear her beautiful 'meow'. It was like a musical note.

When I was anxious, she would come to me, give me kisses and sit with me and purr until I felt better. We had been together for about three months by this point: the happiest and most joyful moments of my life. There is not a single day that I don't think of her and I do miss that 'meow' in the morning.

But even though my mental health was starting to improve, I was still unable to work and so there was no way for me to pay my rent. I was given notice by my landlord to leave the place. Just as I was beginning to feel better, suddenly my whole world came crumbling down. It felt like the end of the world: completely bleak, a huge void.

When they heard my news, some folks at the community centre offered to look after Kitty for me. I felt torn, and in despair. I was apprehensive about giving her away – what if people didn't look after her very well? I couldn't live with that. Yet somehow deep inside me I knew that she could survive. I had seen her take on cats twice her size: she was streetwise. I guess she was a survivor like me.

Finally the day came where we had to say goodbye and part our ways. That morning, my heart was heavy. I made sure that she had enough food and water for a few days and we kissed and hugged for the last time. I felt uneasy, but she was so calm as if she was telling me that everything would be fine and that I shouldn't worry. There was still a sparkle in her eyes, just like the first time we met on that stormy night. It is kind of ironic. The song 'Angel' by Jimi Hendrix plays on in my mind: 'Angel came down from Heaven yesterday / She stayed with me just long enough to rescue me.'

I remember my Nana used to tell me, 'Our loved ones are never gone. They live through us. When we feel sad or in times of trouble, we can always call upon them. They are always with us, in here.' And she would point to her heart. In true essence Kitty never really left me: she is always with me in my heart and I will always cherish the good memories of us together. I guess I was blessed with the best gift: she helped me regain my sanity.

As I left the building that day, I went around to the side where my bedroom window was – the same window I had once tried to jump out of – and I called Kitty. She came to the window ledge and sat, looking at me. Tears rolled down my face. I think she knew it was time for me to leave, because I was healed.

Kitty will always be in my heart and will live through me. I am sure we will meet again my little Angel. I love you and to this day, you still make me smile. We are all worthy but it's easy to forget that. Sometimes you have to go through the storm to see the rainbow.

OUR LOVED ONES ARE NEVER GONE, THEY LIVE THROUGH US WHEN WE FEEL SAD OR

IN TIMES OF TROUBLE, WE CAN ALWAYS CALL UPON THEM. THEY ARE ALWAYS WITH US.

Hamahoullah Diallo

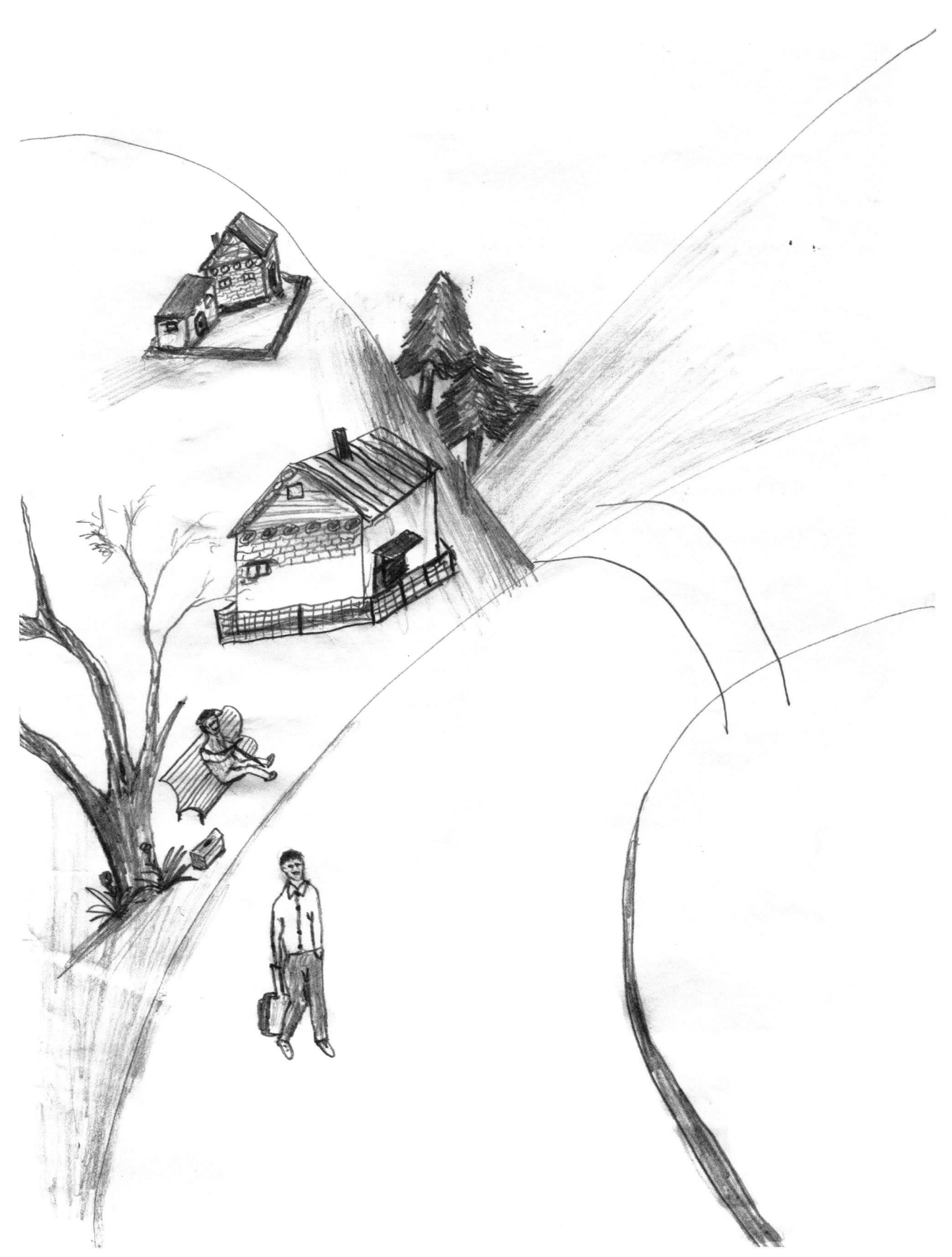

I WAS BORN IN GUINEA, IN MY HOME VILLAGE OF FOUTA DJALLON: I SPENT MY ENTIRE CHILDHOOD IN THAT VILLAGE.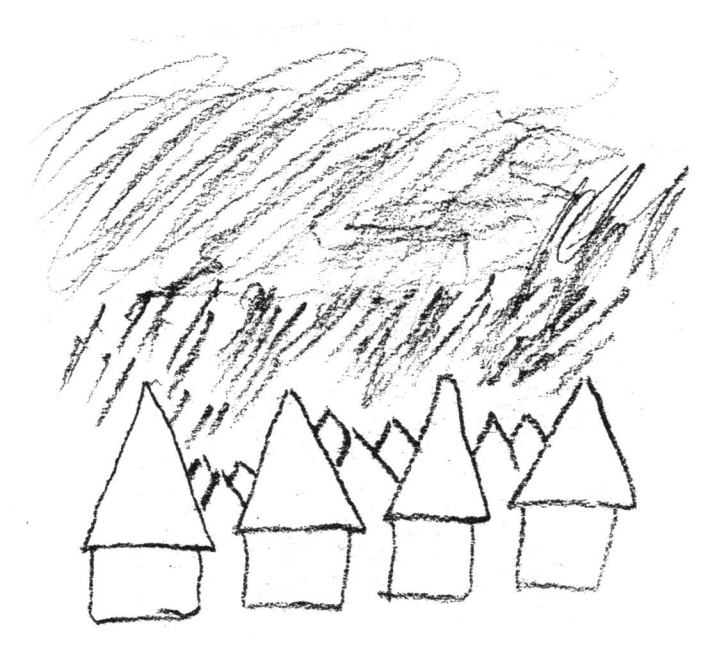
MY PARENTS WERE FARMERS AND BREEDERS OF LIVESTOCK. I WAS A VERY HAPPY CHILD, AMBITIOUS AND FULL OF HOPE.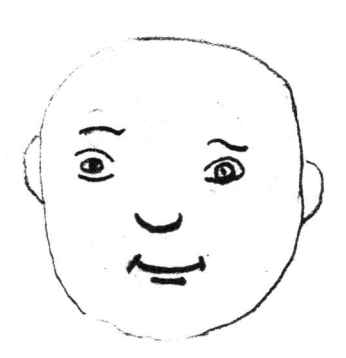

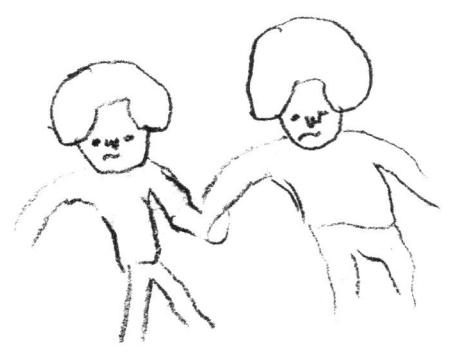
IN THE VILLAGE, I FOLLOWED MY STUDIES, JUST LIKE ALL THE OTHER CHILDREN, IN ARABIC AND FRENCH. OUR PARENTS AND GRANDPARENTS TAUGHT US LESSONS VERY SIMILAR TO THOSE OF THEIR OWN TIME; TO BE SOMEONE WHO IS GENEROUS, HOSPITABLE, WELCOMING AND RESPECTFUL.

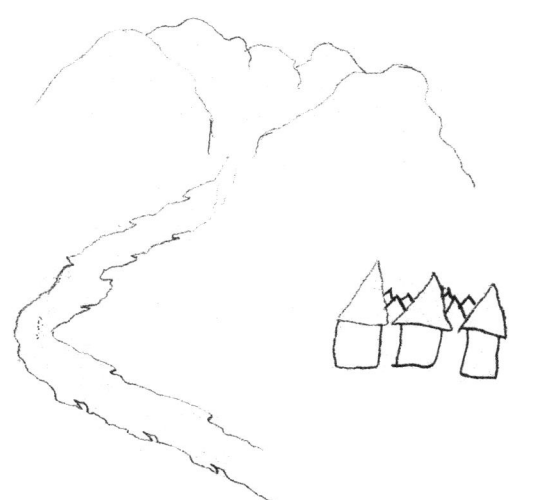

All of this prepared you to understand the culture of being a farmer or breeder of livestock and to better understand your family traditions and customs.

I was very excited by farming and breeding. From time to time my brother would tell me, 'First, your studies, you must first finish your studies.'

Once I had finished my BEPC – the National Diploma – I was transferred to Conakry, near to my mother. There, a new life began.

Once I was in Conakry things started to change as I tried to adapt to life in the capital.

After two consecutive failures of my Baccalaureate, I was put in a vocational school in the capital. Over the course of four years in this school, I studied to be an electrical contractor. In this school, just like any other, we had a habit of organising parties at the end of the year.

Sometimes we welcomed guests, but on the understanding that they were politically neutral. But on this occasion, our director of studies introduced a minister as our guest of honour. We were asked to wear shirts with party slogans on for the end of year festivities: it was turning into an electoral campaign.

Some of us, myself included, were opposed to the idea of the shirts and the filming of the event for broadcast on national television.

And this cost me dearly. Because of this, I was deprived of two years of my studies and so were the friends who followed me. In addition, we were threatened and intimidated in all sorts of ways.

Thanks to the help of a friend whose parents were high ranking within the state, we were able to take up our studies again. But the threats and intimidation never stopped: it was nothing but punishment after punishment.

14TH OF APRIL 2015, THE DAY OF MY ARREST:

On this day there was a demonstration and my mother had asked me if I had any money in my little kiosk to help us get something to eat.

Let me tell you about this kiosk. It was a small kiosk where I sold recharge cards, phone cases and phone accessories. This kiosk generated money for my personal needs, paid for my studies and my school supplies.

I arrived in the centre of Kaloum with my friend Saliou: I brought some money. During our journey back to the house we got caught up in an ambush. In this ambush, my friend was shot in the back. There were lots of people covered in blood on the ground. For a minute I panicked: it was the first time I had seen people in agony.

...When I got back up on my feet, I lifted Saliou, who was bleeding heavily, and carried him on my back in the direction of the hospital. We stopped in the middle of the road – there were the Red Berets – the presidential guard. I wanted to hide among the garbage on the side of the road. The moment I got behind the garbage a guard stood in front of me pointing his gun at me. He told me to get in the military truck and we were driven to the Samori Touré camp.

In the camp we were taken to a detention room. In this detention room we went three days without eating or drinking.

My friend and some other people in the room died from a lack of water and food. There were more than 30 of us in the room. In that room, breathing was very difficult: we were dehydrated. After three days of being held in that room and three deaths, we were driven to a secret place in the same camp. There I experienced the most atrocious treatment of my life. I was tortured mentally and physically in this military camp. This left mental and physical scars. I don't know how long I spent in this camp. I just know I was driven there on the 14th of April 2015.

After the camp we were driven to Security... otherwise known as the central prison which is located, like the camp, in the commune of Kaloum. It was in this central prison that I wanted to commit suicide because of the lack of food, water and above all, the isolation.

My exit or my 'escape' from prison was thanks to the bravery of my older brother who never gave up and fought tooth and nail to get me out with the help of a soldier who worked in this prison. The soldier asked him for a large amount of money, which my brother paid. He called me by my name and, in front of all the others, he told me it was over for me. At first I resisted, then he pulled me towards the door, put my arms behind my back, put handcuffs on me and pulled me towards him. Once we had left the prison he drove me to a room where there were two agents in uniform. He told me not to be scared, he was going to get me out of there. They gave me a military uniform and I followed them into their car. After a while, he stopped the car, someone got in, and we continued on our way. Along the way, the person called me by my first name and I responded. He replied, 'It's me: your brother'. My brother gave the soldier directions to our house. There, the soldier parked the car and told my brother that I would stay under his guard and that no one should be made aware that I was out of prison, not even parents or family. Then we continued along the road to Lambanyi.

We arrived in Lambanyi that night and he gave documents to me and my brother, who opened the door. We went inside.

For three months I was locked in this house alone, and only two people visited me; my brother and the agent.

It stayed like that until one evening the agent arrived, panicked, confused and sweating a lot. He then asked me where my brother was, I told him he had just left. He called my brother on the phone telling him to come back and that it was urgent. When my brother arrived the agent introduced him to a man who was with him. He said 'Diallo, talk with your brother about getting you out of the country, it's urgent. In the central prison there is a big investigation which is happening right now.' My brother and the man agreed on a price and my brother went to the Medina to get a loan from his friends. When he returned I asked him to ask the agent to let me go and say goodbye to my mum; the agent refused categorically and threatened my brother. Some time later — minutes? hours? who knows? — the man returned to find me, and I spent the night at his house.

On the 5th of September 2018 I left my country for an unknown destination. When I arrived at the airport here in the UK I made my asylum request. After finishing my interrogation, I was driven to a hotel near the airport.

It was in this hotel that I contacted my family for the first time with the help of a man who came from Iraq or Afghanistan: he lent me his phone.

Using this man's phone I wrote to my sister Ramatoulla. She replied to me instantly: I called her straight away. When she answered she heard my voice and started to cry. My brother took the phone and asked me where I was: I said I was in England.

He passed the phone to my mother. My mum and I had a sort of password and when I said it, she knew it was me. My mother told me about the death of our maternal grandmother.

After our conversation my brother told me not to call their phone again because of the police.

My brother lost all his money and was forced to sell some of our family's land in Mamoun to get me out of prison. I am never in my life going to forget that, never never never. Most of all I will never forget the courage they showed for me. And what's more I want to thank all those who supported me be it morally, physically, mentally or financially and many thanks to Medical Foundation, particularly Maid Showell.

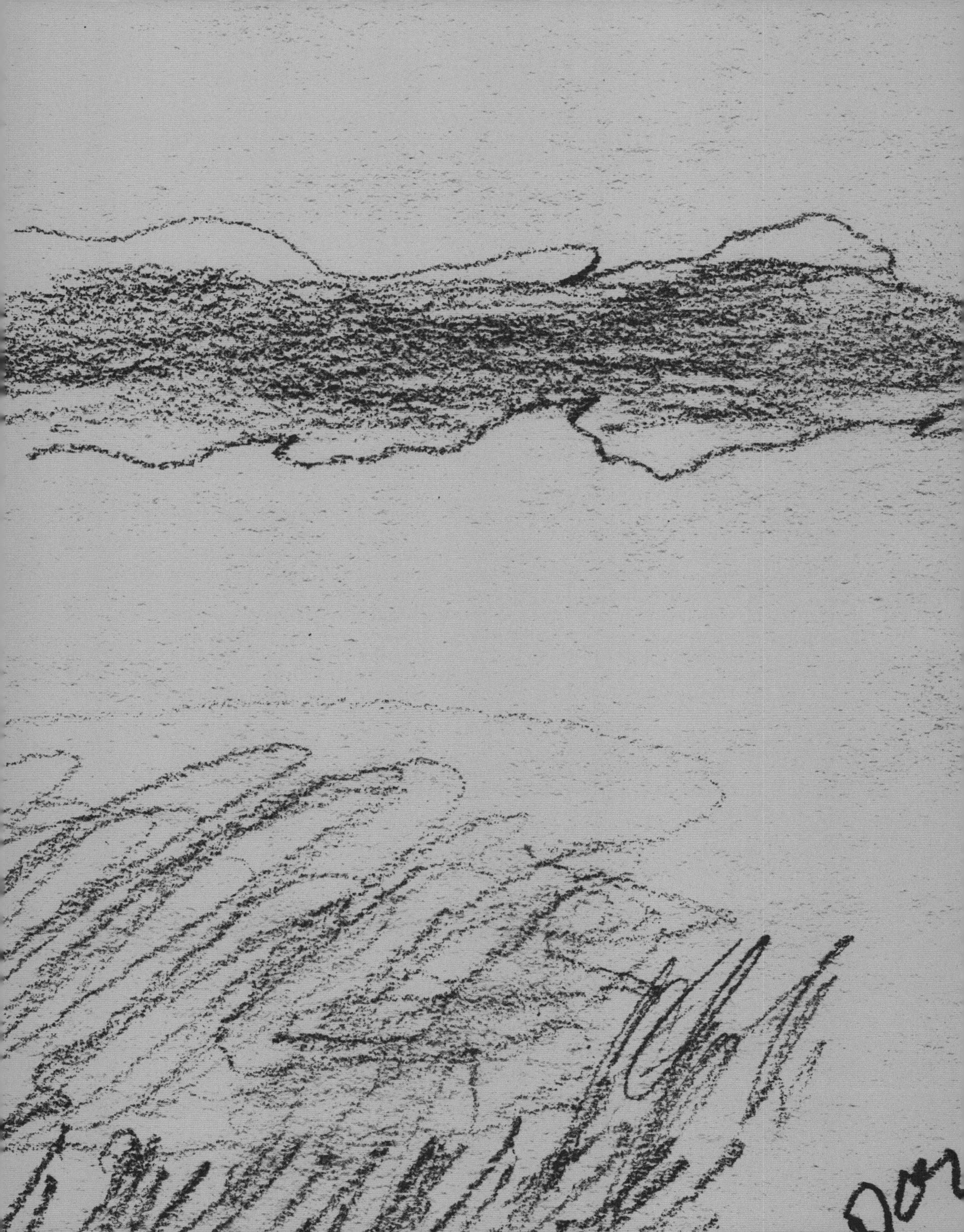

ON THE 5TH
OF SEPTEMBER
2018 I LEFT
MY COUNTRY
FOR AN
UNKNOWN
DESTINATION.

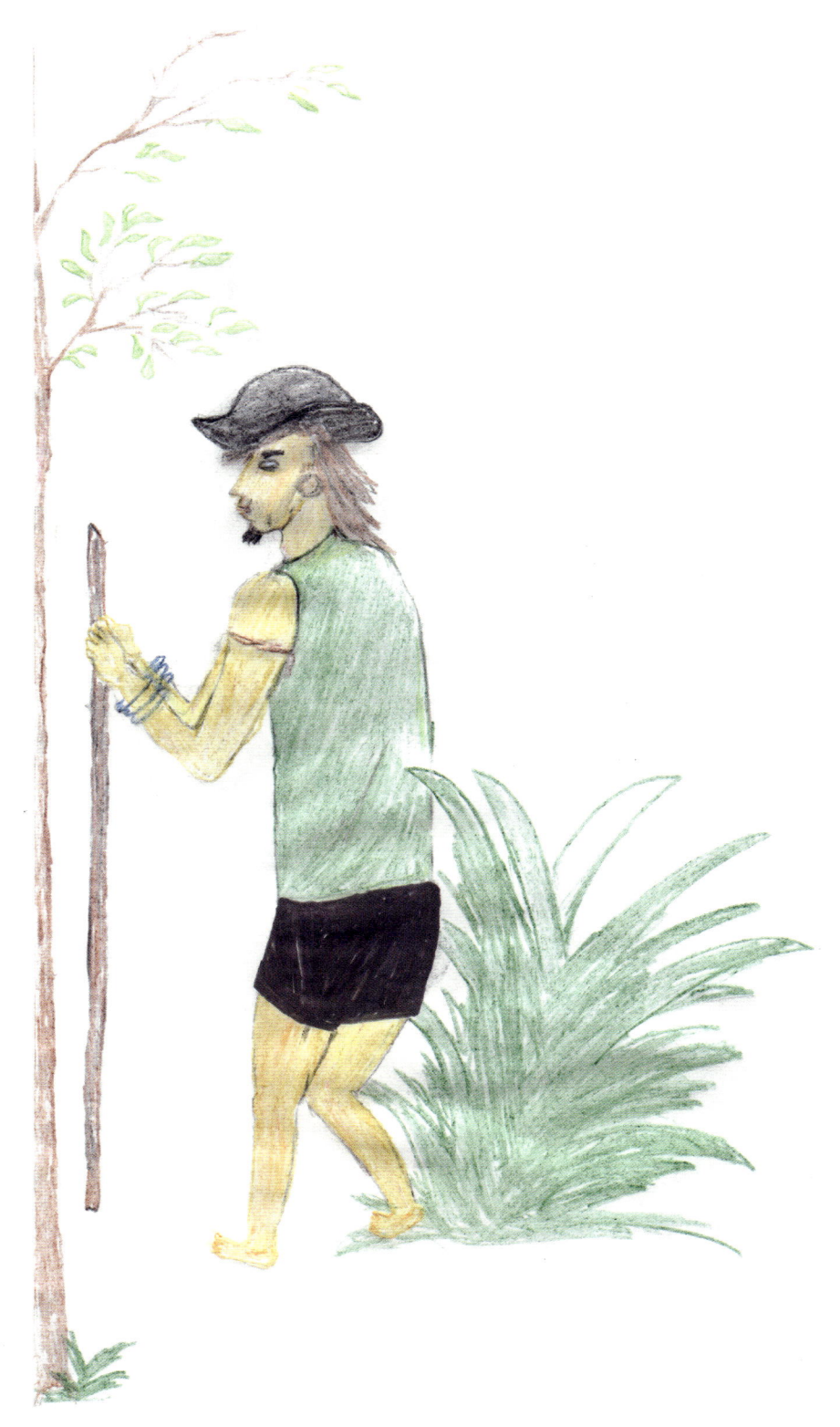

LAST NIGHT I WOKE UP IN THE DARKNESS OF MIDNIGHT. I WANDERED AROUND THE HOUSE LISTENING TO MUSIC, THEN WENT OUTSIDE INTO THE LIGHT OF THE FULL MOON. TWO GUYS APPROACHED ME. THEY ASKED ME WHY I WAS OUTSIDE IN MY UNDERWEAR. 'ARE YOU NOT COLD?' THEY WANTED TO KNOW.

Eyitayo Babatola

MEET TAYO. YOUNG, HAPPY, FULL OF HOPE. HE IS THE FIRST OF HIS SIBLINGS TO GO TO UNIVERSITY. HE CANNOT WAIT TO GET THERE MEET NEW PEOPLE AND AQUIRE MORE KNOWLEGDE. WITH HIS DEGREE IN STATISTICS, HE IS GOING TO HELP HIS COMMUNITY, CITY AND COUNTRY.....

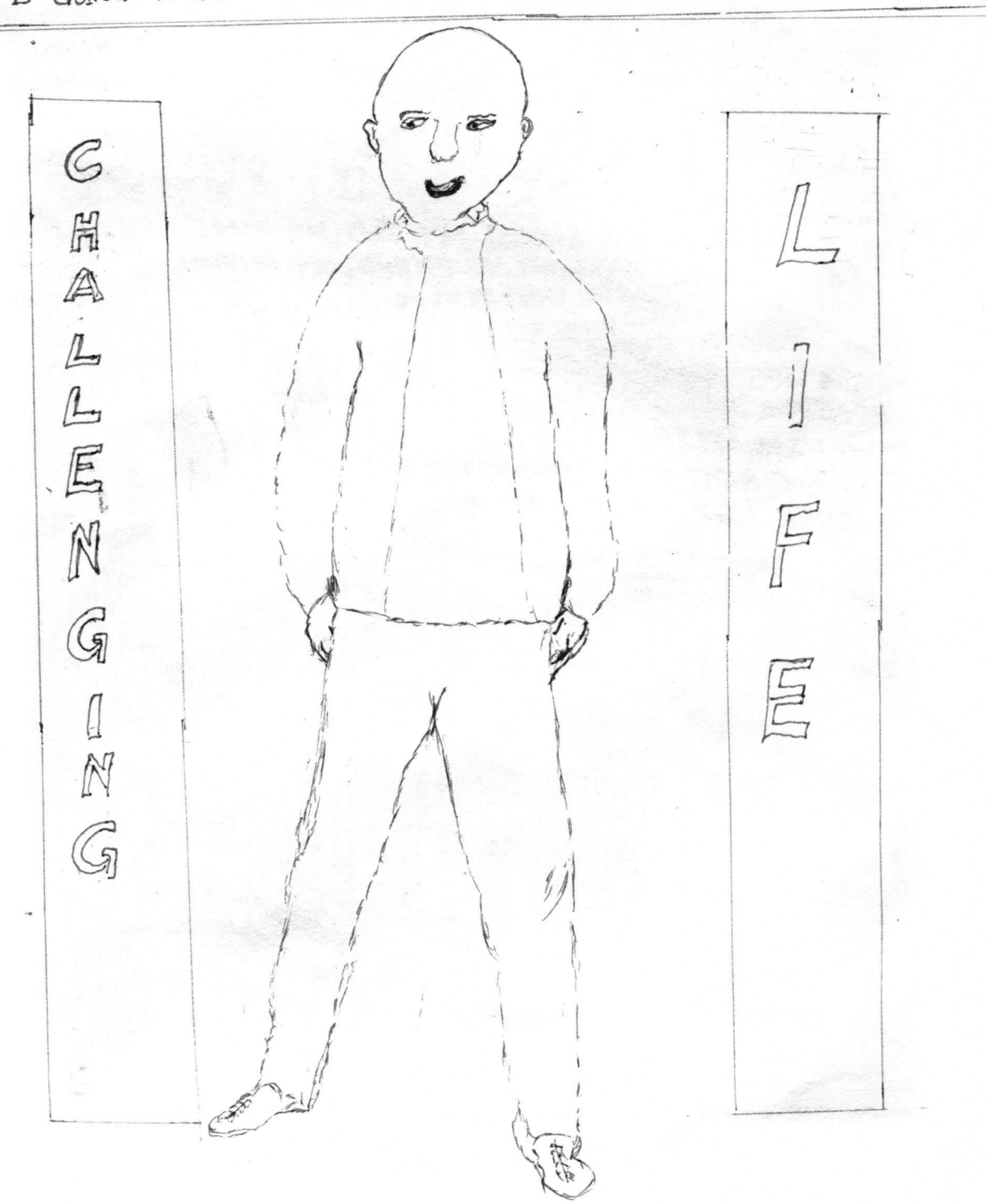

CHALLENGING LIFE

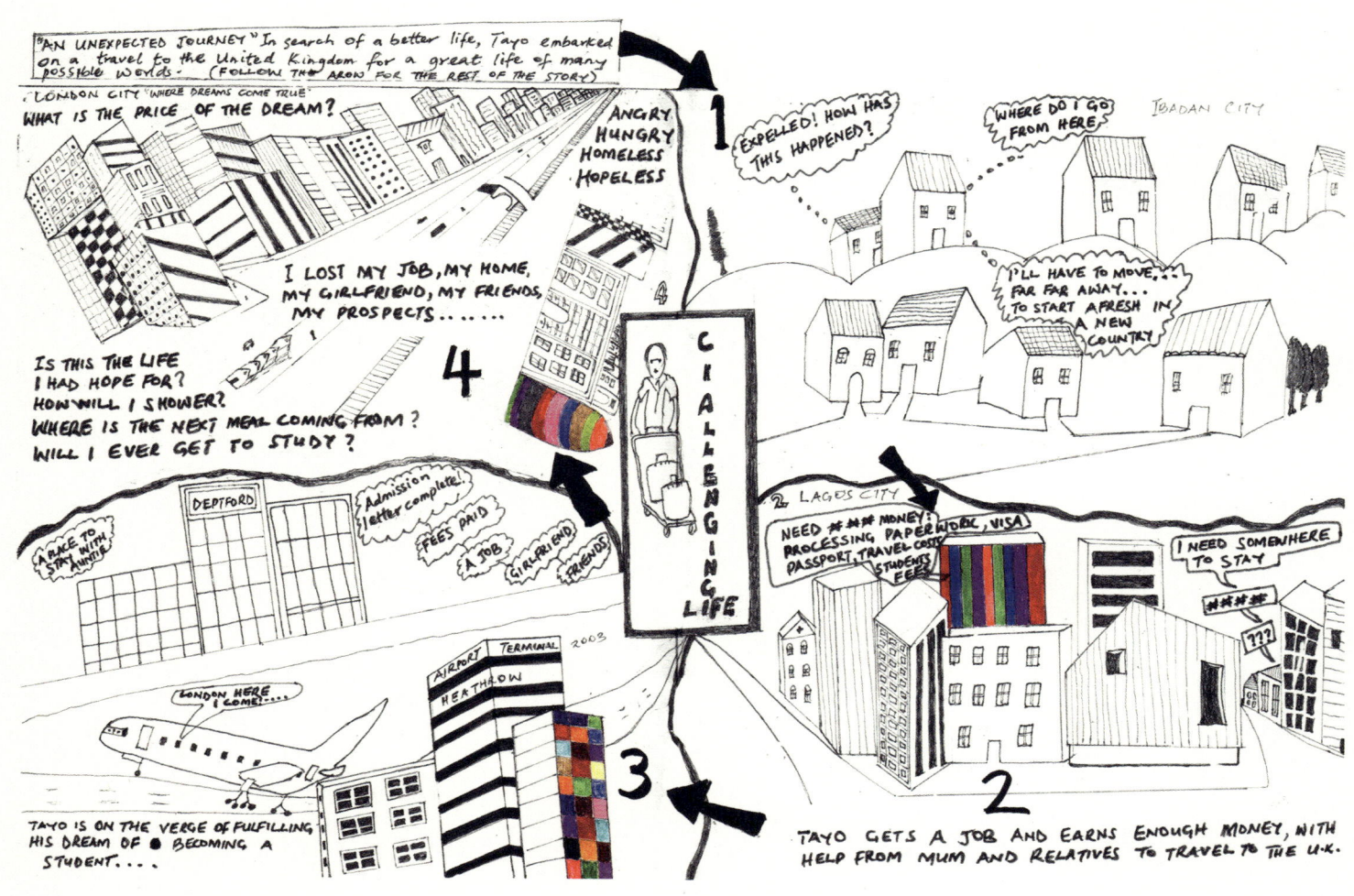

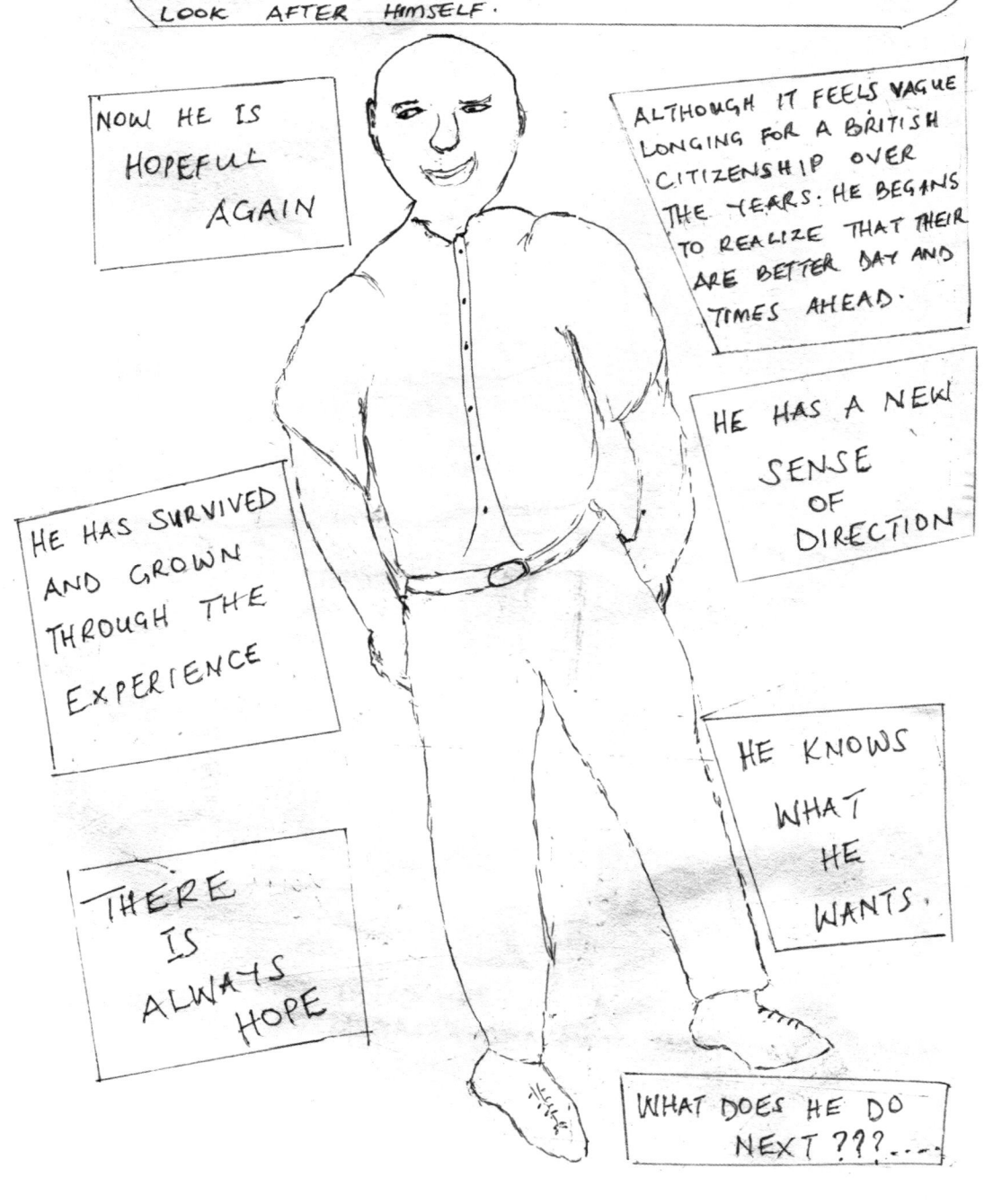

TAYO IS BUILDING HIS LIFE BACK UP AGAIN AFTER HITTING ROCK BOTTOM

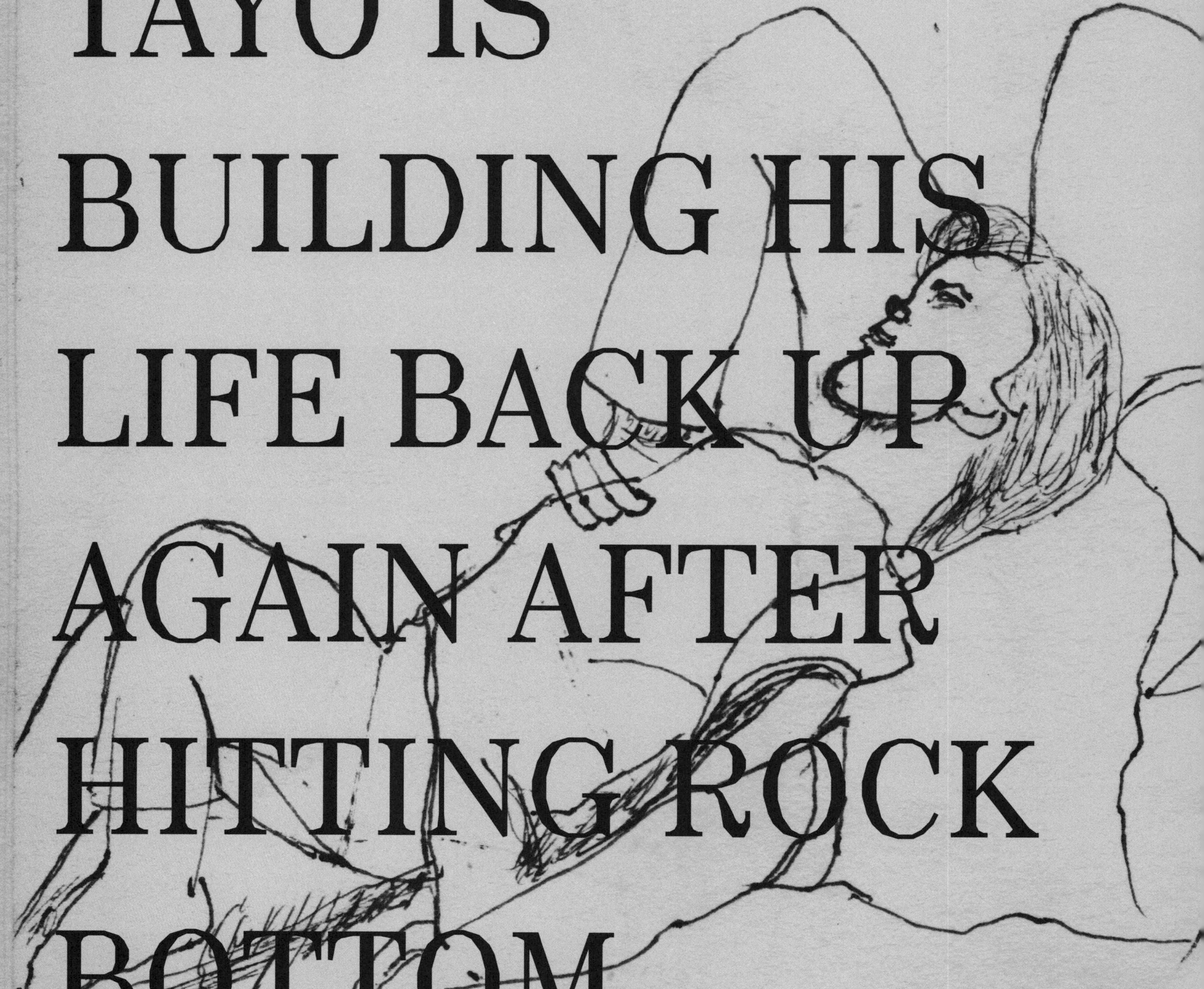

Pg 183

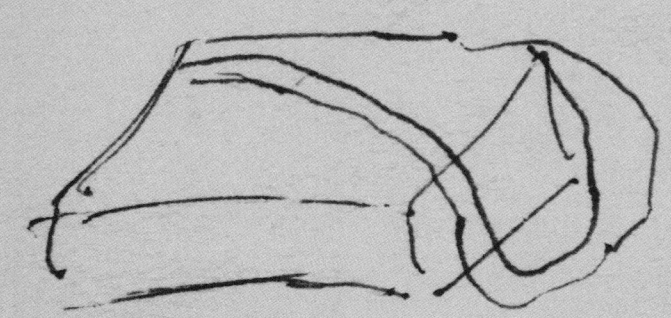

HE FOUND
HELP THROUGH
HOMELESS
AND MIGRANT
CENTRES
RUN BY
VOLUNTEERS.

Farahnaaz Roshan

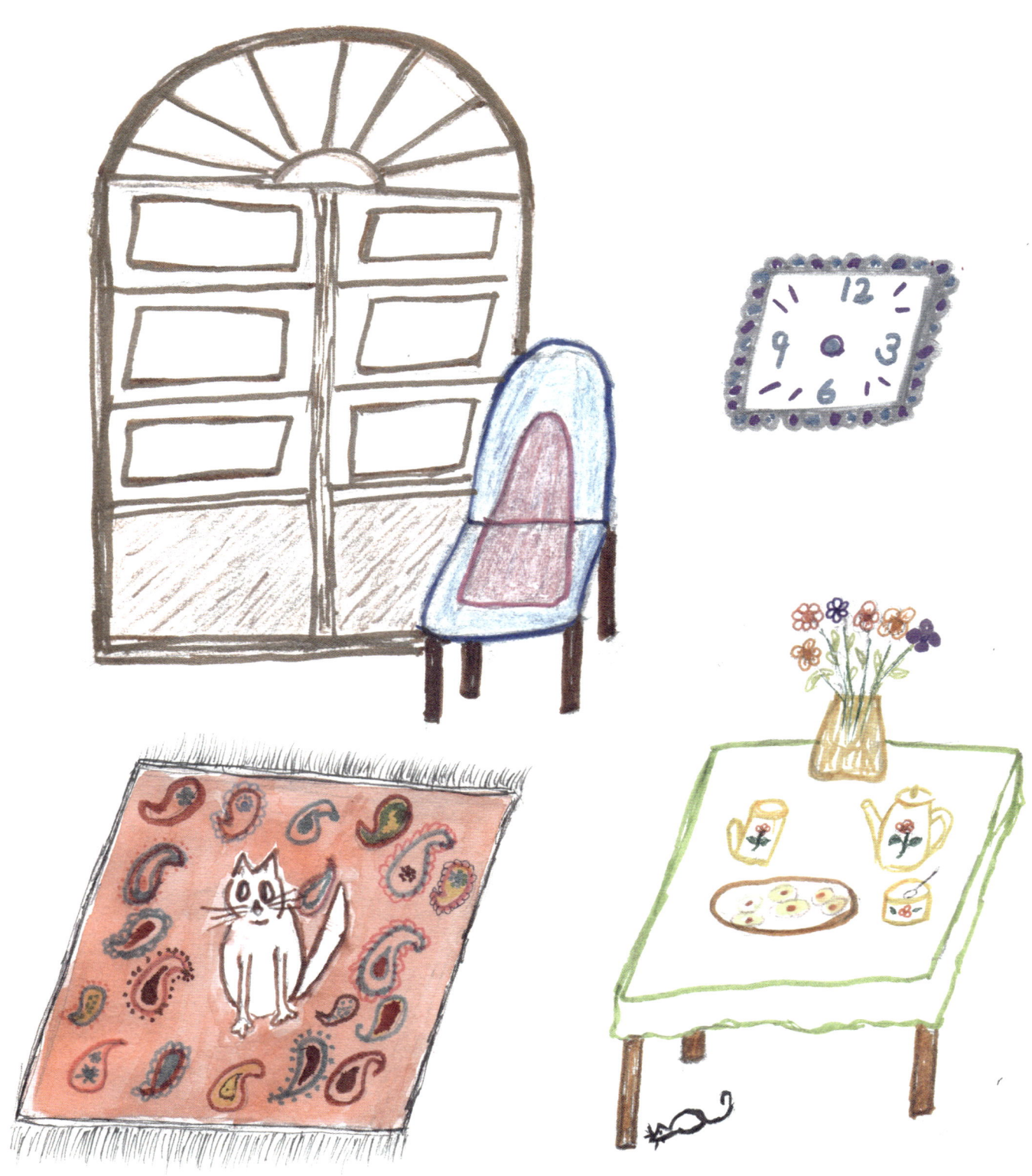

It was after breakfast when Parie's friend told her, 'We would like you stay here with us until you get a job and then a place to live, but as you see this flat is too small for four of us, particularly as my son is just a toddler: he needs more space.'

Parie looked at her with sad eyes and simply nodded her head in silence. She had been hopeful that they might let her stay in their flat for a couple of weeks longer.

After packing her scant possessions, and a sad but very quick goodbye, she left the house.

All day she walked, sometimes sitting on a bench or standing at the corner of the road watching people quietly. It was almost sunset when she ended up in Central London. Victoria Station: overcrowded, so noisy. For a little while, Parie sat on a small wall near the station.

As she sat, watching people, Parie thought about her past: it was saddening and depressing. She tried to visualise the future but could not see any clear bright picture there. Around her, crowds of people, old, young, children, were rushing, walking together, talking together, laughing. Tourists and visitors with their suitcases seemed excited and happy, more than anyone else. So many women, of all ages, dressed formally, smart suits, high-heeled shoes: they caught her eye and held her, fascinated, for a while.

Parie saw herself, an island, isolated in the midst of the huge wave of people who had somewhere to go or something interesting or exciting to do. For her part, she had nowhere to go. Eventually, she went to the information desk in the station and asked about nearby hostels where she might be able to stay the night. The man at the desk was kind, polite. He gave her a couple of addresses of women's hostels that were within walking distance. She chose one and followed the map to find it.

When the lady opened the door, Parie asked, 'Can I stay the night here? I have nowhere to sleep tonight.' The woman let her in, and led her to the desk where she gave her a form to fill in. While Parie was filling in the form she brought out a large transparent plastic bag, sealed across the top. Then she took the form from Parie and looked over it quickly. She told her that any medicines or painkillers should be handed in to the office: whoever was in charge would give them back at the time they should be taken. 'Now go to Room 31: there are two bunk beds in the room: yours is the lower bed on the left hand side.'

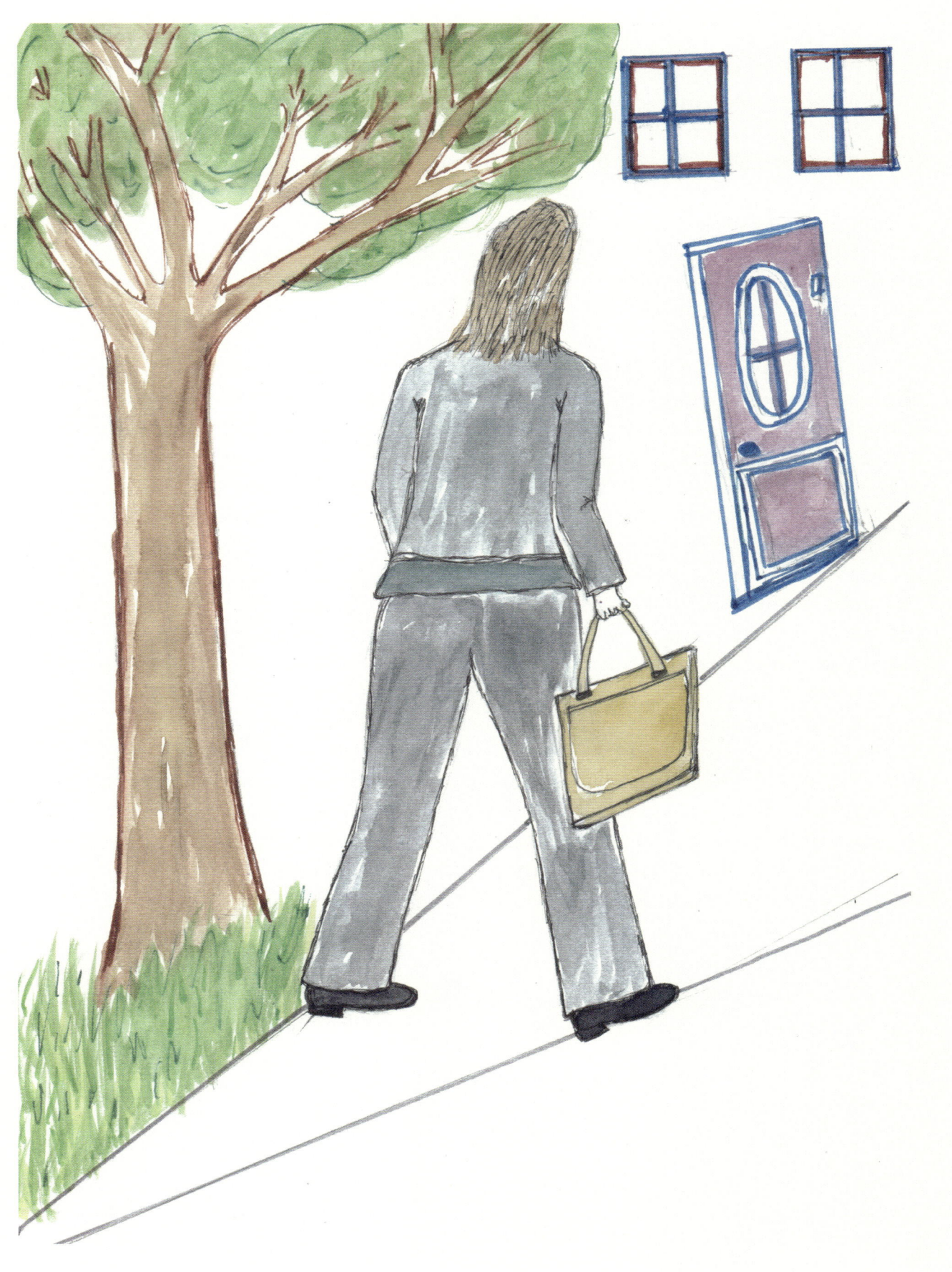

When Parie went up to the room, no-one was there. It was a small room, with bunk beds on each side, a tiny window with no curtain, and a little table with two chairs. She put down her things. In the plastic bag, she found a set of bedding, two towels — one large, one small — a toothbrush, toothpaste, a bar of soap and a small bottle of shampoo.

Then she laid down on her bed. It wasn't too uncomfortable. Parie thought to herself, 'Who slept here last night? Who will sleep here after me? Who knows, or even cares? No-one is thinking of them, let alone keeping a record...'

She tried to sit up, but the space between the two beds was not high enough: her head knocked against the underneath of the bed above. Something tugged at her head: some of her hairs had got caught in the springs. With her fingers, she gently tried to free them, but some of them came out in her hand. She turned her head and saw the hairs, caught there: not just hers, but so many others too. Long hairs dangling down, short hairs twisted up amongst the metal springs. So many different colours: blond, black, brown, even grey.

Here was the record of the women who had slept in this bed. Maybe some stayed for a long time: others, like her, just for one or two nights. Where did these women come from? Where did they go? What were they doing right now?

She looked again, closer, but this time she could not find her own hairs: they were lost amongst the others. So too were those poor lonely women: unseen, lost in the heaving waves of busy life, drawn down into the depths of society until they disappeared. Only this bed, with its springs, has taken a record of them, a keepsake: something to remember them by.

I've always believed that inanimate objects have character: now I'm wondering to myself, do they have feelings too?

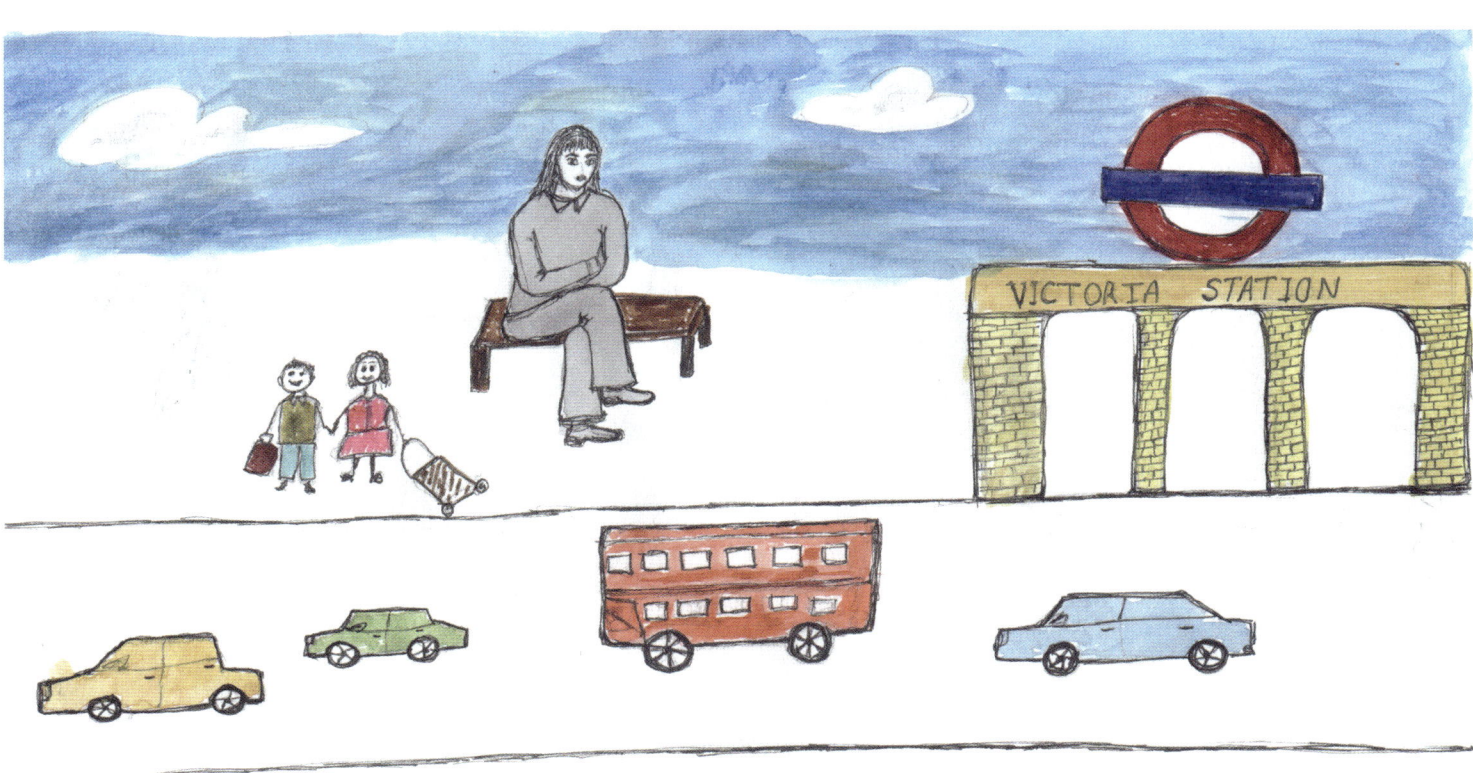

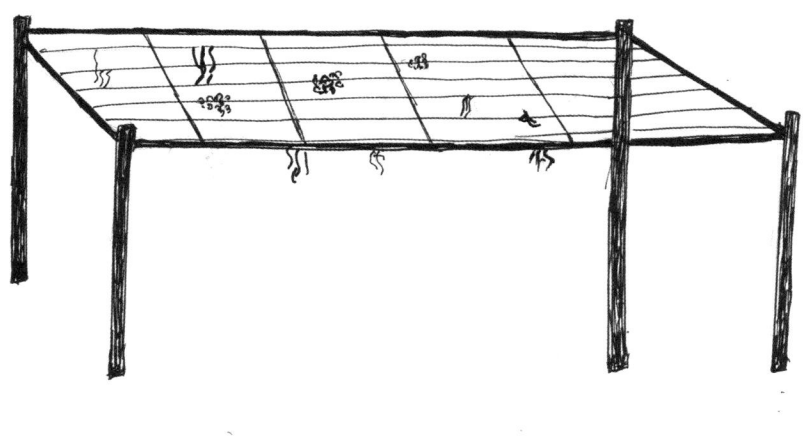

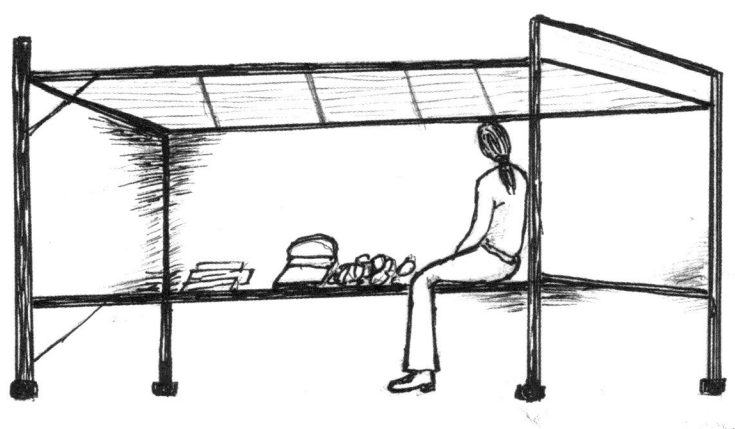

Jade Amoli-Jackson

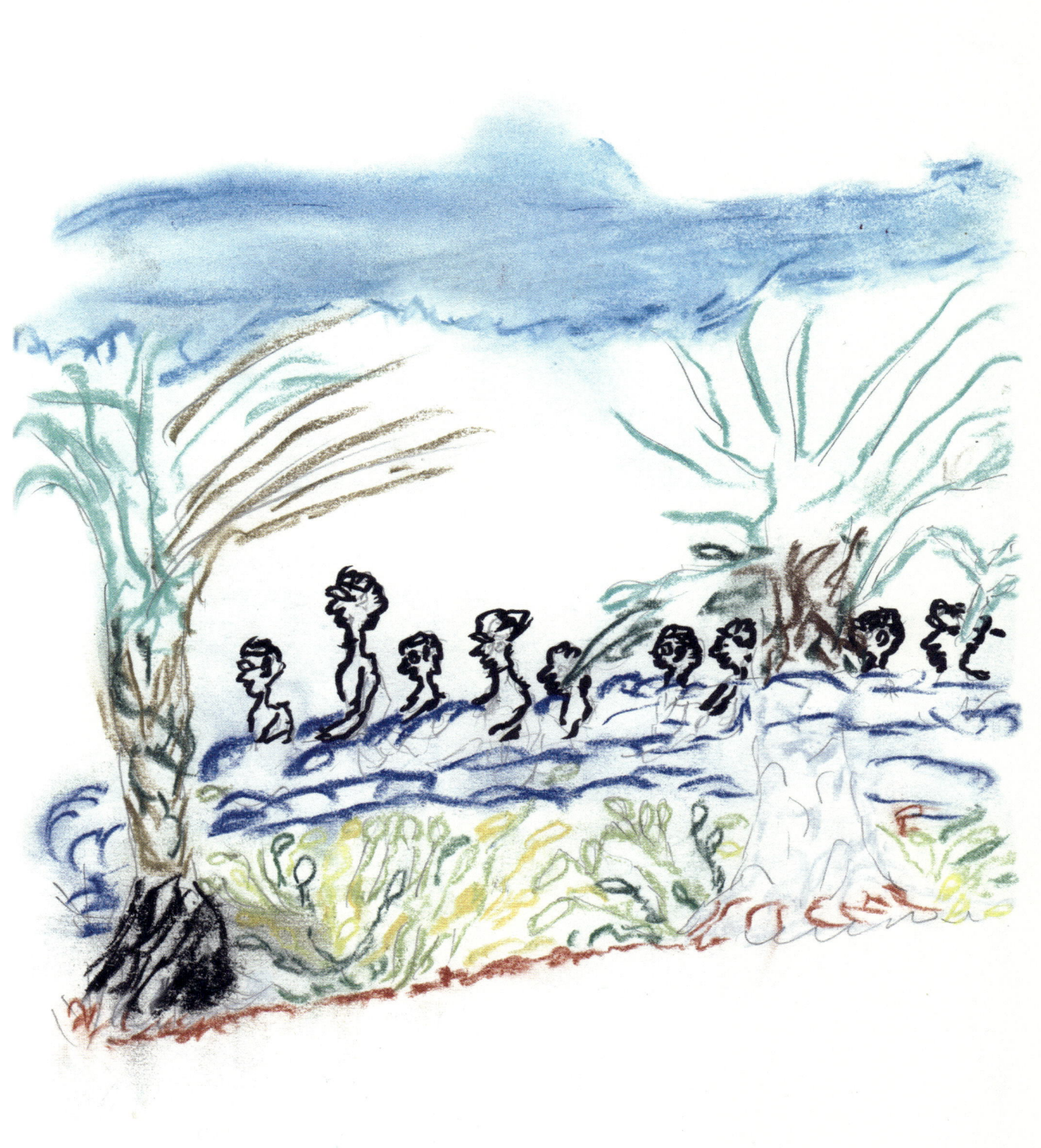

TORTURED BY MY OWN BROTHERS

Growing up, we had it all: a loving mother and father. Our mother came from a very rich family. Our father was a schoolteacher and a farmer: he later became a head teacher and a Reverend. Our mother's elder brother, Uncle Laban, thought riches were everything. Our father was earning his own money from teaching and from his livestock, but it was not enough for our greedy uncle's lifestyle.

One day, when we were very young, Uncle Laban drove to our house when Dad had gone out to get his teacher's salary from the head office. Uncle Laban came and took my mum, my brother, my twin sister and me, to my grandparents' home. We were made to live there, leaving our father alone. We lived with our grandparents until my sister and I were three years old and my brother four and a half years old. One day, our father came and took us back home without our mother. She had been forced to marry a police officer and live in the city. We didn't know where she was.

We really missed our mum and knew that she might never come back to us. Dad was the best dad he could be, even though he was looking after three little children. He provided us with all the good things a parent can give to his children, including love and support.

We lived with our dad until I was five years old before he remarried a woman we nicknamed 'Stepmother from Hell' and 'Wicked Witch' — she deserved those names. When our dad was around or came in the kitchen and talked to us, she would speak gently, all Miss Nice, telling us to eat or wash ourselves. As soon as Dad left to go to the sitting room to mark children's homework, Miss Nice went out through the roof and Evil arrived in a flash.

She treated us like slaves. Though still just small children, we worked from early morning to late at night, we were given very little food, and we were beaten regularly.

During meal times, we were only allowed to take one mouthful of beans each. My twin sister and I would chew for ten minutes to make it last while my stepsisters ate like hungry lions. Our brother used to keep food in his pockets for us whenever he could because he ate with our cousins while the girls ate separately.

On school days we found ways to be happy: we got up very early in the mornings to go and fetch water from Lake Kwania or Lake Victoria. The Lakes were more than five miles from home, so we had to run to and fro making sure we got to school early: we feared punishment for being late. We did our homework at school because our stepmother did not allow us time to do it at home: we were punished if she caught us trying to study. One day she caught us doing our schoolwork and it angered her so much that she threw all our schoolbooks into the pit latrine toilet. That night, we cried ourselves to sleep.

Our father, a head teacher who respected study, decided to let us keep our school books locked up in the cupboard at school.

In the meantime, we continued to work hard around the compound. My twin sister and I cooked ground millet and our brother kept the compound clean. He took the goats, the sheep, and the cattle out to graze. The drinking water was five miles away from home. Luckily we had cousins who helped him with that, otherwise it would have been too hard for a little boy alone.

Our two stepsisters were grown women, but we never had any help from them. We shared a big bed with them, which had been our mother's. I think our dad didn't

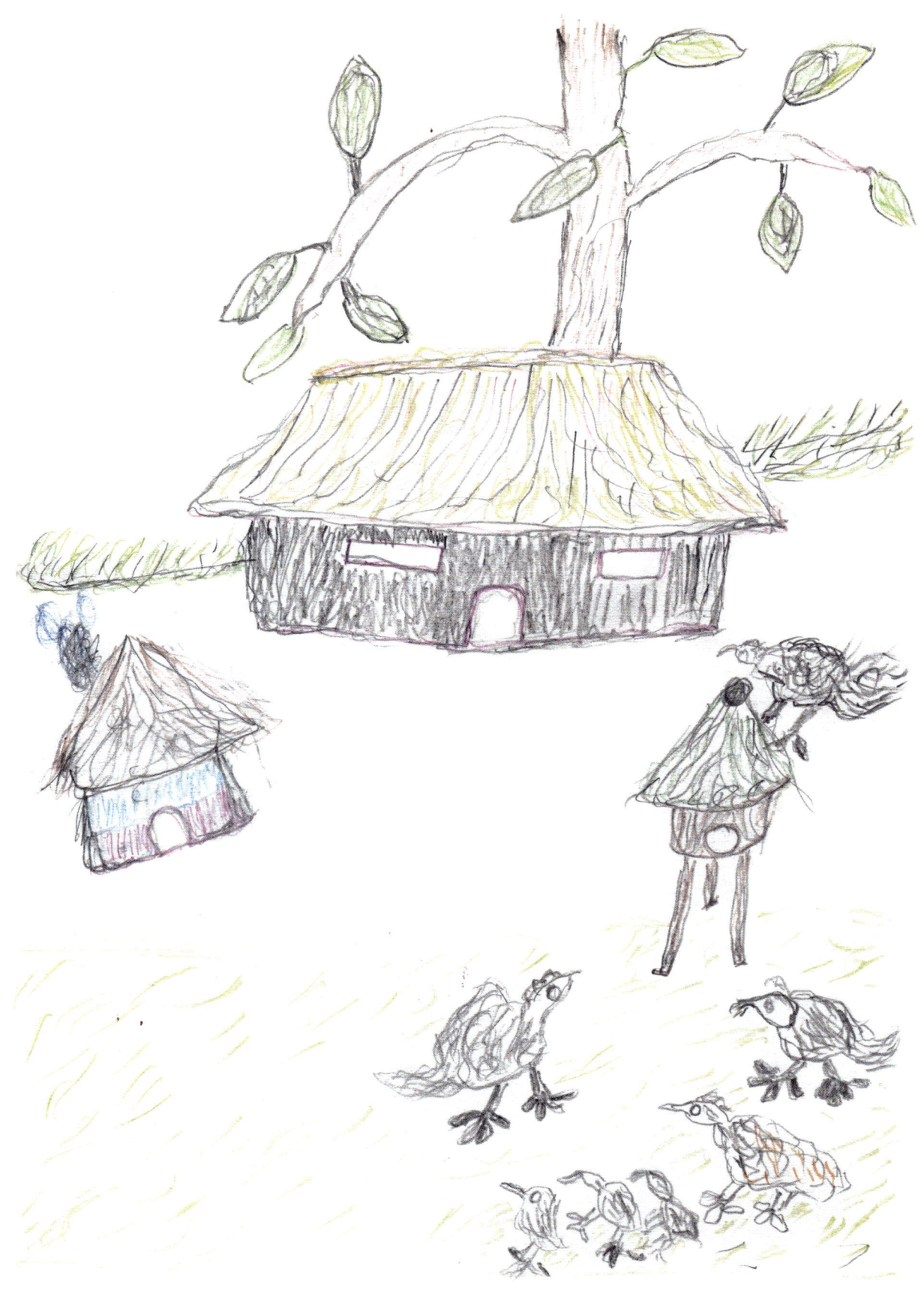

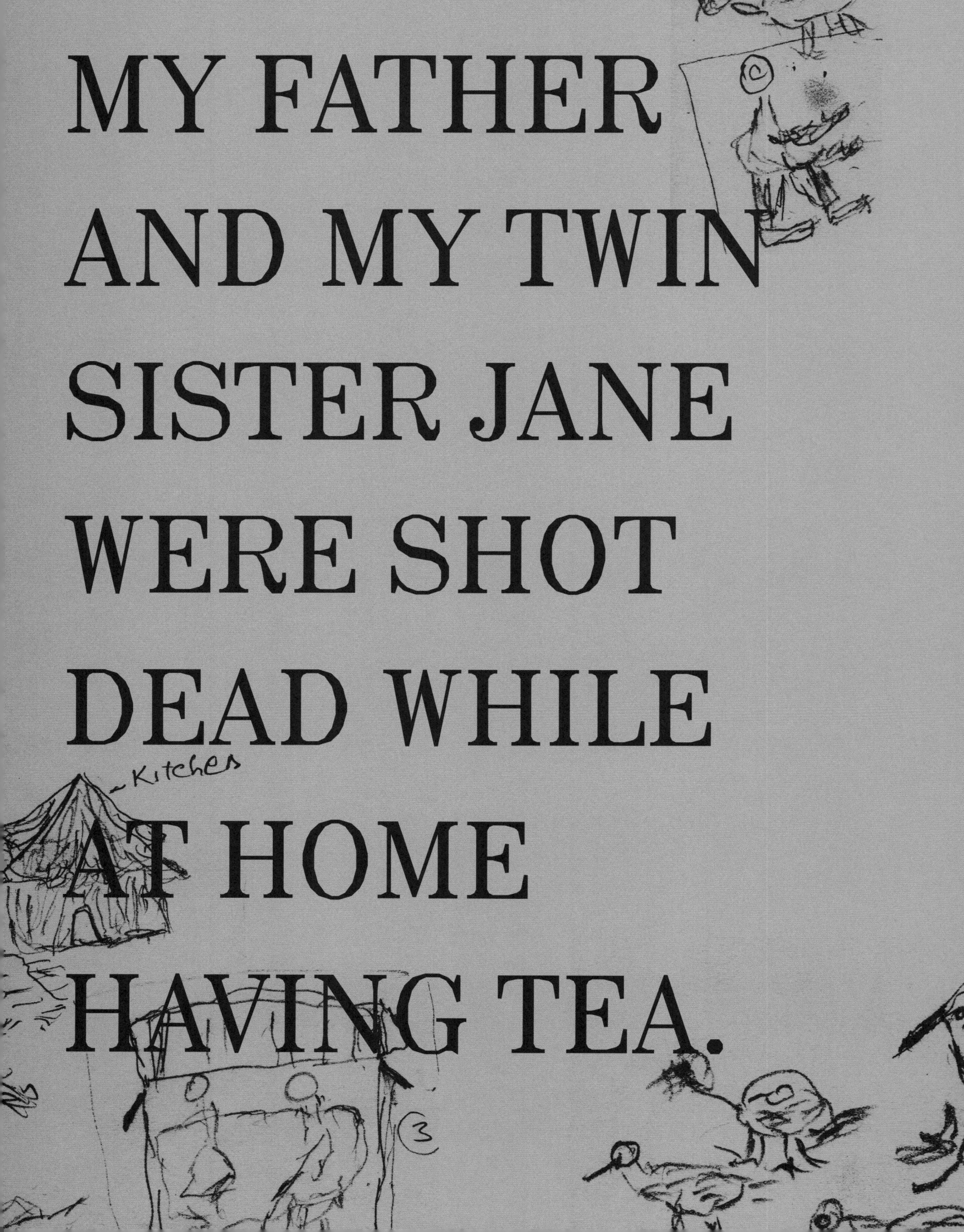

MY FATHER AND MY TWIN SISTER JANE WERE SHOT DEAD WHILE AT HOME HAVING TEA.

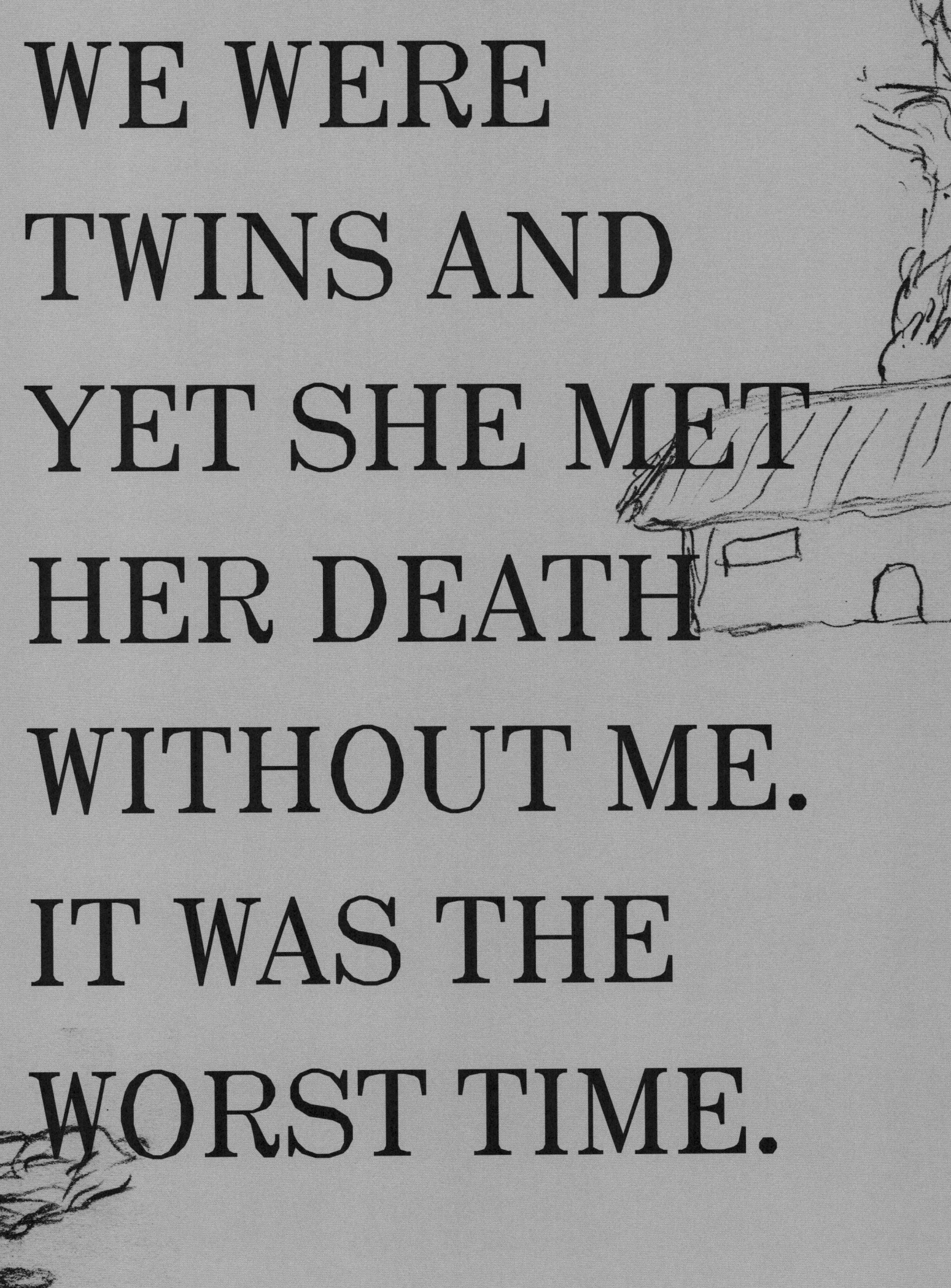

WE WERE TWINS AND YET SHE MET HER DEATH WITHOUT ME. IT WAS THE WORST TIME.

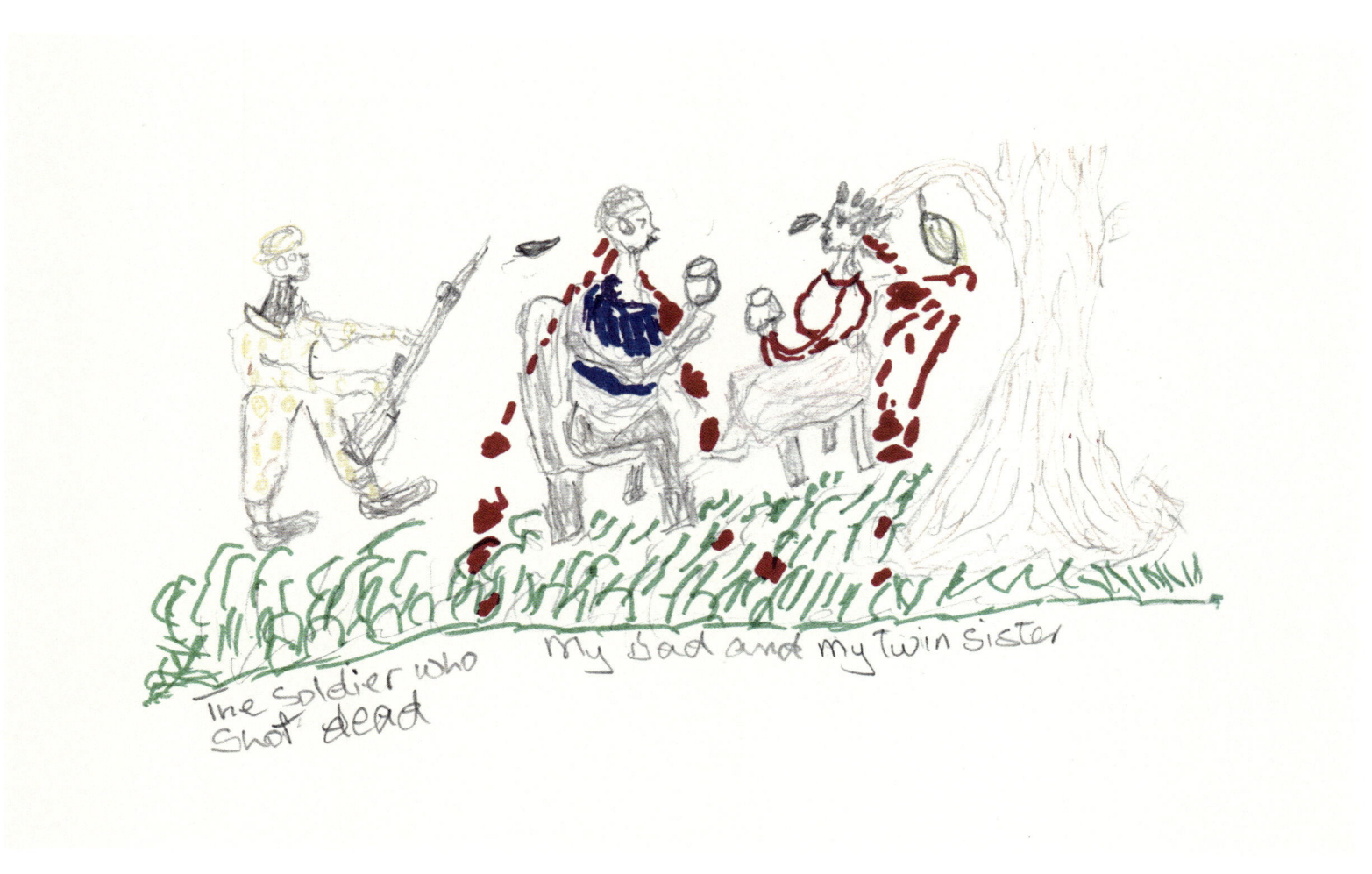

want to share it with our stepmother. My sister and I were forced to sleep on a hard board at the bottom of the bed. Our stepsisters would sleep with their feet on us, kicking and farting — another punishment.

Sometimes it seemed they only knew how to eat and sleep around. Soon, both of them were pregnant and our stepmother, because of shame I think, sent them back to live with their grandmother. We celebrated it quietly, talking with signs. These signs we had invented for the three of us: not even our dad understood.

This life went on until we were eight years old and passed our exam to go to junior school: by then our brother had already left for boarding school. We went to live with Aunty Rebecca, who spoilt us rotten — we were free from our stepmother!

For the first time, we were truly loved and happy, just as we had been with our mother and father before our greedy uncle split us all up. Our uncle Milton became a president and we would go and stay with him and his family from time to time during the holidays. After suffering for so many years, we were at last free. We finished university and got good jobs. My sister was an engineer, I worked in television and radio and our brother worked in agriculture, got married and had children. Even our parents had found each other again and Mum was still wearing Dad's wedding ring after all those years apart.

When my husband refused to join the present government, I gave up my job with the television and radio and we went to live in the town where my husband was born, Gulu. We started many businesses and we had many acres of land. We kept livestock and had over two hundred herds of cattle, plus goats, sheep, chickens and ducks. Life was good and we started a family. I gave birth to a beautiful girl followed by a son and again another son.

But then, everything began to change. My husband refused to work with the soldiers who had taken power illegally and were killing so many people: he was taken to the army barracks and killed.

My father and my twin sister Jane were shot dead, while at home taking tea. Jane had gone to visit Dad and I was supposed to have gone too, but my daughter wasn't well, so she went alone. We were twins, and yet she met her death without me. It was the worst time.

My sister had always been my pillar. If it hadn't been for her children and my kids, I would have committed suicide. I struggled on and my mother was there to give a hand and love, though it was difficult for her too. She was also suffering: she had lost her daughter and our dad, the love of her life.

Back when he was alive, my husband and I had started a group looking after orphans, widows and widowers, who had nothing left. So now I was looking after my own family and these extended families. People's lands had been taken and their homes destroyed by the army so I took them in and helped them. It was not expensive to build huts, so together we built homes for them and they helped around the farm: we were simply a very big family.

One day in April 2001, I had gone to buy things for my shops from the city as we shopkeepers used to. The following day when I was on my way home in the lorry, we were stopped at a road block. A man approached the lorry and told me not to go back home as 'they' would kill me as soon as they saw me. Then he disappeared before I could speak.

I had to walk to the village, which was a good ten miles away from where I was. What had happened to my children? What had happened to everyone in my household? What had happened to our village? I tried to find family and friends, but no one was talking for fear they would be killed.

Very few escaped. Nearly everyone in our town had been killed, everyone in my home was dead, my own children were dead.

One night when the village was quiet, we were rounded up and taken to the bush. I was there for two and half months. We were all tortured and raped: everyone, including the children and the men. They would tell us, 'Today you're coming to my tent': that's where you'd be raped and tortured. We lived in the swamp, which was our bed. We lived on mud: it was our food and drinking water. My friend was raped and her three-month-old girl was raped too. One evening I was looking for her and I found her hanged together with her daughter. The monsters forced us to dig a shallow grave to bury them. We were all skeletal as we were eating only mud. We were heartbroken.

One day a young man told me to go to his tent. I knew what he was going to do with me. I went to his tent, he gave me water to bathe, and then he gave me hot meal. I ate like a dog because I had not eaten food for such a long time. For a moment I forgot that this young man was going to rape me. He gave me a mattress and blanket to sleep on. He told me that I had helped his parents and brothers and sisters cross over to Kenya. That I had not taken any money from them for this. He told me that I had saved their lives. I could not remember a thing because I was so scared: I still thought he was going to rape me. Then he reassured me that he was going to help me get out of there. I was not even listening but he kept his promise. The following morning he said he would take me to pick up fruits and vegetables for lunch. We walked for a long time but as we approached a house, he told me to keep walking and never look back.

I walked to the house and asked for drinking water but no one was willing to talk to me, so I limped on. Within a short time, a man came along on a bike and told me to sit on the bike. I couldn't: I was too fragile. He lifted me and put me on the bike and gave me water. I drank like a cow because I was so thirsty. He took me to a friend's house where they brought a doctor to treat me as I had wounds all over my body and was so underweight. They thought I would not make it. I did, though. I made it because I was with humans again. Not those monsters: animals were better and kinder than they were.

When I recovered a little, they drove me to Kenya. I lost consciousness as I was still very sick. When I woke up, I saw a white man and thought that I was dreaming and I dived back under the duvet. He was talking to me very gently and so I looked at him and he told me that his name was John and that I would be well looked after by him and his girlfriend Juliet. When Juliet came into the room, I saw that she was black and I almost took off: if I had had the strength I would have, because she brought back all the bad memories of my black torturers and I did not know that I was in London.

John and Juliet looked after me for two weeks before taking me to Croydon Lunar House to claim asylum as it was illegal to stay without letting the authorities know. I made my claim and they treated me like a human being again. I am so grateful to all the British people: above all to Juliet and John for taking me in.

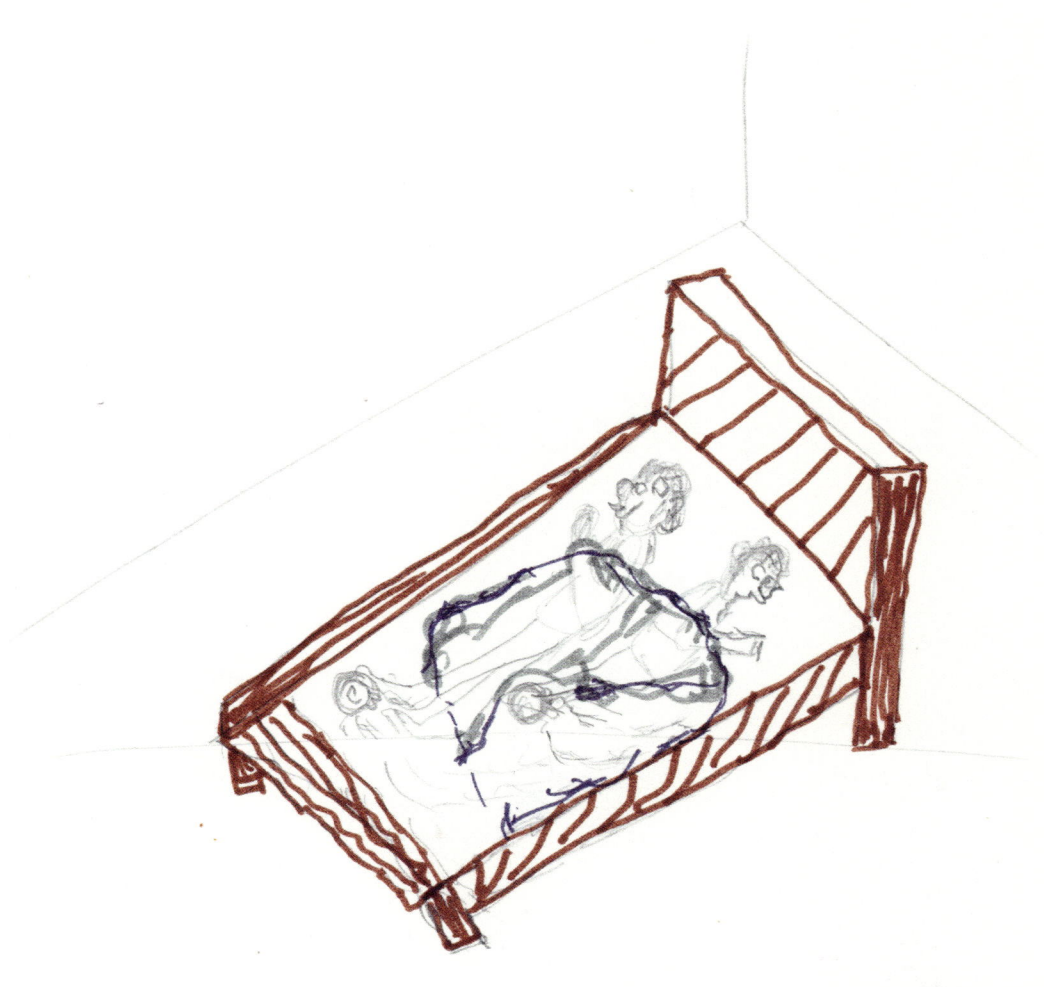

Lida Mansourian

MY NAME IS LIDA. I AM A 58-YEAR-OLD WOMAN FROM IRAN. I HAD TO LEAVE MY COUNTRY ILLEGALLY AS AN IRANIAN POLITICAL PRISONER WITH MY TWO CHILDREN: MY DAUGHTER AGED NINE MONTHS OLD AND MY SON AGED TWENTY TWO MONTHS. 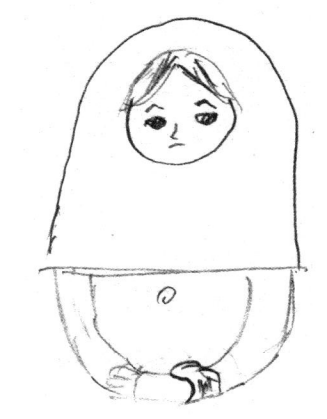 THE SEARINGLY DANGEROUS JOURNEY WE HAD TO UNDERTAKE WAS 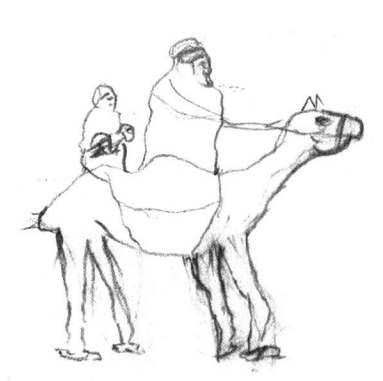 VIA IRAN'S BORDER CITY, ZAHIDAN, TO AFGHANISTAN TO THE FIRST SAFE CITY IN PAKISTAN AND ITS U.N. OFFICE. MY THREE DRAWINGS TELL THE STORY OF THE THREE DAYS OF OUR JOURNEY.

1

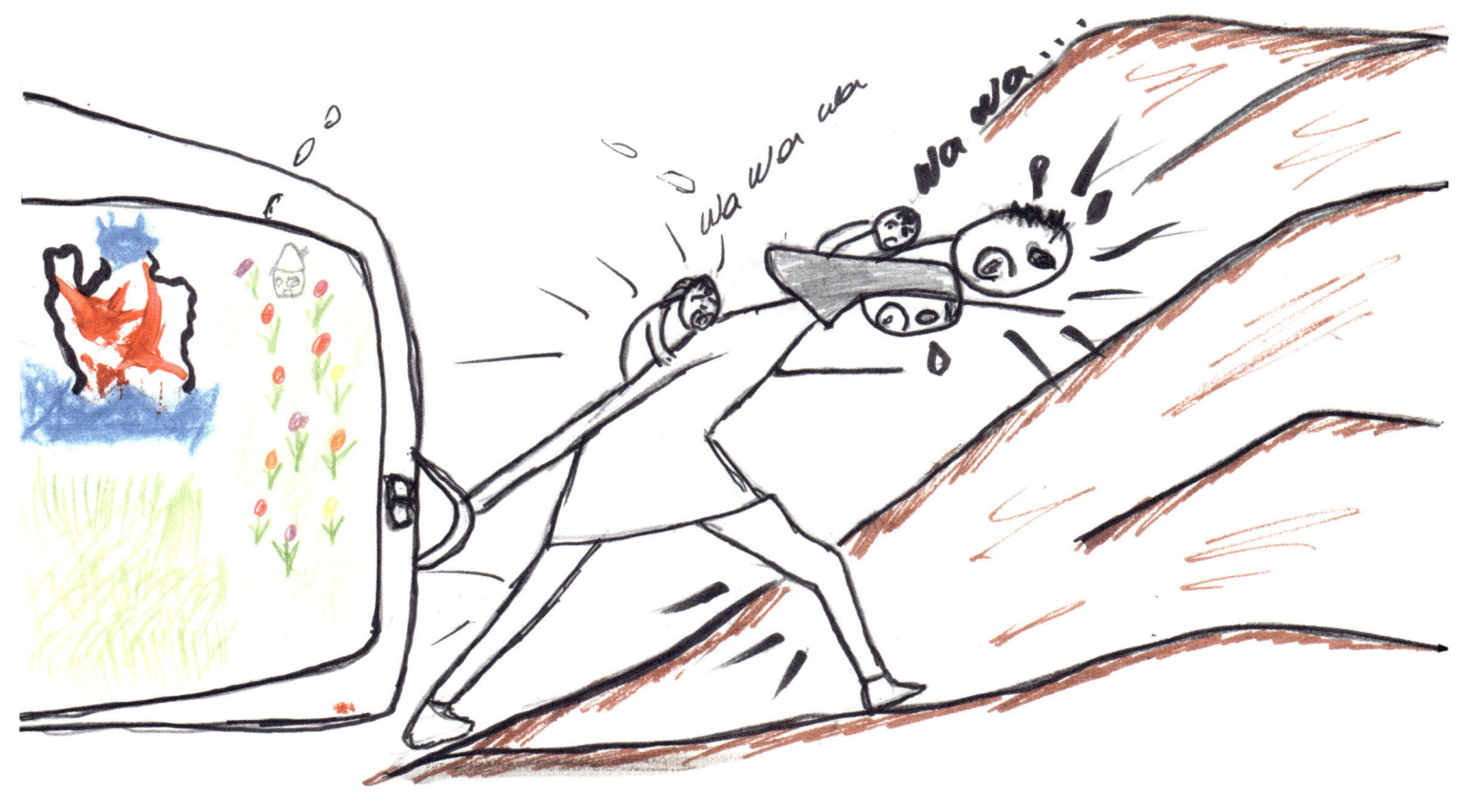

ESCAPING FROM IRAN. PULLING MY MEMORIES, GOOD AND BAD, INTO AN UNKNOWN FUTURE

2

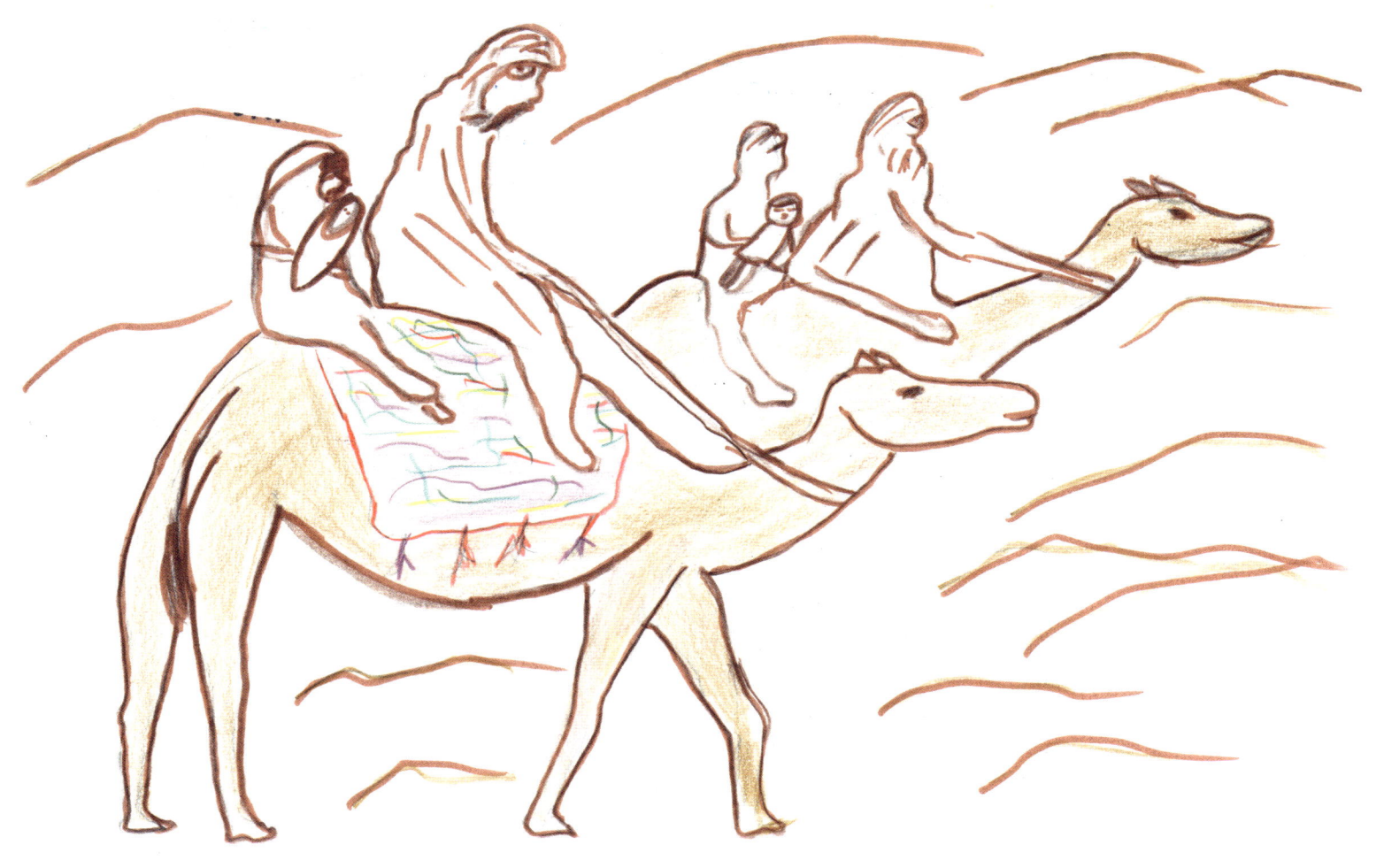

WE HAD TO TRAVEL AT NIGHT BECAUSE IT WAS TOO RISKY AND DANGEROUS DURING THE DAY

3

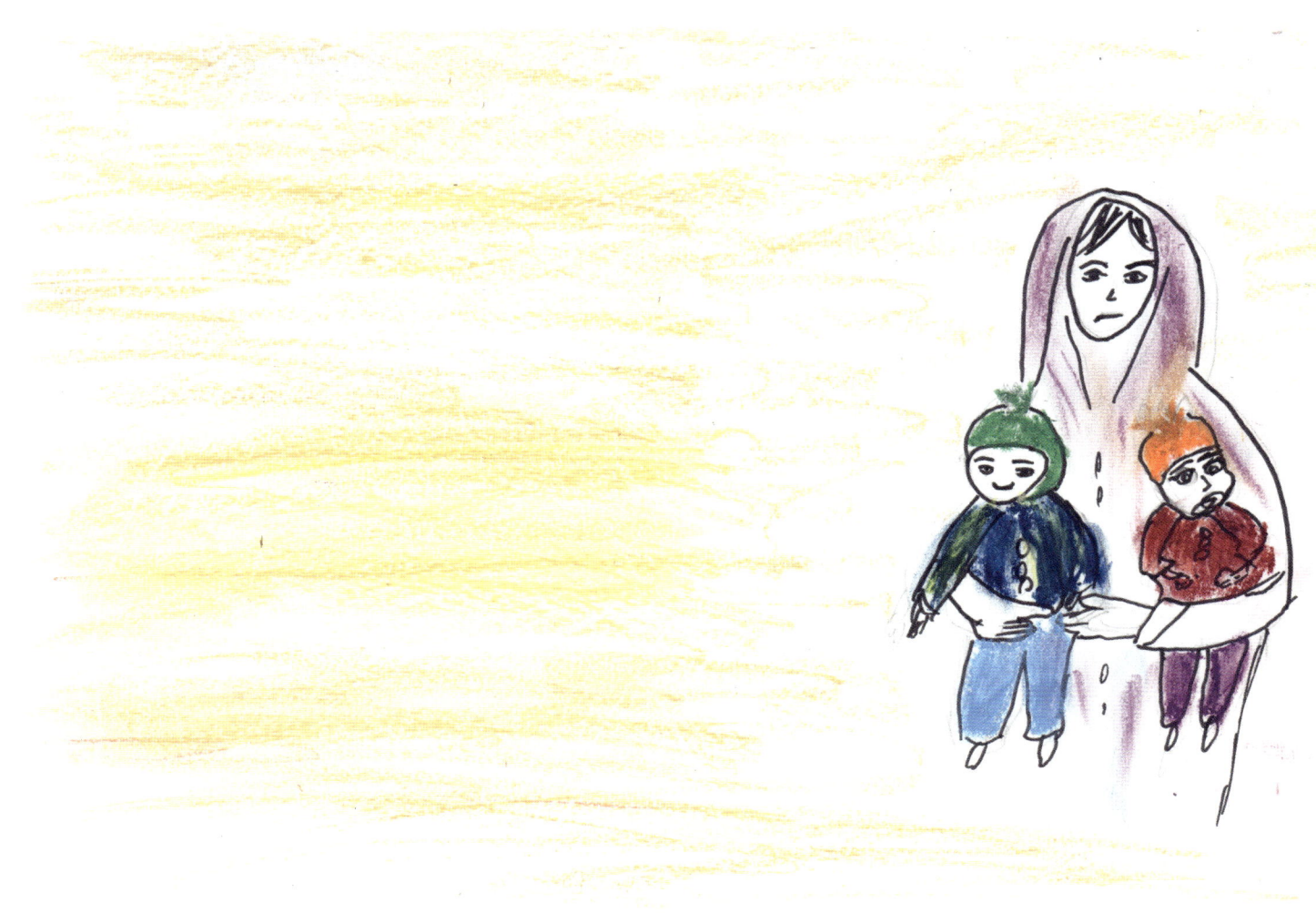

THE ROAD FOR A REFUGEE IS AS LONG AS YOU MAKE IT

Luke Smith

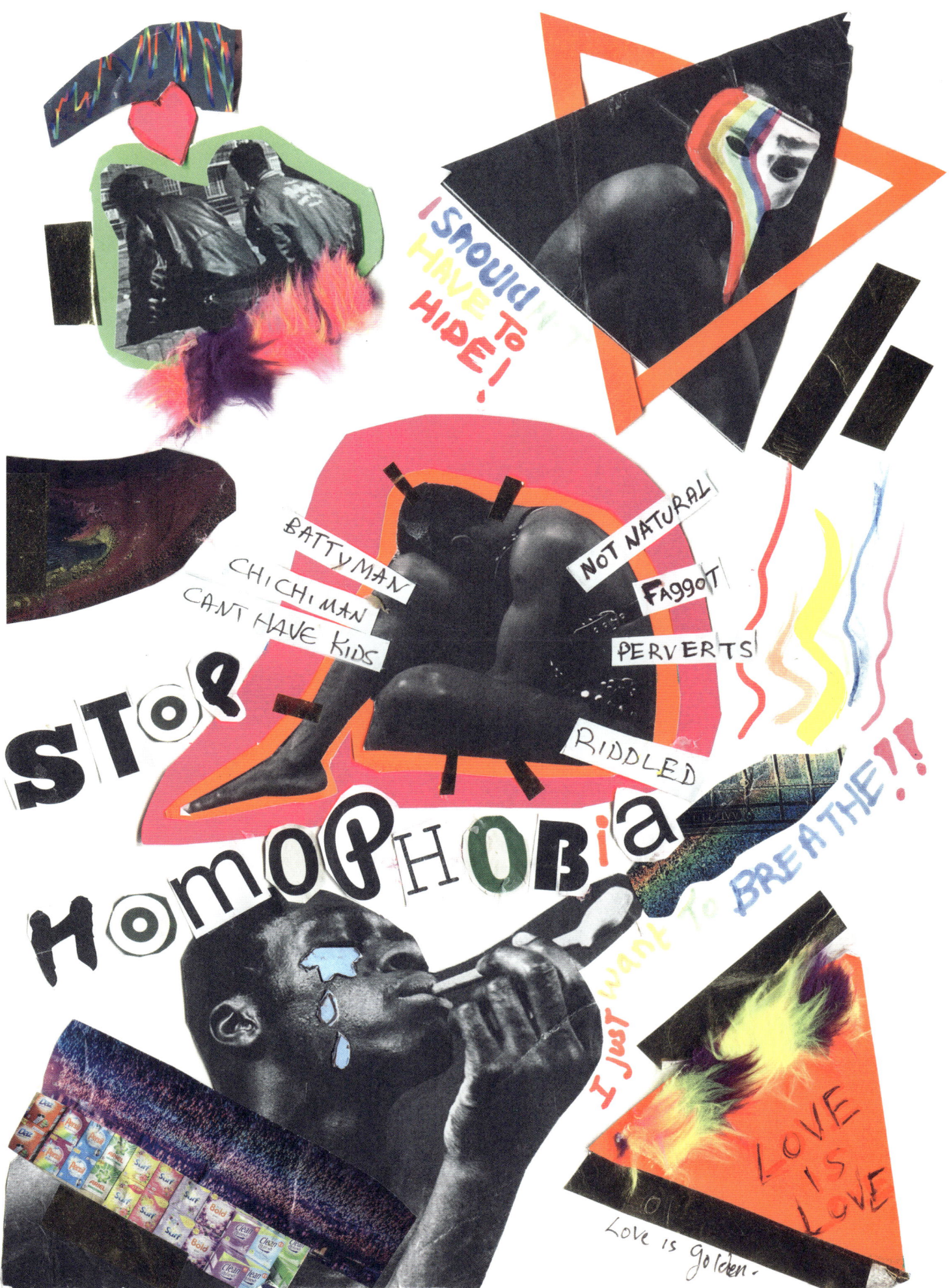

THE LOOPY LIFE OF LUKE IN LONDON

I lived in a small seaside town, where nothing happens. Just fields of greenery, and water. Yes, for most people it's nice but for me, well, I felt out of place. Especially since throughout school I was constantly bullied for being flamboyant. And more OTT than everyone else, with my crazy hair colour choices and daring outfits. It was clear this town wasn't for me.

Growing up I always loved music, fashion, and anything relating to the arts. I had an interest for the camera, and I have been singing for as long as I can remember. But growing up in a town where everyone lived under a rock and never set foot outside the village, I always wondered how I could ever pursue all these things, especially as my confidence had been totally knocked over the years.

As I got older the verbal abuse from other people got worse: it was about my sexuality, about the way I dressed and presented myself. I felt I couldn't tell anyone as I felt judged by nearly everyone.

The only people I could rely on were my mum and dad, who, luckily, were great about the way I was. However, I didn't want to worry them. So I would cover up my bruises and carry on as normal.

As I got into my twenties the village never changed. Opinions never changed. Everything was always the same. Then I was attacked. Outside my mum's house.

After broken ribs and black eyes, and absolutely no cooperation from the police, I knew I needed to leave. I knew I needed to chase my dreams, and socialise with people that understood me. But how was that going to happen? So many questions on my mind.

And then, out of nowhere an old family member who I hadn't spoken to in years gave me a chance to move to the big city. It was like all my dreams coming true at once.

So I packed up and headed to the big city. I was scared and nervous as I'd always lived with my parents until then. And I was sad to leave them. But they knew and I knew that this was exactly what I needed. I don't think I could have expected what was going to happen over the coming years.

As I settled in and started to make friends, I began planning — what auditions was I going to do, what creative industry was I going to get into? I was in the city — the world was my oyster! I landed a job in a gay bar. It was crazy to me: I had never seen so many people like me all in one room.

Although I was a fish out of water, I mingled and made more friends. It was the first time I had found people that got me, that understood me. However as I started going out more and more things became slightly cloudy.

I got myself a job in retail during the day and a job in a nightclub in the evenings. This nightclub opened pretty much all weekend, and eventually it took a toll on me.

As months went by I found myself at random parties. I hardly had any sleep from one day to the next. The people around me I thought were part of a community. And whilst I never did think that it would be all rainbows and unicorns, somehow I never imagined that it would get really messy.

I couldn't have been more wrong.

As days and nights blurred, my perceptions of everyone and everything grew fuzzy: my dreams and ambitions got pushed to the back of my mind.

I had to move out of the house I was living in: the daughter of the woman who owned it needed to move back in. That's when things started to spiral out of control. I wasn't ready to leave and move back home – London was my home now, wasn't it?

As the months went on, I ended up staying on people's sofas, rough sleeping around London. I wasn't giving up. However my choices during this time were not the right ones.

Then I met someone. An older guy. I'd never been in a serious relationship, or even met many people like me in my town. It was fun for a while. I felt like I was escaping, but I was just making more bad choices.

After a few months of dating and sleepless nights, I could tell the guy had some issues, especially with his sexuality. I knew how it felt to be isolated so I wanted to try and help. That's when he decided to take it out on me. I was being attacked again, and this time by someone I liked.

Luckily things ended with the man I was dating, however I was still not in the right frame of mind. I shaved off all my hair and felt I needed to start again. Obviously my mind wasn't all there: I was still sofa surfing and still trying to survive the tough life of the London scene. Not really knowing which people were my friends or who was really there for me. I had to try and be strong and continue with my original plans.

I didn't know then how vulnerable I was, especially after everything that had happened. Then, unusually, I met someone new. Charming, handsome, manly: I thought this was the one to protect me. I felt like I was falling in love for the very first time. I thought this was a new start. Wrong again.

The first few months were great, at least I thought so at the time. Nights of walking around the streets because we had nowhere to go. I wasn't allowed at his because he hadn't yet come out of the closet to his family, so we would go to parties all night, stay on people's sofas… It was a really unhealthy situation and I was oblivious at the time.

I had completely forgotten about my hopes and dreams, and instead focused on moving closer to the person who I thought was 'The One'. I had never met anyone that was so nice to me and someone who I thought understood me.

However, I started to notice friends turning into enemies. He had put it in my head that I couldn't trust these people. And to be honest no one had given me any good reason to trust them.

About a year passed and things started to change. After sofa surfing, walking the streets for many nights, losing near enough everyone I knew, things started unravelling about the guy I thought was my saviour. Things like him lying about his name, me discovering he had been to prison.

I wasn't one to judge: I know everyone has some sort of past, but unfortunately – due to either my stupidity, trust or naivety – this was just the beginning.

We started living together and this was when things got really nasty. I ended up having no money and had to rely on him. I wasn't allowed to see any of my friends then the abuse started happening. He controlled when I left the house and where I was going. I had no one to tell as he smashed all of my phones.

I was so angry with myself. What had happened to me? What had happened to the fun, loud, eccentric, happy Luke that once was?

In any domestic relationship, you always think they will change. He didn't change. It just got worse. Knowing full well what happened to me in previous years still didn't stop this monster from doing the things he did. From the moment I first fell in love he had me right where he wanted me. I was locked in a room for days and I would wake up to being strangled, having belts whacked across my legs. I was repeatedly told no one liked me because I was gay, that my family and friends didn't care or they would be there with me.

I started to believe all this.

Time went by and we began to fight, daily, on the street, on the train. There would be blood, bruises and scratches. I hated myself and the person I had become.

Then one morning I was staying at his parents' house. I went downstairs to make a coffee and I was shaken by my partner and his brother fighting.

Then out of nowhere I hear 'I'm going to cut your boyfriend' and a big kitchen knife plunged into my leg. I didn't notice at first, but my leg was stiff. I walked out into the garden, looked down and I was soaked in blood. I ran out of the house, down the road and collapsed. An old man and lady saw me and brought me to their house, wrapping a blanket around me.

The police and ambulance came. All I kept saying was 'I am not dying, not here and not in this outfit!', to which the police called me a tart. Even in the worst situation I was still trying to be funny and keep my spirits about me.

I was rushed to Whitechapel hospital where they deal with stabbings. I had twelve stitches in my leg and they put me in a wheelchair. The brother was arrested as they found him hiding in someone's garden a few streets away from his house. However I was too scared to pursue charges. Even after this I stayed with my partner: I felt bad for him. After all, it was his brother who had stabbed me, not him. A friend, the only one I could talk to when I got a chance, told me I needed to leave him or I'd end up dead or in prison.

Time went by, and months passed, with me on crutches. I finally plucked up the courage to leave him. I couldn't have been prouder.

However the emotional damage it had done had taken a toll on me.

I moved into a hostel not far from him, where I made some friends and tried to get over the damage. For months and months via text and phone calls I was still getting abuse from my ex-partner: he was even getting people to follow me in shops. It was hell!

And then suddenly it all stopped!

I knew something had happened… that's when I saw he had been put behind bars, yet again! Although I was scared, it was a huge relief.

I moved into a house share which turned out to be totally unsafe. I ended up being attacked again due to my sexuality. People used my name to get cabs out. And I would pee in bottles in my room so I didn't have to leave the bedroom. The police were useless. I kept thinking, how did it come to this?

One day I came home and the whole house was smashed to pieces — everyone had left.

I moved back into my mum and dad's but I wasn't ready to give up on the city just yet. I hadn't done anything I had gone there for. Instead I had just partied, got caught up with the wrong crowd and fallen in love with the devil.

I got help from domestic violence refuge organisations that support LGBT people as it wasn't really spoken about back then. I took the opportunity to move back to London, and after trying different hostels, I moved into one named Evolve.

And now things started to change for the better. I got involved with different projects. I worked on radio at the Brit School, and won an award. Then I found a leaflet for a photography course and decided to give it a go. I remember turning up to the Strand and meeting Marice from Accumulate. There were so many people there from different backgrounds, with different struggles. And everyone was here to get into creative arts. It was just what I needed

Weeks went by and I dedicated myself and stayed focused on the photography course. Our final exhibition show was in a gallery in The Guardian building in Kings Cross. My work was there on display — it was such a great moment for me and I never thought it would happen.

Then they announced I had won a scholarship to study at Ravensbourne University London.

I couldn't believe it. All this hard work and passion had paid off. I had never been to Uni or even thought about it due to my grades being so bad in school from the amount of bullying I experienced. So I finally felt like the bullies had not won after all. I felt appreciated and had the opportunity to show people my talent.

I've always wanted to be on TV and have always been into the creative arts, so when we got the chance to appear on Good Morning Britain it was just amazing. We appeared on London Live (twice!) and ITV, to talk about our struggles and show that there is a silver lining if you just focus on your dreams and work hard.

I lasted in university way longer than I ever thought I would, although I didn't pass my degree due to my mental health and issues that I've never actually overcome. But I've done so much that I've always wanted to do, and found creative friends and workshops that have been just amazing.

I am now a member of Crisis and am involved on the creative side, like producing the brochure. I've also made a documentary film about my experiences. I support people from the LGBT community who are fighting for a roof over their heads, but may not have been taken seriously due to their sexuality.

Accumulate really helped me gain my confidence back, helped me regain my creativity and feel appreciated. I've got to see places I never would have, experience different things and really learn about the true nature of creativity and art — all the reasons I moved to the city in the first place. Working at Somerset house, and having an exhibition at a London art gallery are things I never thought would happen. And I can say it's great to know I can help other people along the way.

I'm not sure what my next chapter is, but I feel like this could be just the beginning...

Mitchell Ceney

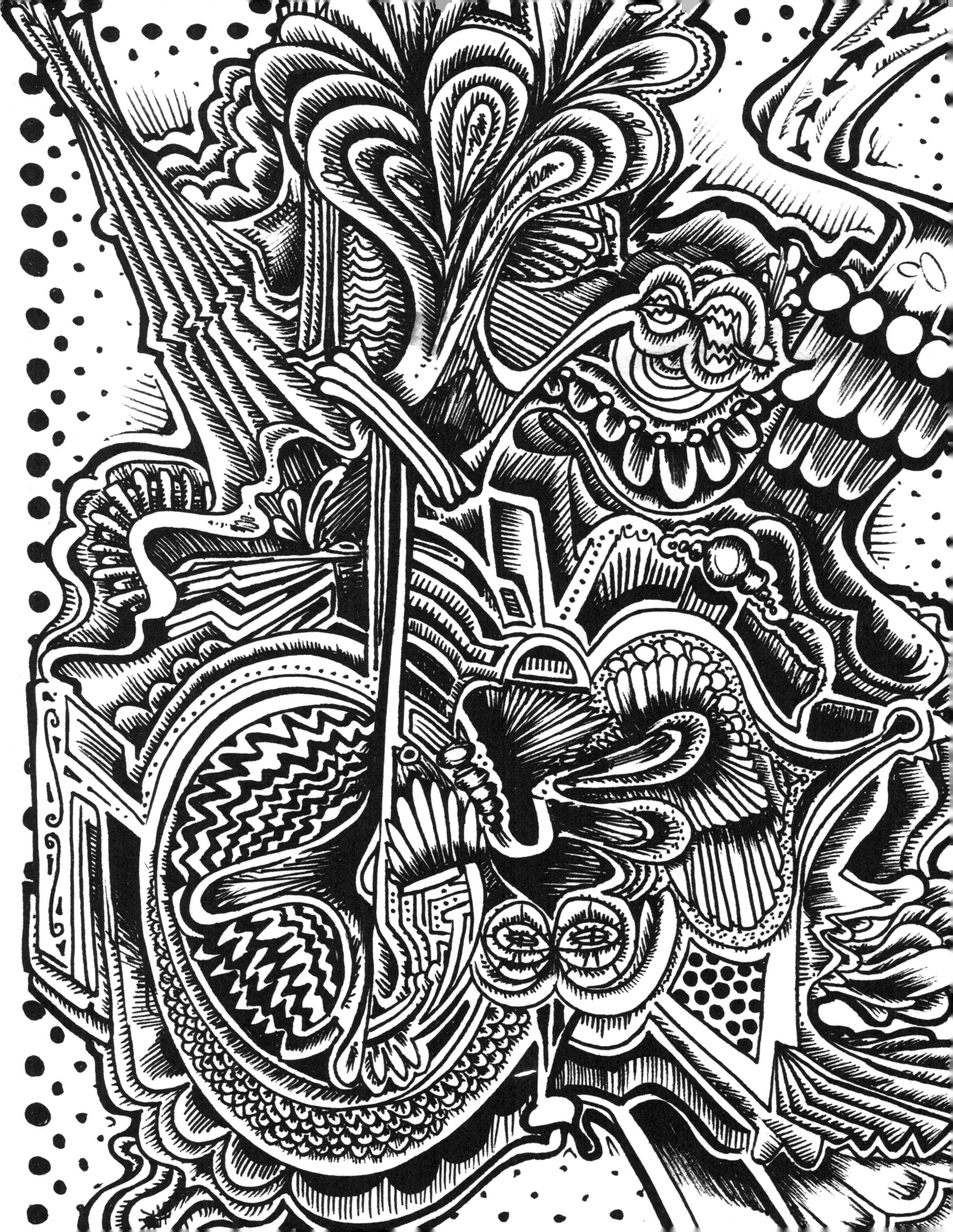

I WANTED TO TELL A STORY BUT I'VE HAD THAT MUCH HAPPEN THAT I DIDN'T KNOW WHERE TO START. THIS IS WHERE I WORKED, BUT THAT'S TOO FAR BACK SO SEEING AS THIS IS A BOOK OF HOMELESS- 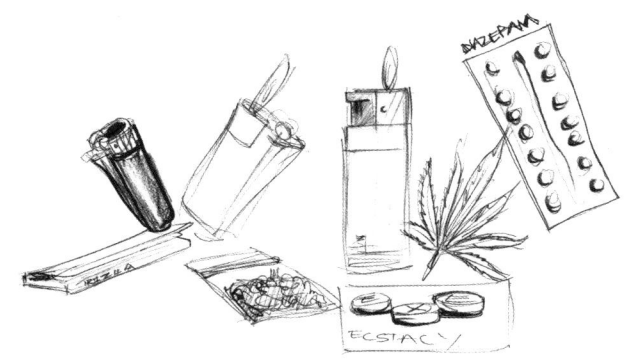 NESS, I'VE GONE BACK TO THE DAY WHEN I BECAME HOMELESS.

THIS IS WHEN I LEFT LONDON. I WAS AT UNI BUT I'D BEEN SPENDING MY MONEY ON SMOK- 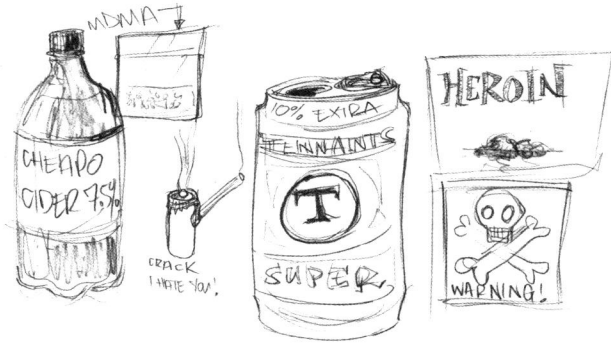 ING DRUGS INSTEAD OF PAYING THE RENT.

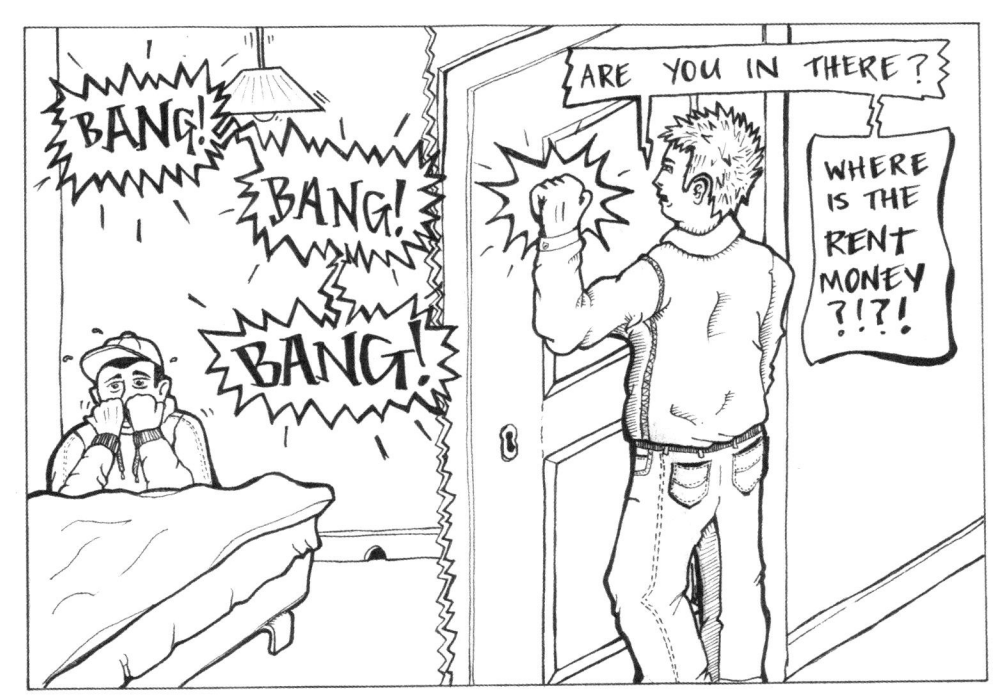

I HAVE PTSD AND A PERSONALITY DISORDER. THIS MEANS I HAVE LOT OF ANXIETY ALMOST TO THE POINT OF NOT BEING ABLE TO FUNCTION. I HEAR VOICES. I HAVE TAKEN DRUGS SINCE I WAS 13 TO GIVE MYSELF SOME PEACE. IN THE SHORT TERM IT HELPS BUT IT COMES WITH ITS OWN PROBLEMS. I WAS ABUSED AS A CHILD AND CAME FROM AN UNSTABLE BACKGROUND.

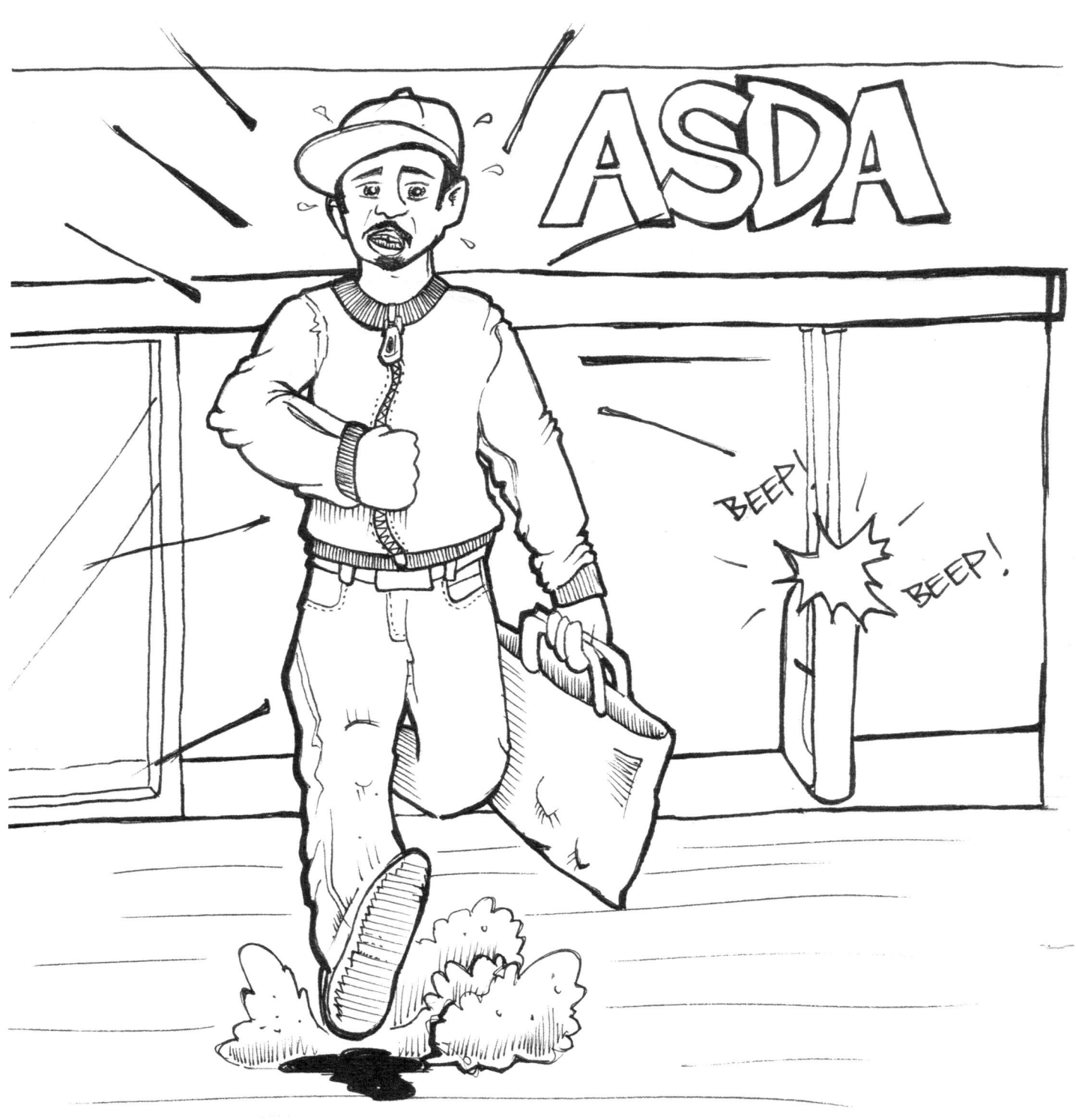

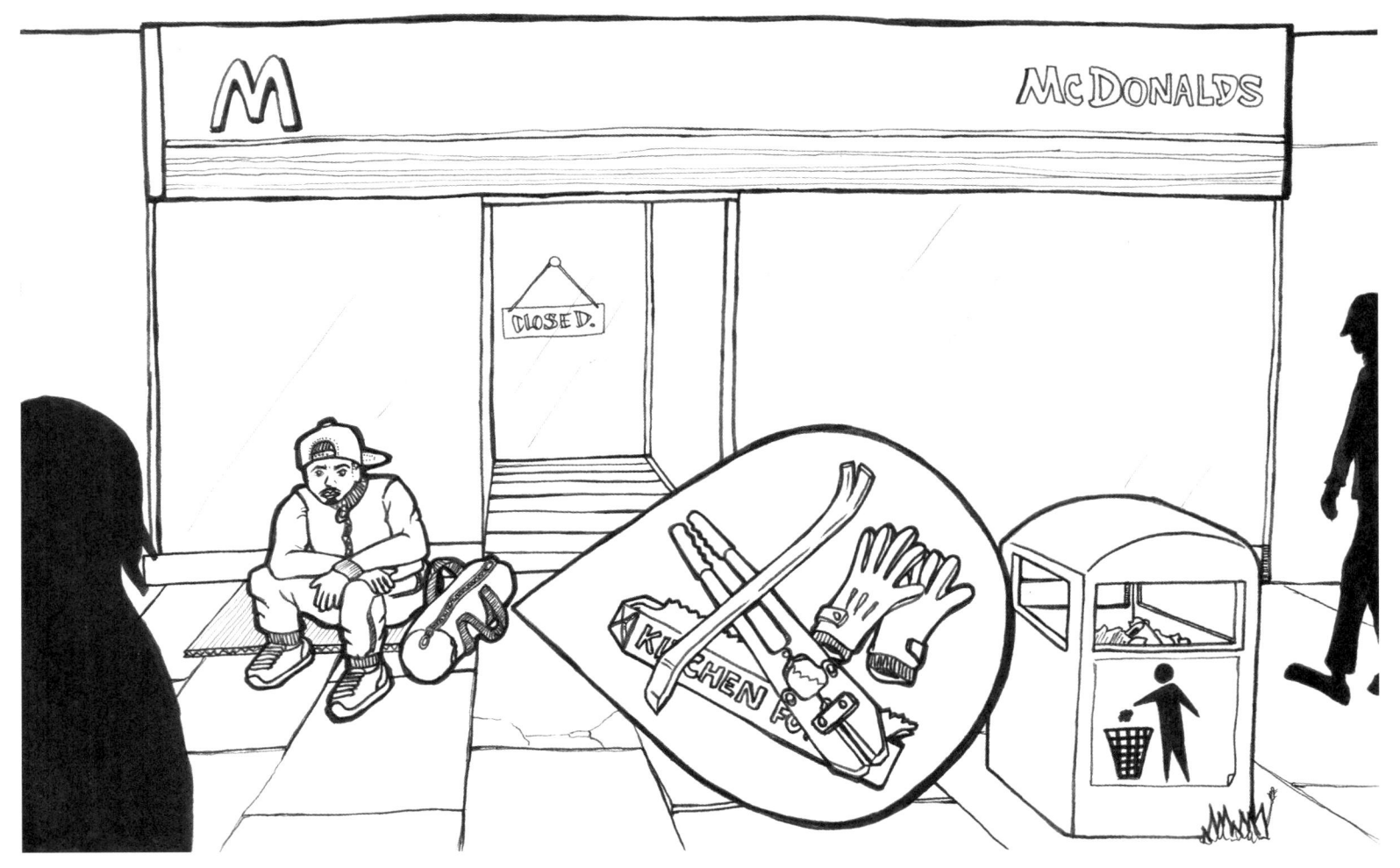

WHEN HOMELESS I ENDED UP SPENDING A LOT OF TIME AT MCDONALD'S. FREE INTERNET, CHEAP FOOD — BUT I WASN'T HERE FOR ANY OF THAT. I'D LEFT MY GIRLFRIEND THE DAY BEFORE. IT'S 7.30AM AND I'M WAITING FOR A DRUG DEALER.

Nikolett Eszes

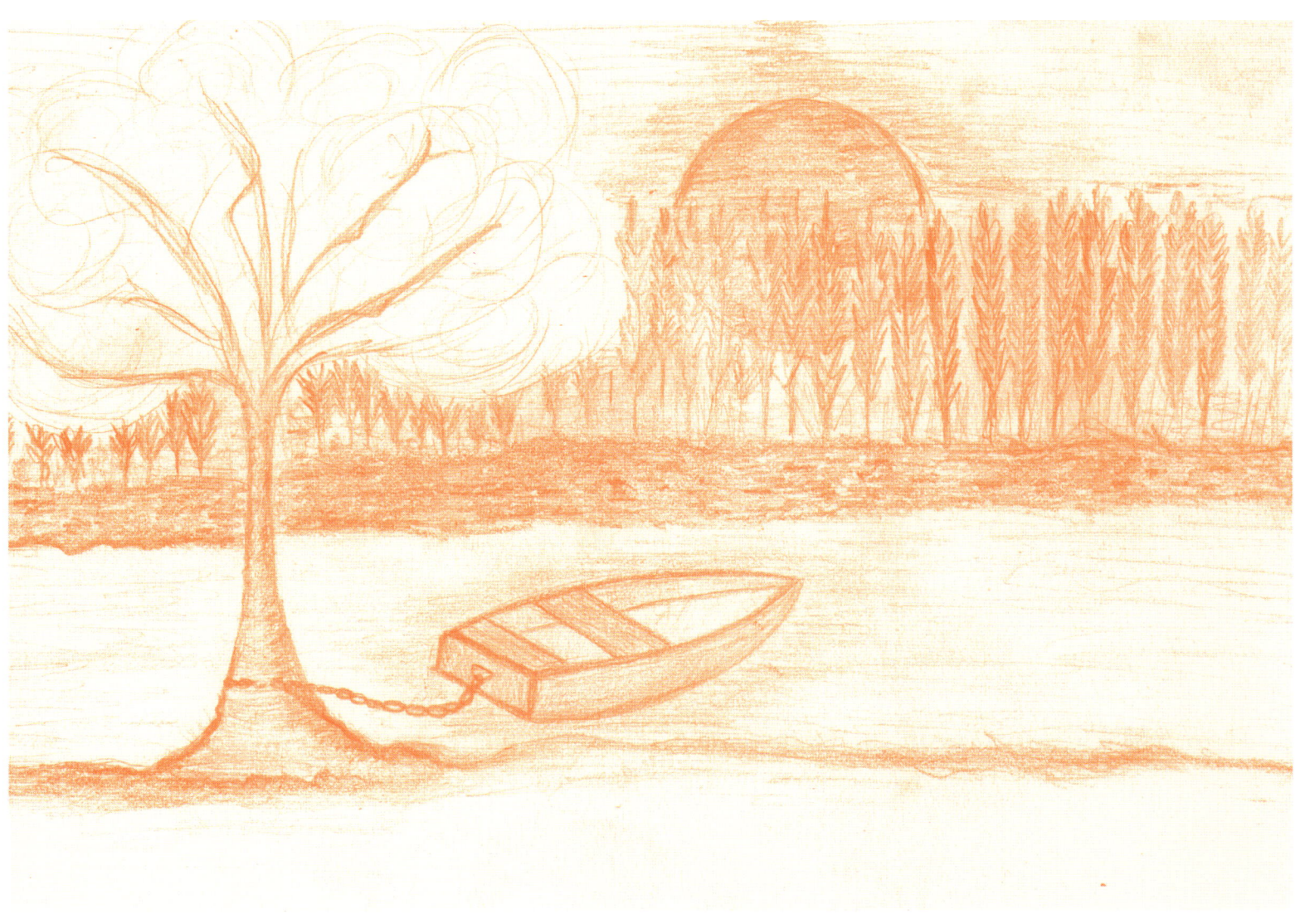

A river in the town where I grew up, at the end of the road where my family lived. We used to go there to walk along the river, to watch the sunset. A warm memory that reminds me of the special time that I spent with my mum and my step-dad.

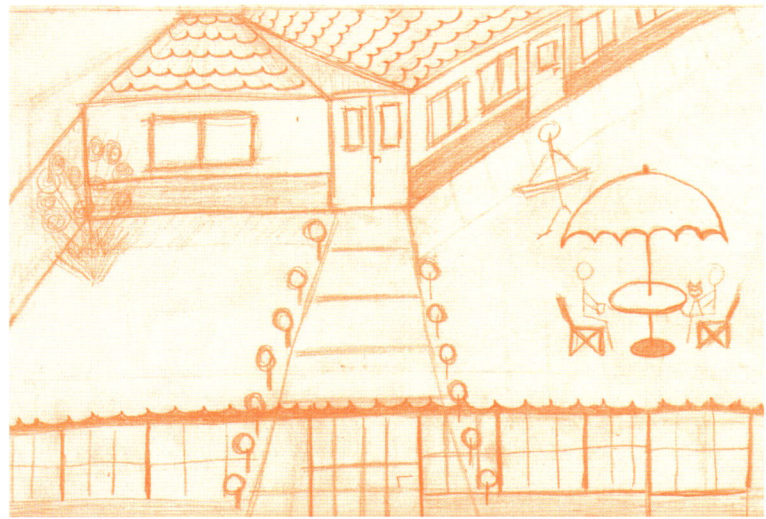

This house was built by my grandpa. Summertime. On hot days I would sit at the table with friends and my mum would bring us sweets and drinks.

This is where I used to play with my friends every day, by the river. We would jump, dive, swim, and play hide and seek under the water. My mum couldn't keep me indoors because I loved playing outside. I wanted to be independent, I loved the sense of freedom so I used to sneak out to play. One time, when I was little, the police found me crossing the bridge on my tricycle and had to bring me home.

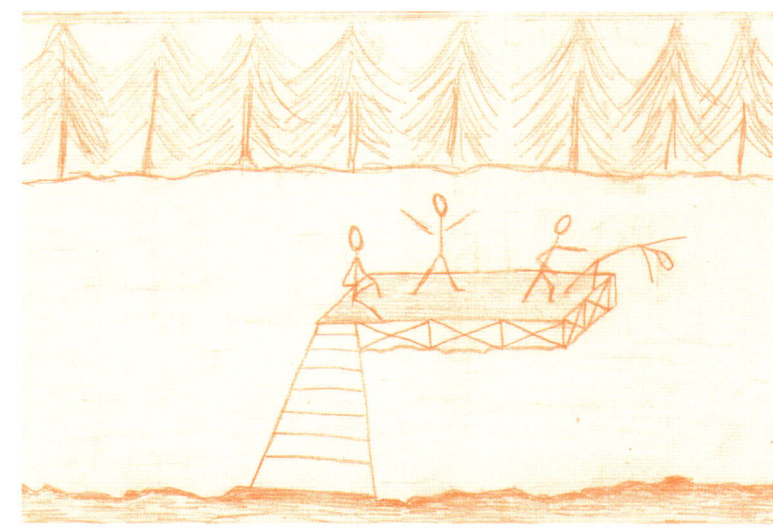

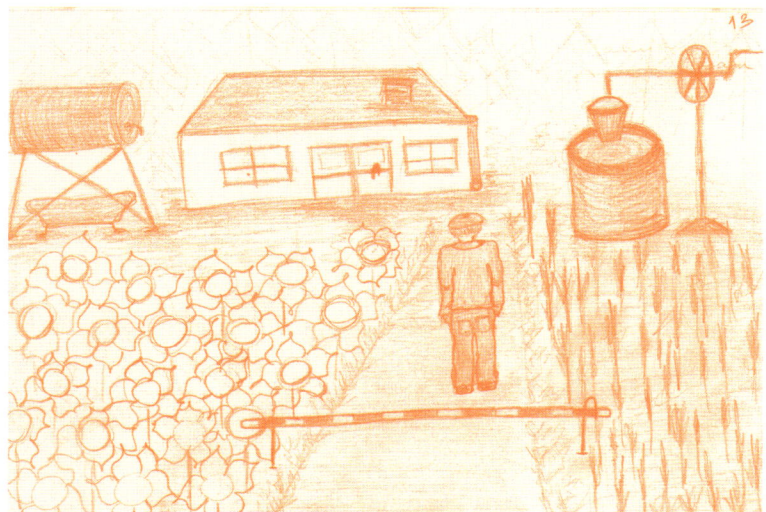

This is my grandfather, my stepdad's father. This is a special memory.

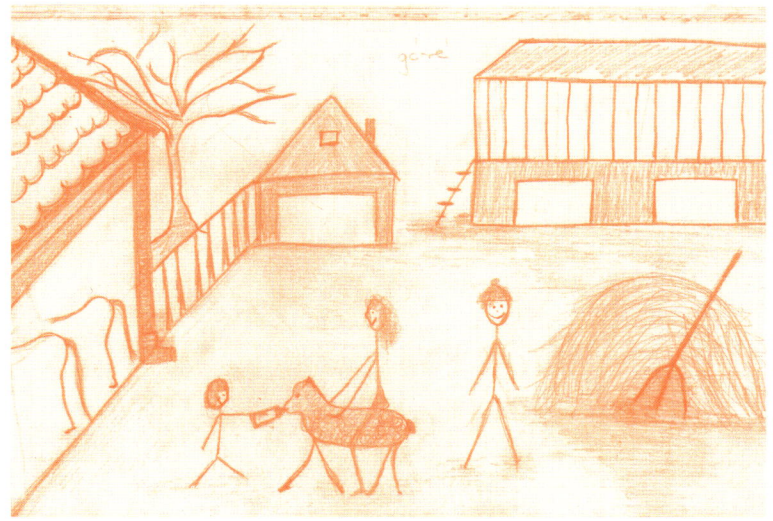

Grandpa kept horses, sheep, chickens — so many animals. Here, I am three years old, still in nappies. I remember being woken in the middle of the night so that I could feed the lamb. My mum climbed on top of it to keep it still, and I fed it warmed milk from a baby bottle. I remember the lights from the house twinkling softly in the darkness of the night. The lamb's wool was so soft to touch. Grandpa would shear the lambs and make lambskin covers for the furniture to keep us warm in the cold winters.

My mum asked my grandpa to teach me how to ride a bike. He came up with the idea of attaching a mop handle to the end of the bike to help me keep my balance. My grandma and mum were so happy and proud to see me learning to ride! From that moment on I never stayed at home. Riding a bike was my pathway to freedom.

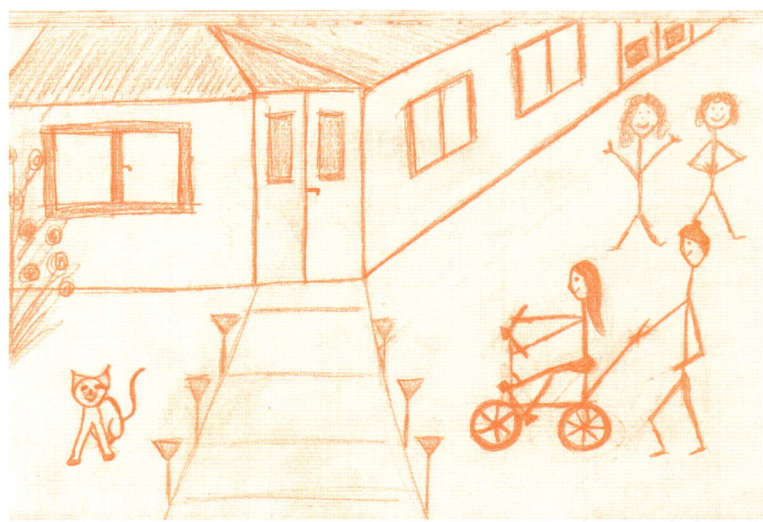

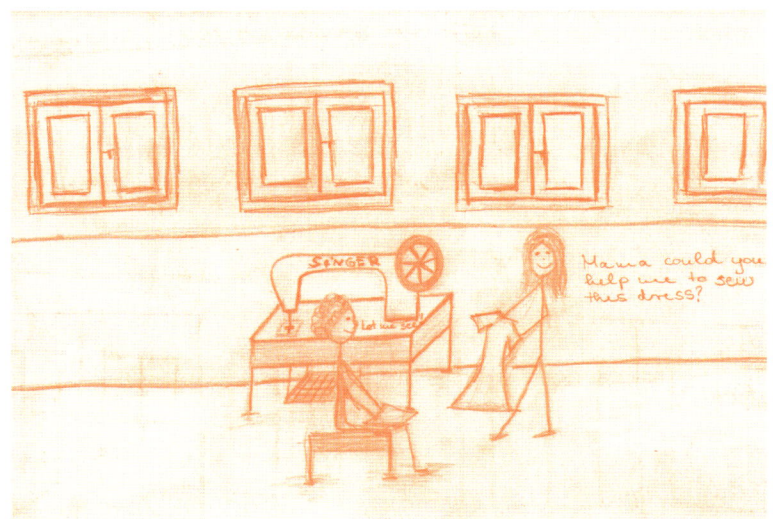

My grandma used to sew clothes and she taught me how to sew. She was diabetic, and needed regular injections. When I was four years old, I asked her if I could help her with her injections so she taught me how: I really loved doing that for her.

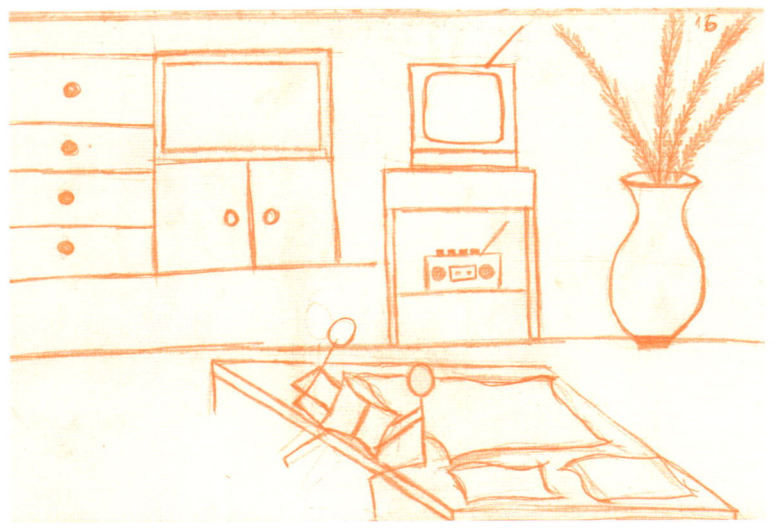

We would ask my stepdad to go into town and to buy us chocolate. While he was out we would sneak into his room and explore, opening each and every drawer to see what was inside. One day we found a beautiful book all about elephants. When we had finished reading it, we tidied everything away carefully as if nothing had happened.

I used to love watching my grandfather work outside. He would go out and spray the fruit trees and collect the twigs and prunings. I would gather hazelnuts from the tree-lined path.

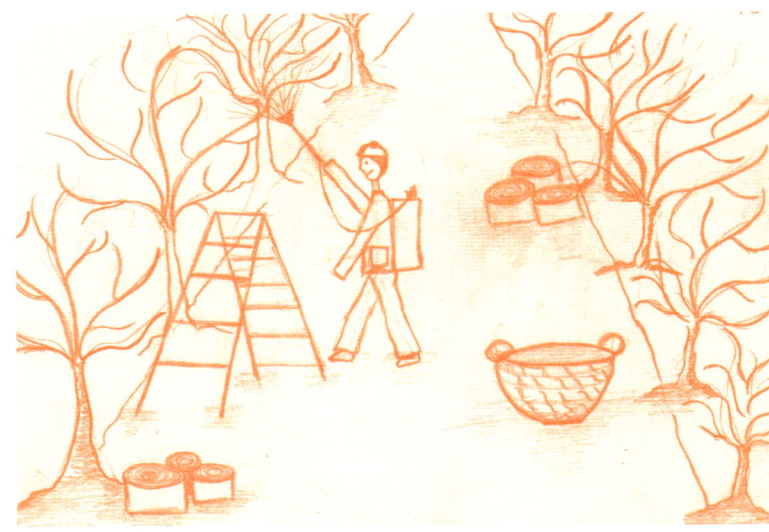

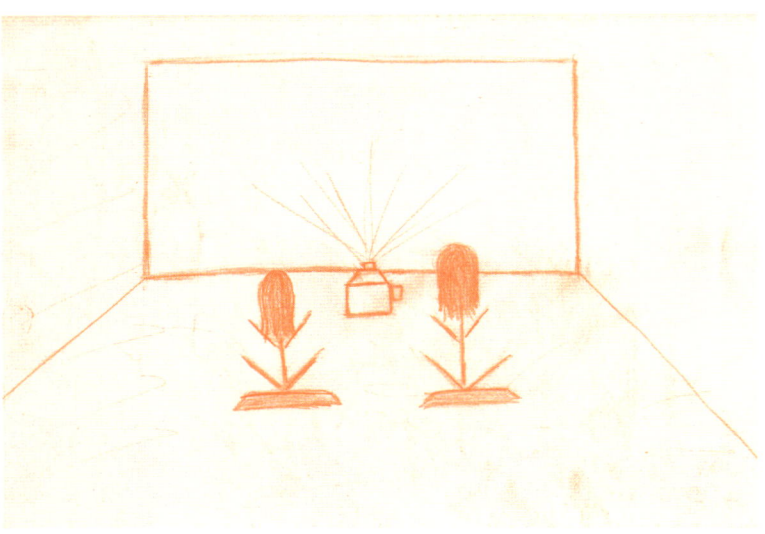

My mum tried to keep me inside sometimes. She came up with the idea of putting a bedsheet on the wall. She found a small projector and brought animated films for me to watch. The screen was huge — bigger than a cinema screen! She would narrate the stories for me while we watched together. I loved it, but after an hour or so, I would be off outside again...

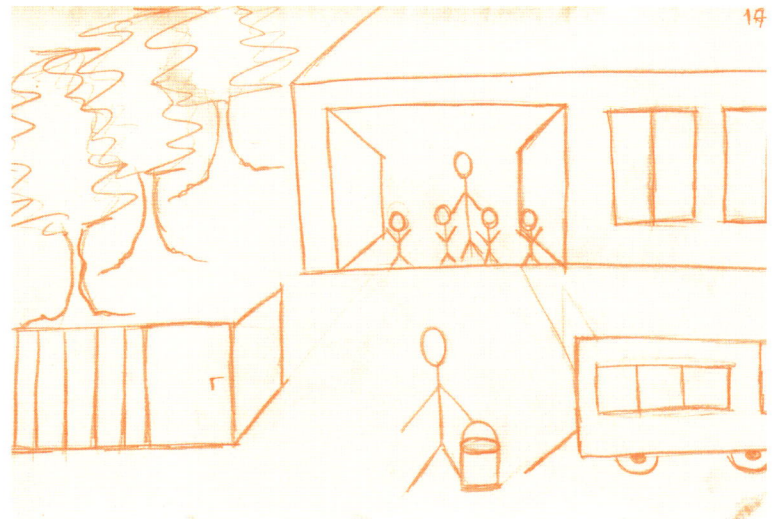

When I was tiny, I was so excited when my stepdad used to drive to my nursery in his red Mitsubishi and bring us all food for lunch. I was so proud. My stepdad used to joke that he only stayed with my mother because of me. He was more than a father to me. I don't know what would have happened to me if I didn't have him in my life. We are still very close.

In my first year at secondary school I was asked to perform, to sing at the tea afternoon: a social event to celebrate the end of the year. I sang a Hungarian folk song, accompanied by my music teacher.

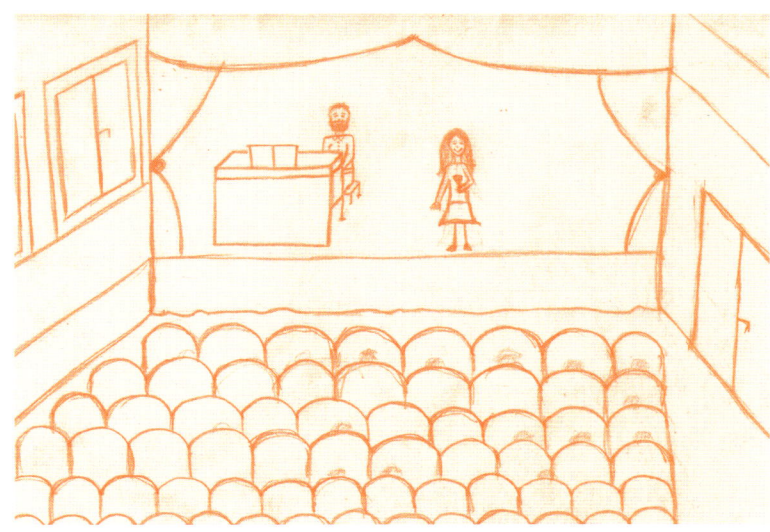

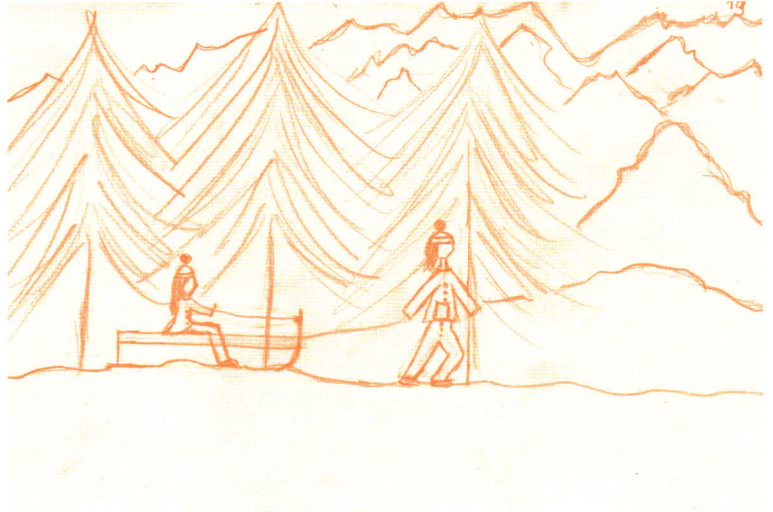

In the snow, my mother and I would take a sleigh out and she would pull me along. I remember losing my dummy in the snow…

Phil Olunniyi

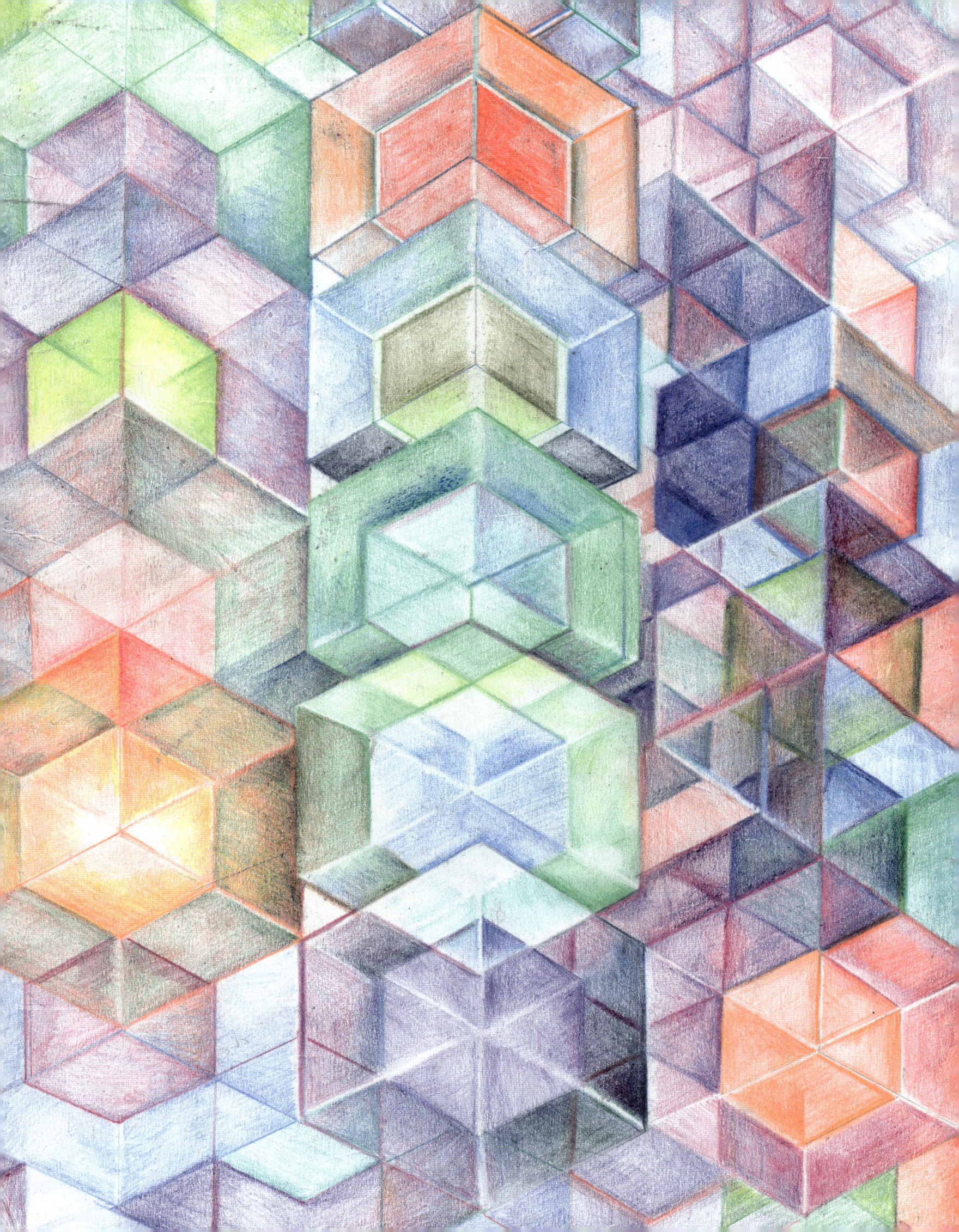

AS THE COUNTRY NEVER SLEEPS AND THE VEHICLES OF THE WORLD ALWAYS NEED FUEL, SO DO WE. WHAT STOPS US FROM GETTING 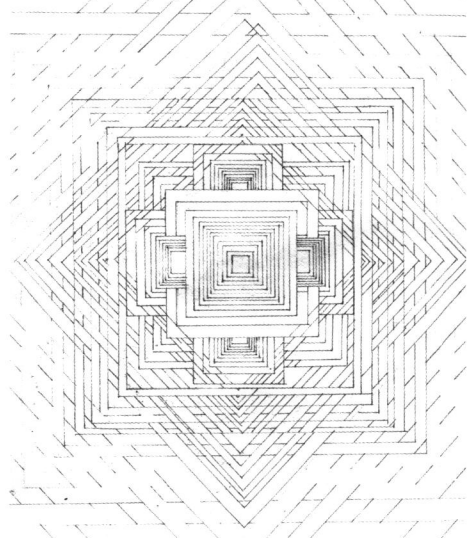 WHAT WE WANT AND NEED? WELL, I'VE SPOTTED SOME- THING SERIOUS THAT CAN CHANGE US RAPIDLY. WHAT IF THE FUEL WE ARE USING IS PUTTING US IN AN EVERLASTING STATE OF DEEP HUNGER? I MEAN PEOPLE ARE ALWAYS DIGGING.

WE HAVE MADE SO MUCH, BUT NOT MANY PEOPLE CAN APPRECIATE AND ENJOY IT AND THERE ARE ALWAYS PROS AND CONS. MOST OF OUR RESOURCES PUT US ON A CARBON AND MOLECULAR LEVEL, RIGHT? I APOLOGISE 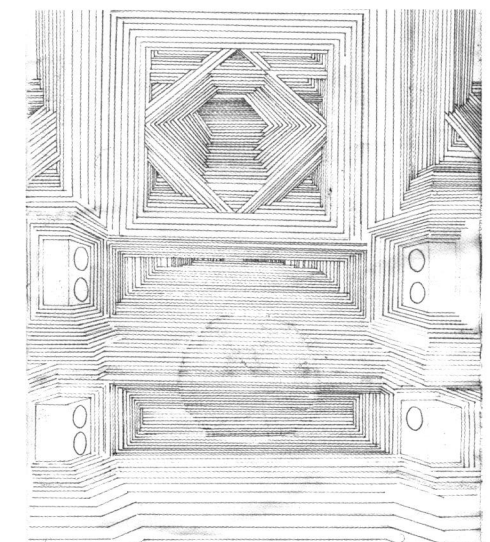 I HAVE BEEN STUDYING THE PERIODIC TABLE. THERE ARE SOME ELEMENTS THAT MAY CANCEL SOME OTHERS OUT, LIKE ADDING AND SUBTRACTING.

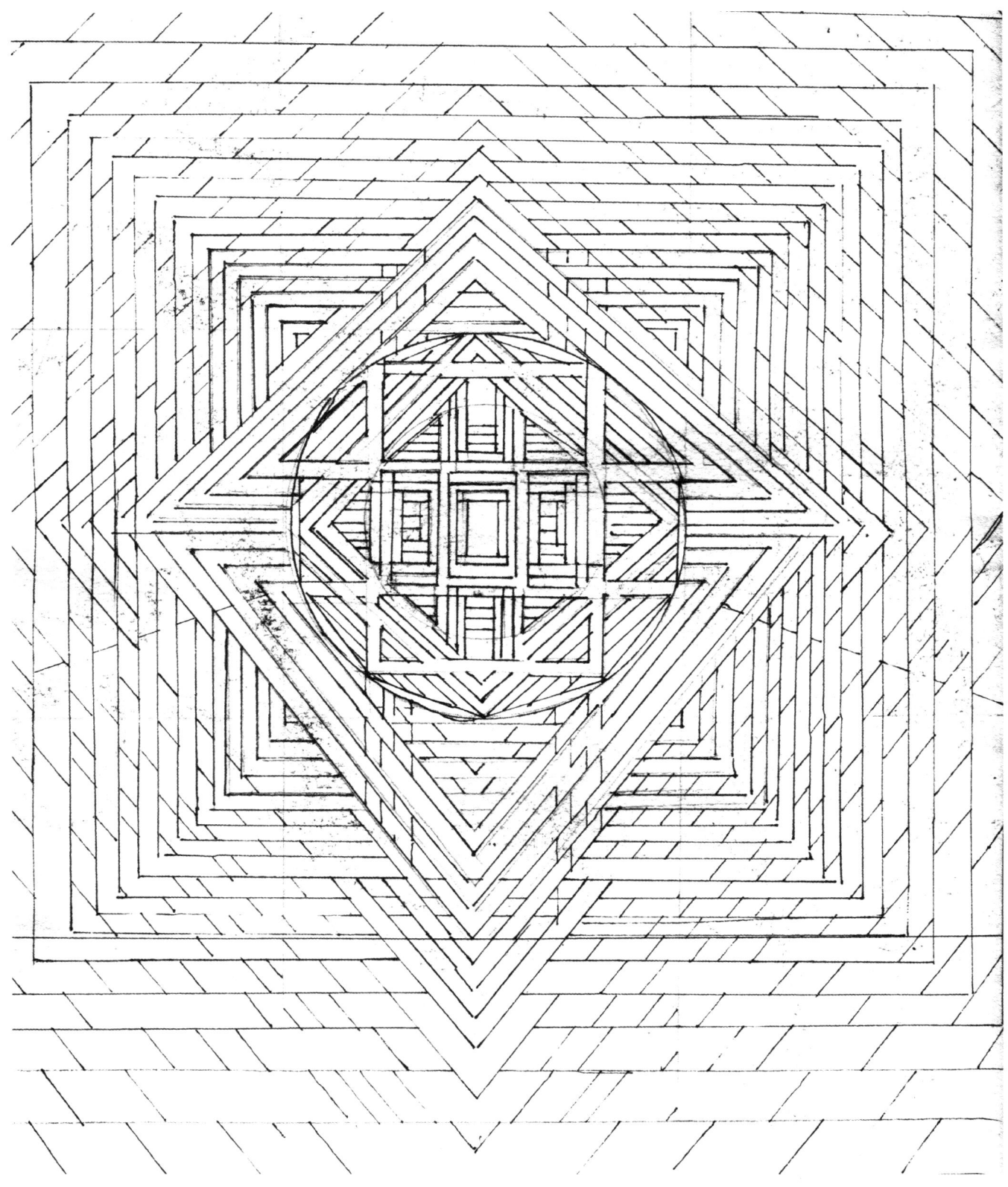

This is a painting done in respect of understanding that music is linked to everything and art itself in this physical spectrum of intellectualised creativity and organised observation alignment playing with sound and vibration.

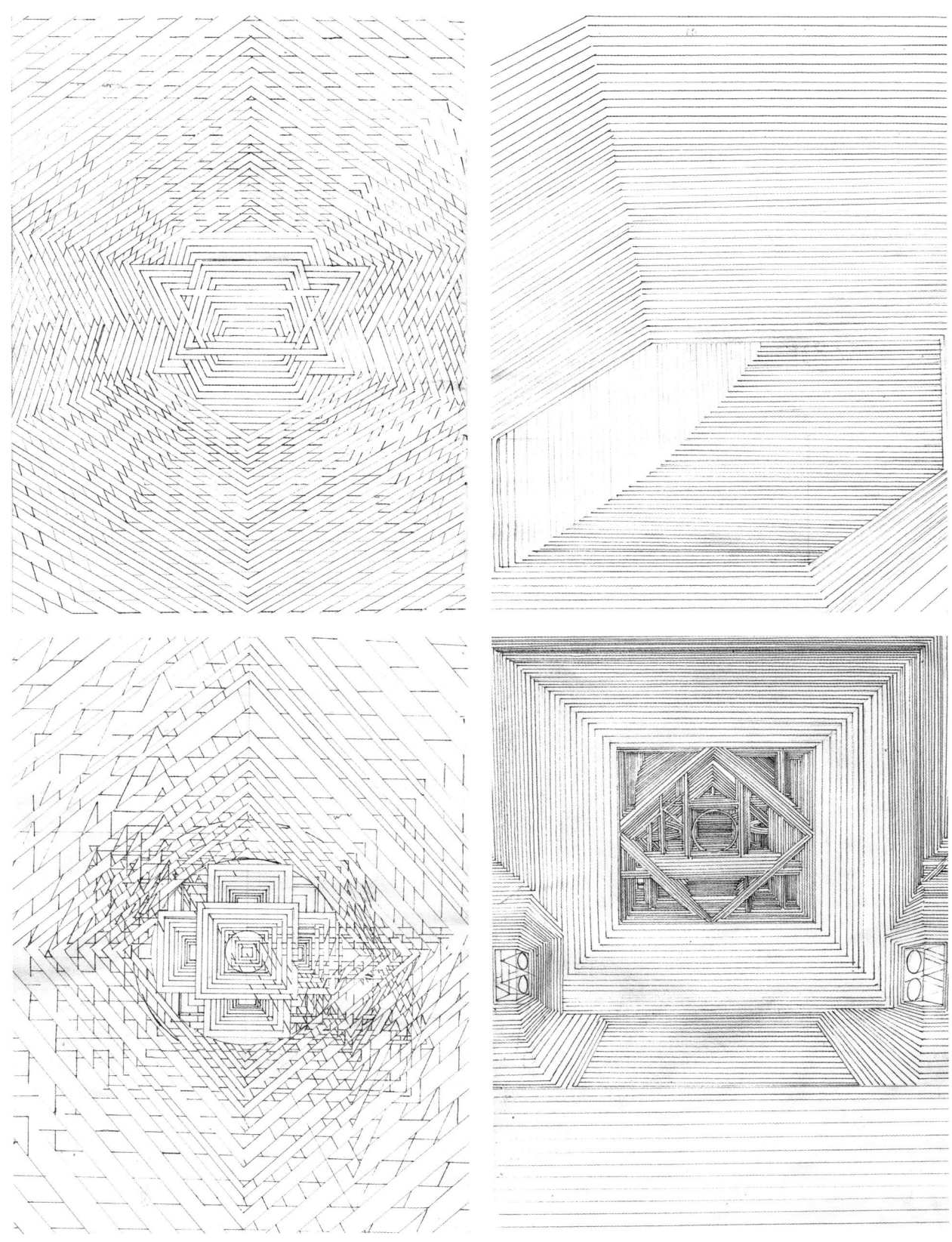

Blinded by an angel. The current void that has been forever expanding and has finally decided to make a demonstration to those that live without purpose and planning. It picks out the slackers, people in the narcissistic, endeavours, indulgers, addicts, people without family orientation (ie those living without parents or who are from a broken family and have a history of violence). It picks out those who are creative and want to pursue a career in their creative practice, such as actors, actresses, TV presenters, craftsmen. People who are prone to psychic attacks and night terrors. I myself have been a victim of this, but my friend had an encounter with it. It is almost like it turned him into Lucifer himself.

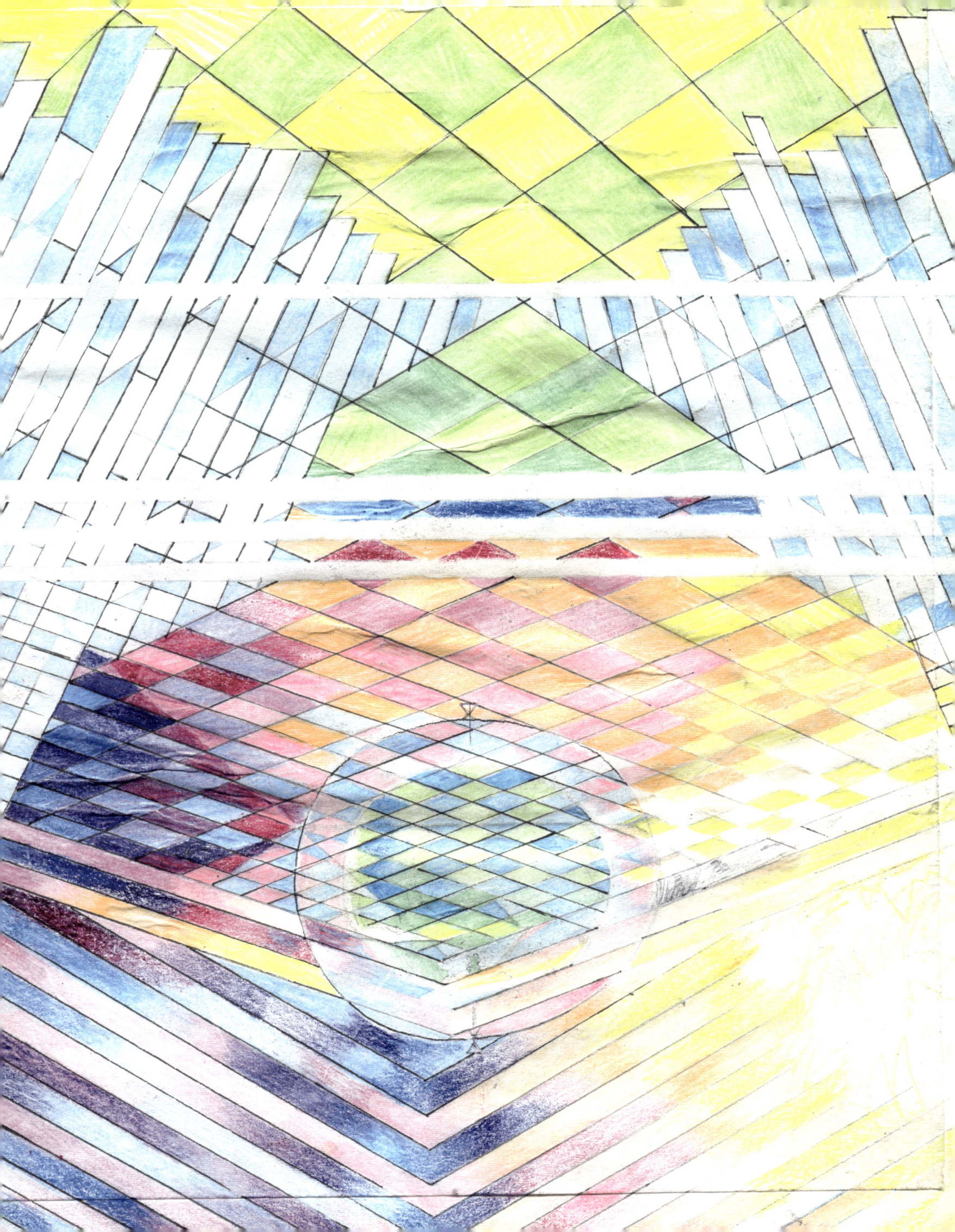

Prosper Kouayep

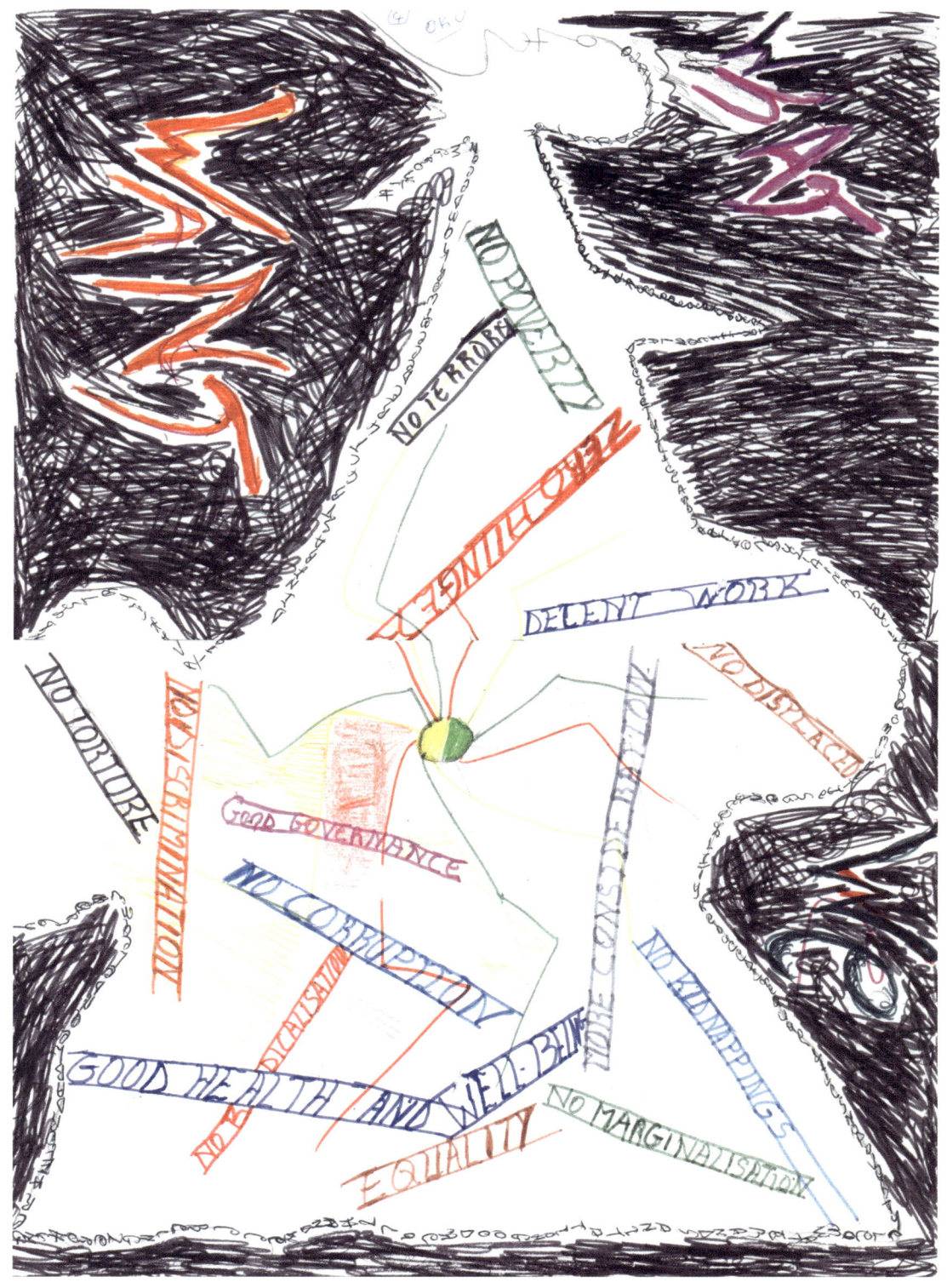

Because what divides us is nothing compared to what unites us:
A peace
A justice
And sustainable development
is 'What We Want' for our beloved Cameroon.

Cameroon has two secular identities from its historical heritage, 'Francophone' and 'Anglophone', who have lived together and used their differences to make it a strong country. That is why, for many years after the struggle for independence, this country was a 'haven of peace' where it was good to live. People of different ethnic backgrounds married, worked and lived together. In short, they shared everything that they would have shared if they were living in the same room. This peaceful society was seen as a model for Africa.

As the country was rich in natural resources, the economy, society and culture flourished. Cameroonians everywhere spoke of their country with patriotism, love and pride. We were then ONE FOR ALL, ALL FOR ONE. From Dja-et-Lobo in the South to Logone-et-Chari in the Far North or from Ngo Ketundja in the North-West to Boumba-et-Ngoko in the East, people moved and travelled freely throughout the country; whether they were 'Francophones' or 'Anglophones'; or whether they were in the country because of the strong sense of national integration. Cameroonians were forgetting that Cameroon had been a federated state: they just wanted to live and build a sense of family. What bound us together was stronger than what divided us.

That is why Cameroon was seen as a model of unity and inter-community integration, an Africa in miniature. This was due to its physical, sociolinguistic and even historical elements. These are its landscape; its two official languages — English on the one hand and French on the other; its having more than 280 national languages; its ideal situation in the centre of the continent, between the Africa of plains and plateaus, the Africa of forests and savannahs, the Africa of Christians and Muslims, Anglophone Africa and Francophone Africa.

Thus in different parts of the country one could feel the full expression of this cultural richness: from North to South and from East to West, these cultural and linguistic identities gave the country its solid foundations. This justifies the migration of certain elites from one region to another for educational or socialisation purposes in order to contribute to the consolidation of these assets and make Cameroon a developed country after the departure of the colonists. Its natural, economic, social and cultural potential was then an asset to be preserved and consolidated.

However, nowadays the vast majority of young Cameroonians live in a state of underemployment for just over two decades, 70% according to the data of the International Conference on the closing of the project for the improvement of youth employment policies in Africa, held in Yaounde, from 20 to 24 July 2019. A real and systemic problem, alongside other dysfunctions that manifest themselves in the omission of the satisfaction of the basic needs of the populations and aggravated by the lack of social

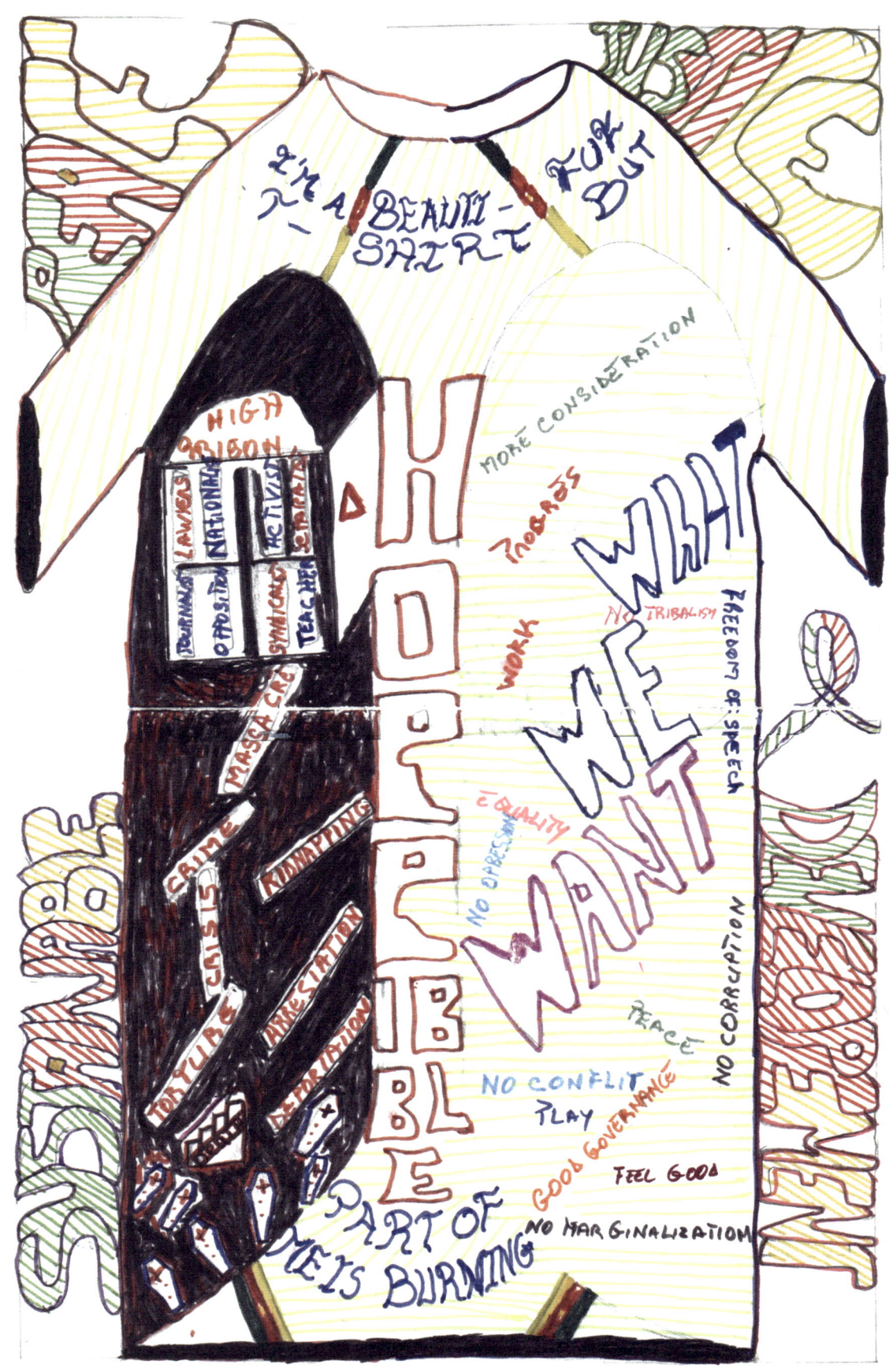

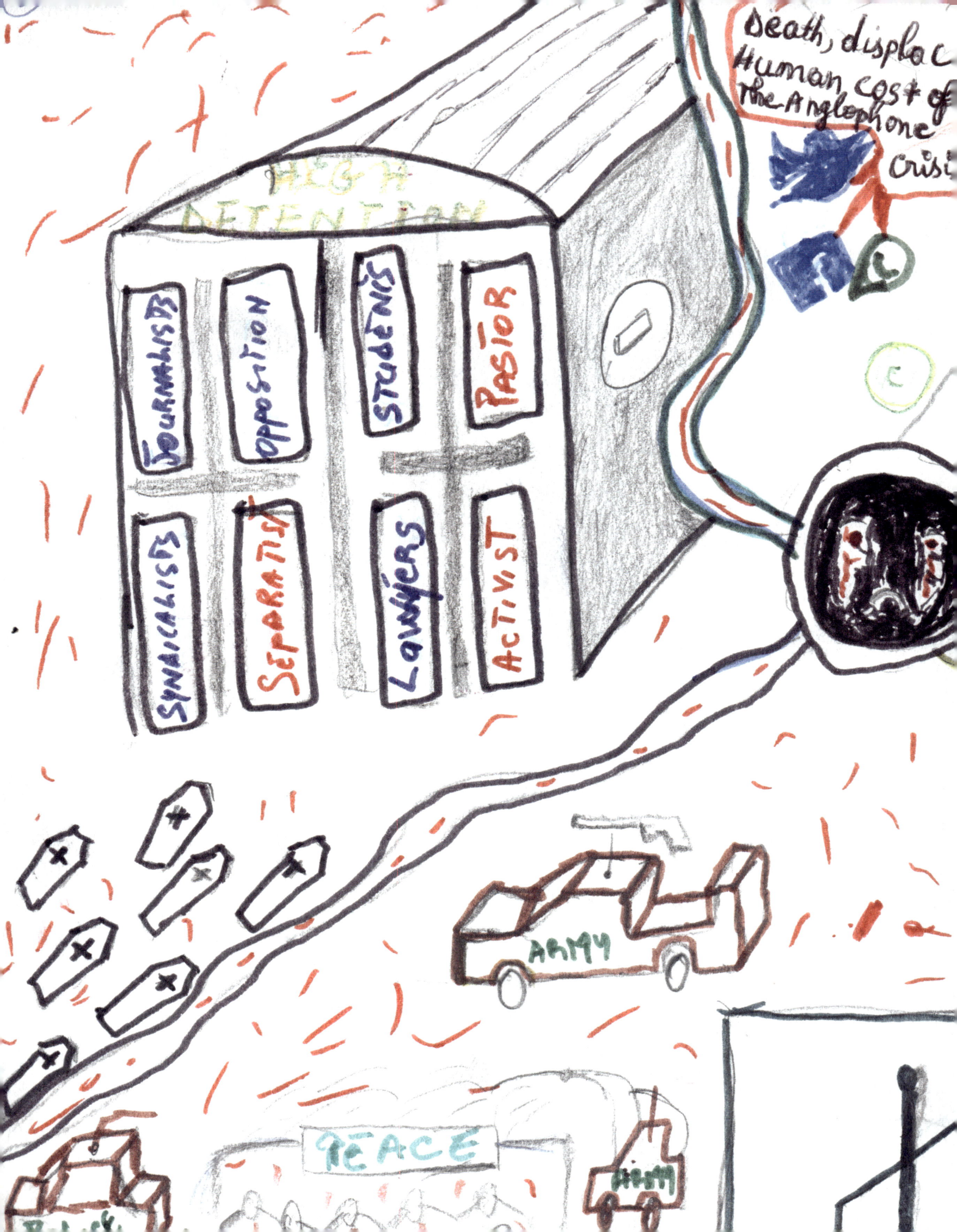

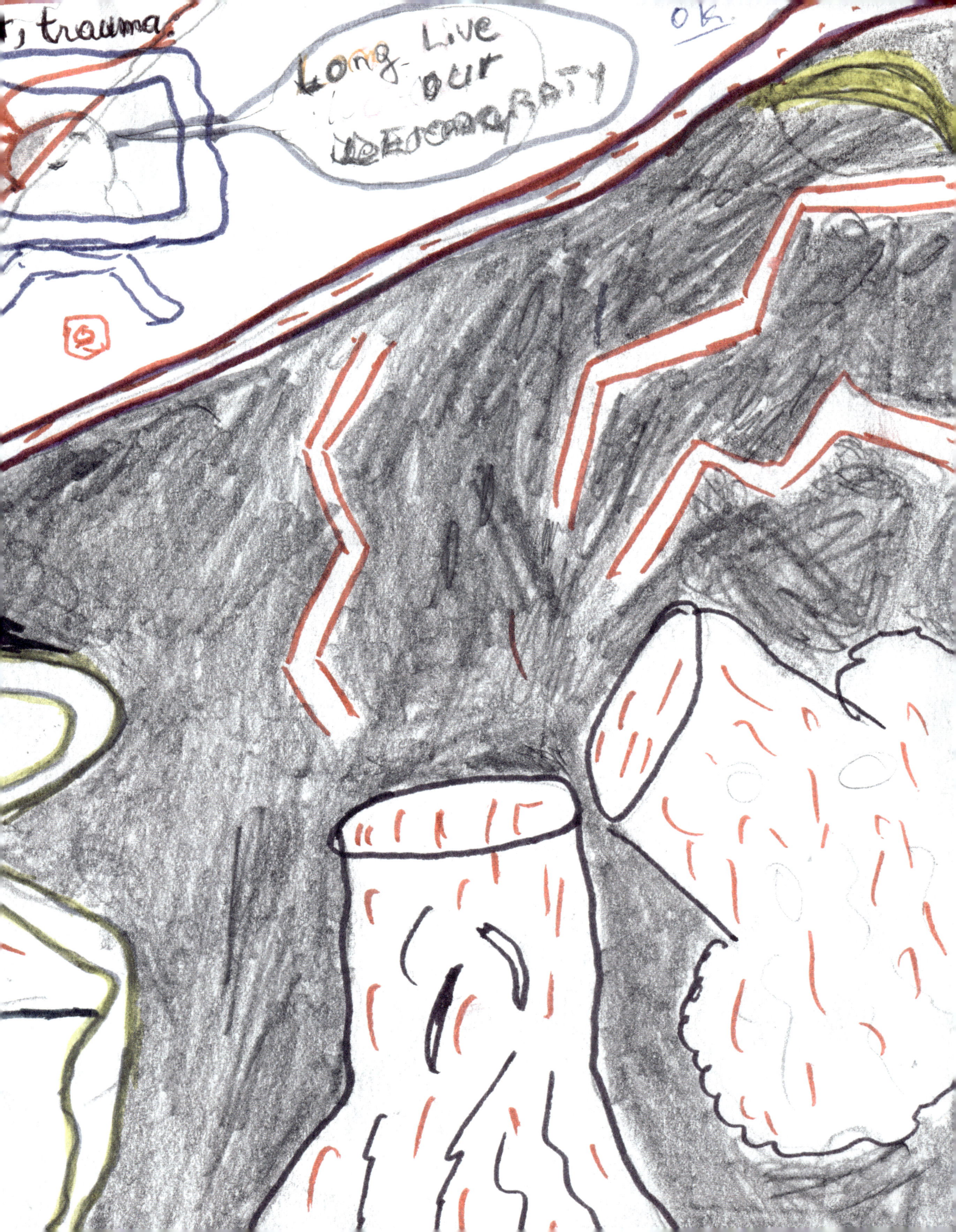

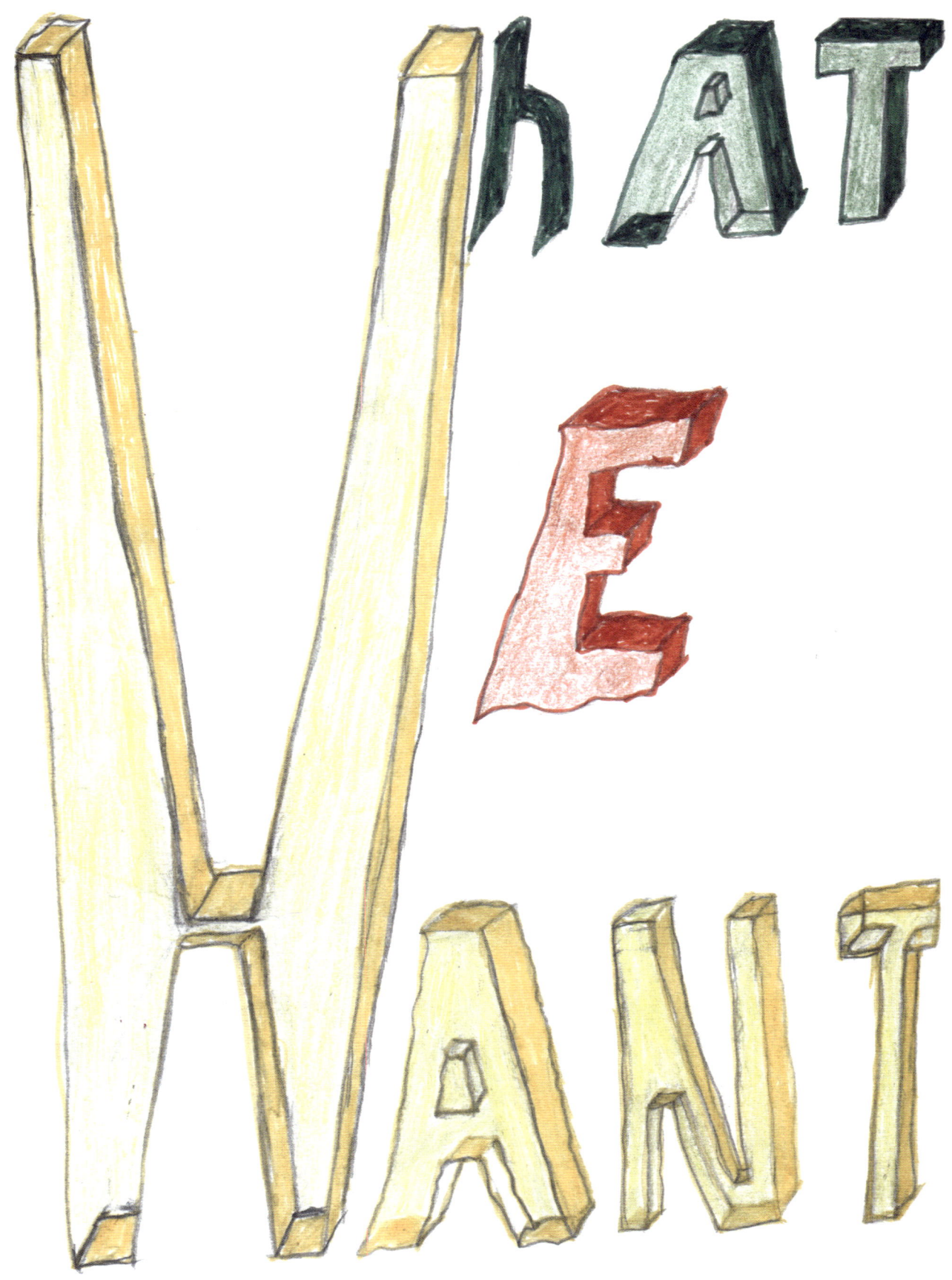

justice in the redistribution of the nation's resources and wealth; Peace Studies speak of Negative Peace. Hence many corporatist demands that are strongly repressed by the system in place. These have been transformed into a civil war in the northwest and southwestern regions, with demands that are more than republican, as observed. In view of these circumstances, the future and self-determination of the Cameroonian people is increasingly compromised in the face of feelings of revenge and resentment resulting in the collapse of the societal unity of rapidly deteriorating communities.

How then can we understand how our national strength has turned into such weakness? How can we understand how the power that was initially shared among many has become a power that has transformed individuals and communities by setting them against each other? How can we understand that academic qualifications have become for many individuals in Cameroon obstacles to participation in public affairs? In the past, a simple Certificate of Primary and Elementary Studies or a Brevet d'Etude du Premier Cycle assured you a sustainable and decent job. No family or tribal ties or connection with the ruling elite would make anyone either a favourite or put them at a disadvantage.

Moreover, the competitive and glossy image of Cameroon, sold by national and international media, has given way to an image of fear and obscurantism; as in the case of the balance sheet of the NOSO conflict, so heavy that the country no longer presents itself as a popular destination for tourists as it did in the summer a few decades ago. The violent conflict between the Cameroonian authorities and the English-speaking separatists continues to grow. After twenty months of crisis, the toll is heavy: 1,850 deaths, 530,000 internally displaced persons and tens of thousands of refugees, including 35,000 in Nigeria (source: Crisis Group).

Why do our prisons, once regarded as havens for murderers and thieves, have journalists, lawyers, doctors, pastors, intellectuals and activists from opposition political parties as inmates? The only crime they have committed is to have expressed their differences of opinion or declared their position in a so-called democratic state.

'What We Want', in this sense and in view of this state of affairs, taking into account the catastrophic repercussions of the COVID19 pandemic on Africa in general and Cameroon in particular, cannot stand by in the face of the delays now blamed on the victims of the various conflicts and the great pandemic. It is intended to be a platform for the contribution of a new Cameroon and of the present and future generation. For the victims and/or displaced persons as a result of these insurrections inevitably have an urgent need to make a new start. This is in order to build a new Cameroon, where peace, justice and sustainable development can be the unifying themes that move us forward into a common future.

We dream of a new country, built on the basis of available resources, with friends of peace, development partners, volunteers and all the actors whatever they have to give as support. We want a homeland where the dream can become possible again.

Because what divides us is nothing compared to what unites us:

Peace,
Justice and,
Sustainable development
It is 'What We Want' for our beloved Cameroon.

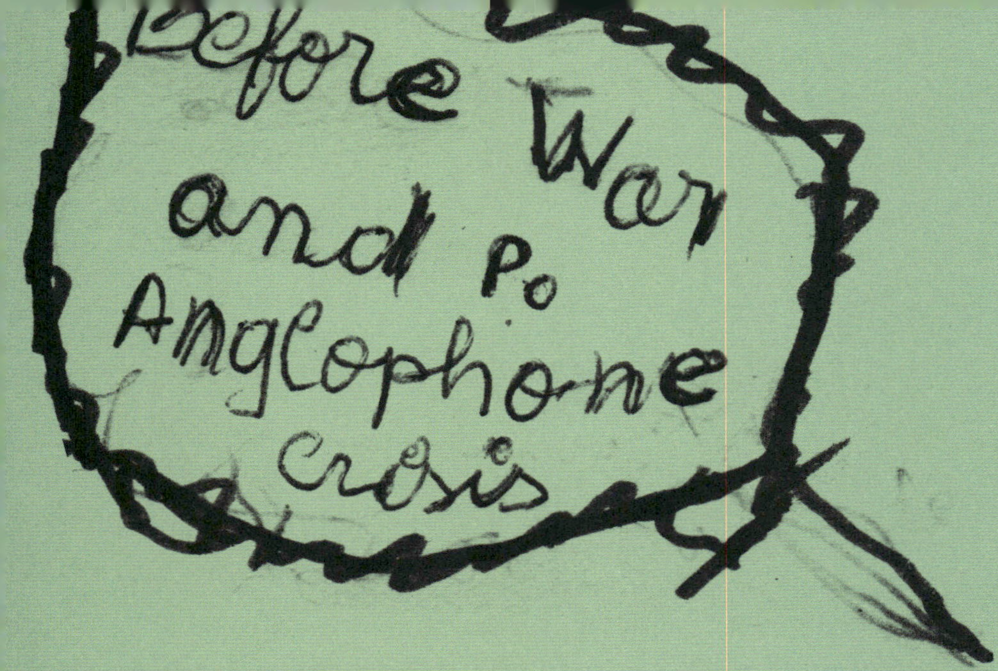

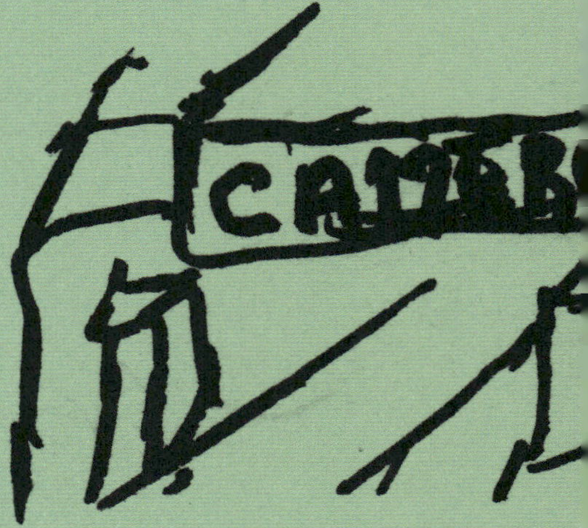

THIS IS MY STORY. THIS IS A TRUE STORY.

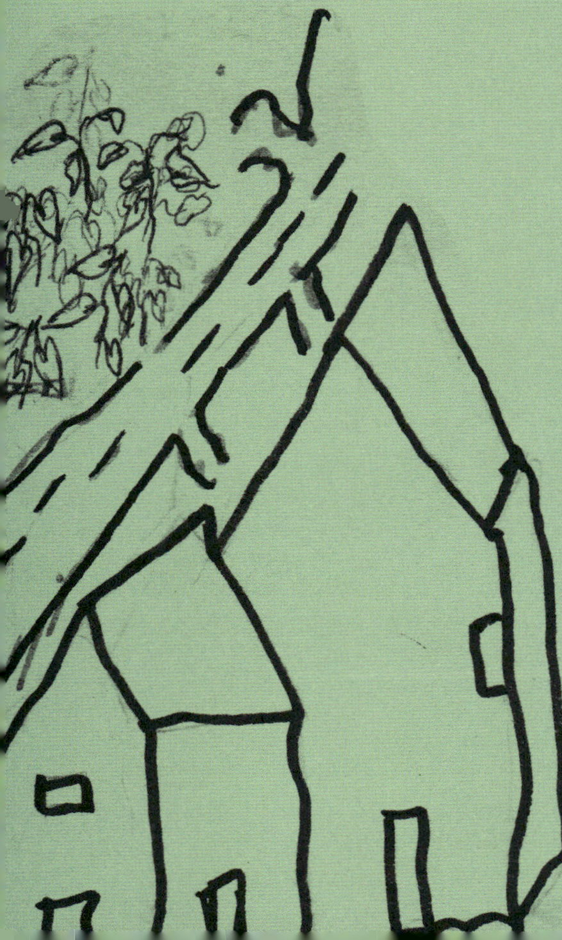

I'M WRITING BECAUSE A LOT OF PEOPLE ARE DYING.

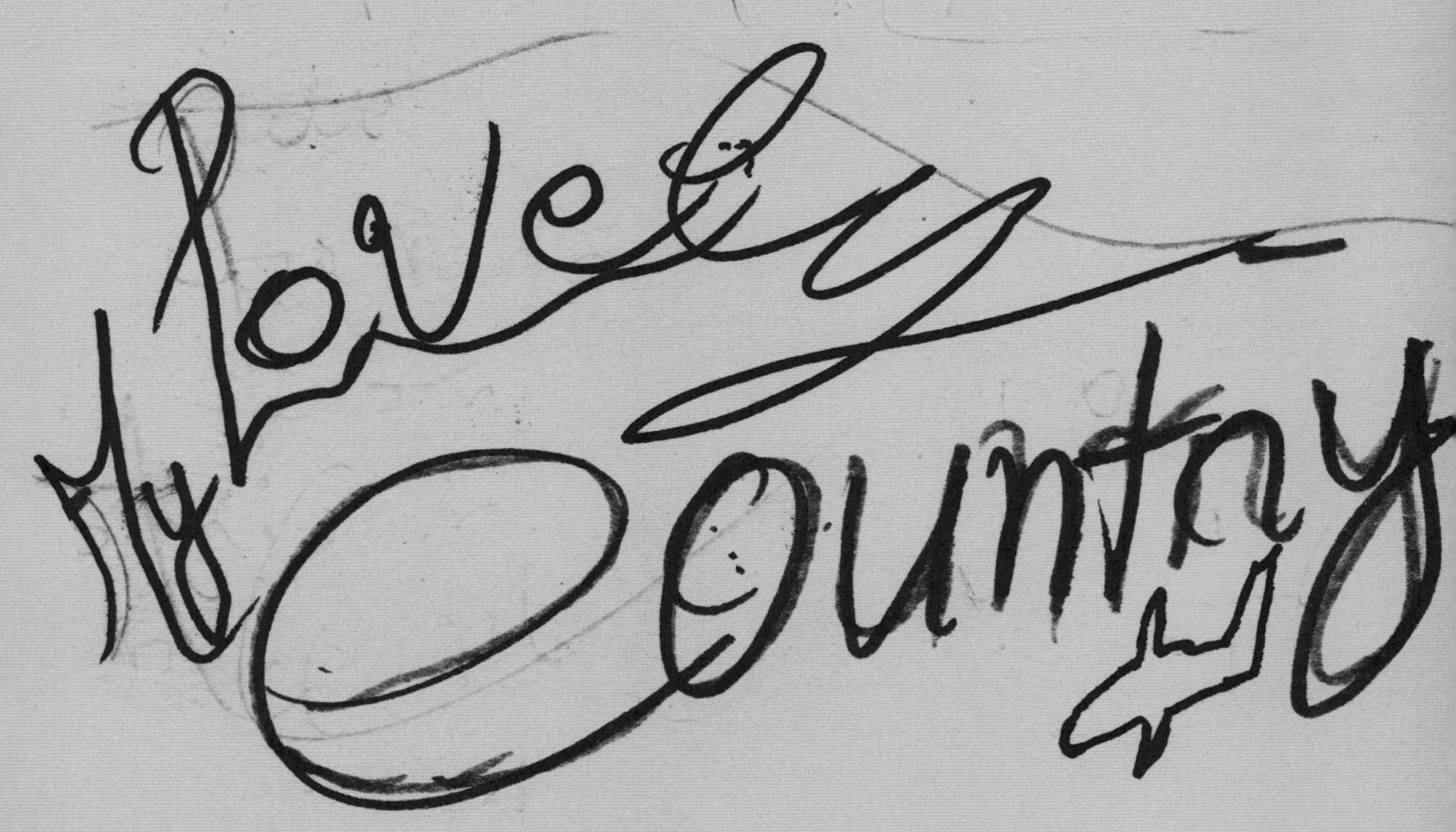

Ria Wallace

In the mind of a little girl it was normal to me. I couldn't see a problem with it.

I looked up to them as if it was my lifes destiny. It was hard for me not to conform with their type of reality but I did it anyways.

For as long as I could remember it was all a game to them, our little secret even.

Don't tell your mum, don't tell my wife, don't tell your sisters, It will ruin your life

And that it did, aged 13 , 2014

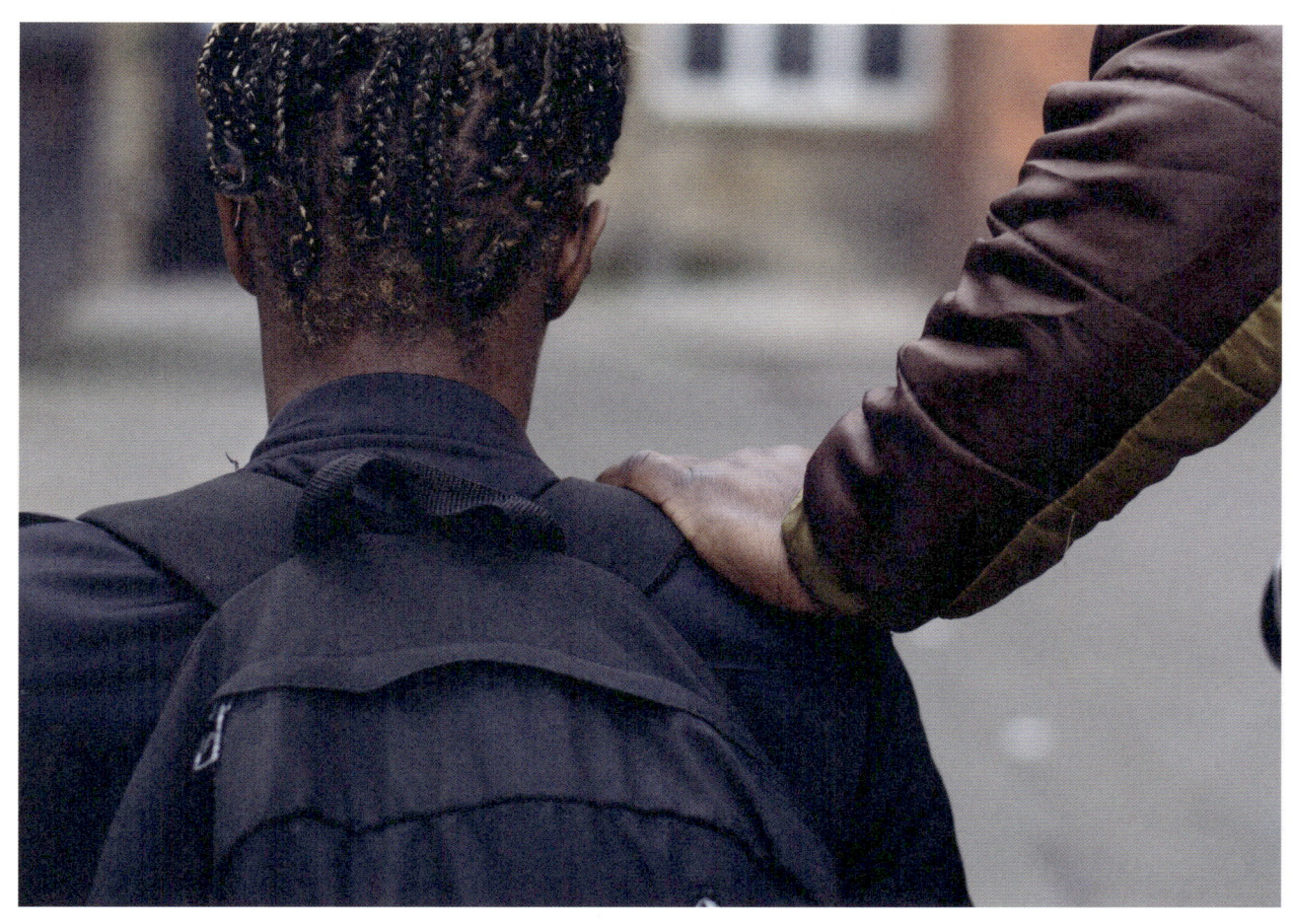

Like it was yesterday it's all in my memory. Waking up knowing I had to tell my mum this tragedy.

Her daughter had been abused and it was no stranger but the very person that helped create me.

4 years go by and theres no sign of my worlds (sisters) – It killed me not seeing them grow.

I missed so much of their lives and it hurts me till this day, I still blame myself till this very day.

But talking saved me...

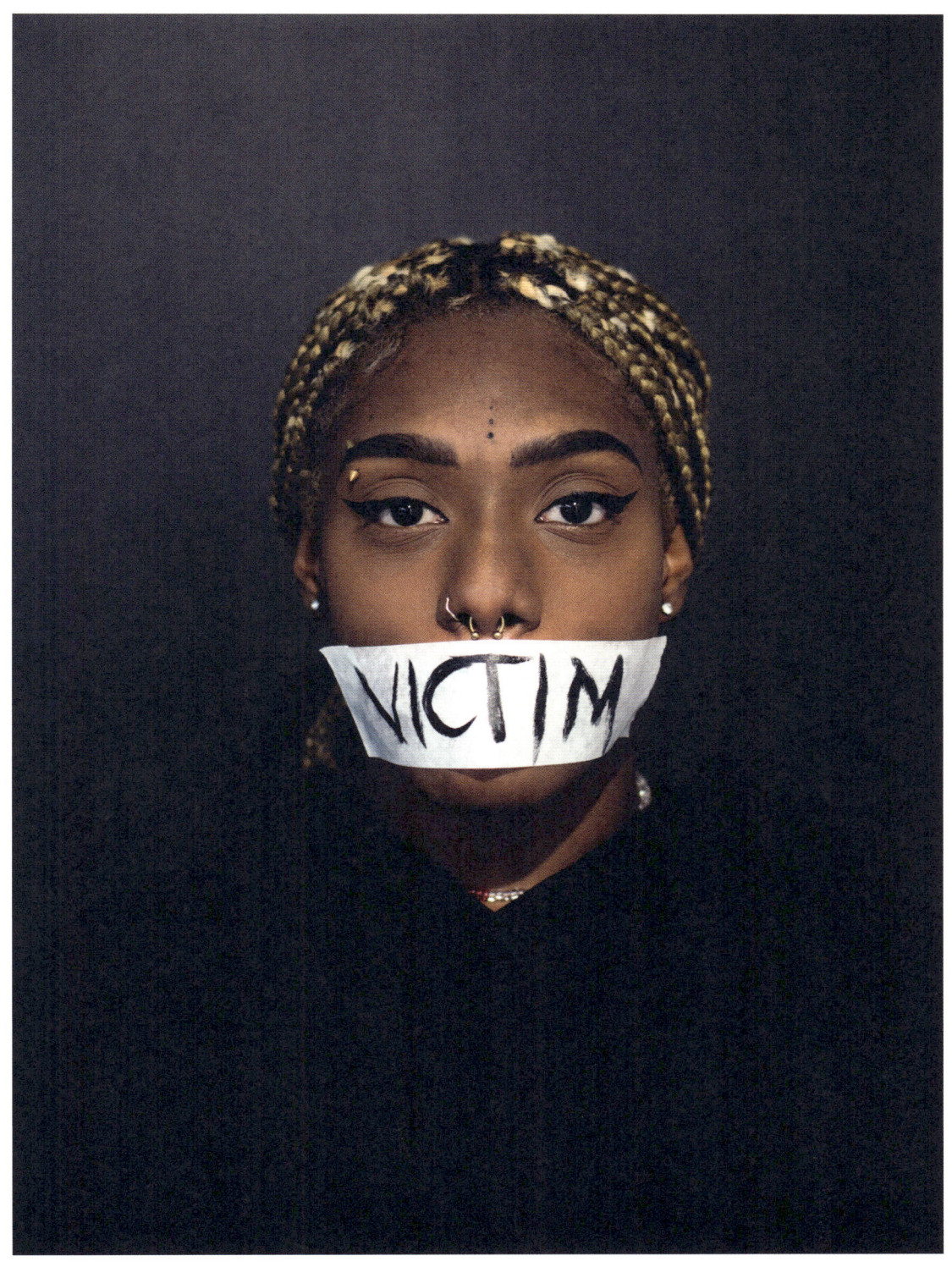

It's a sickening thought but it happens on a daily, we don't say anything for years because we don't want to be labelled a victim.

We are not victims, we are survivors + warriors. We will NOT be called any less but our NAMES

and MINE IS
RIA RENÉE WALLACE

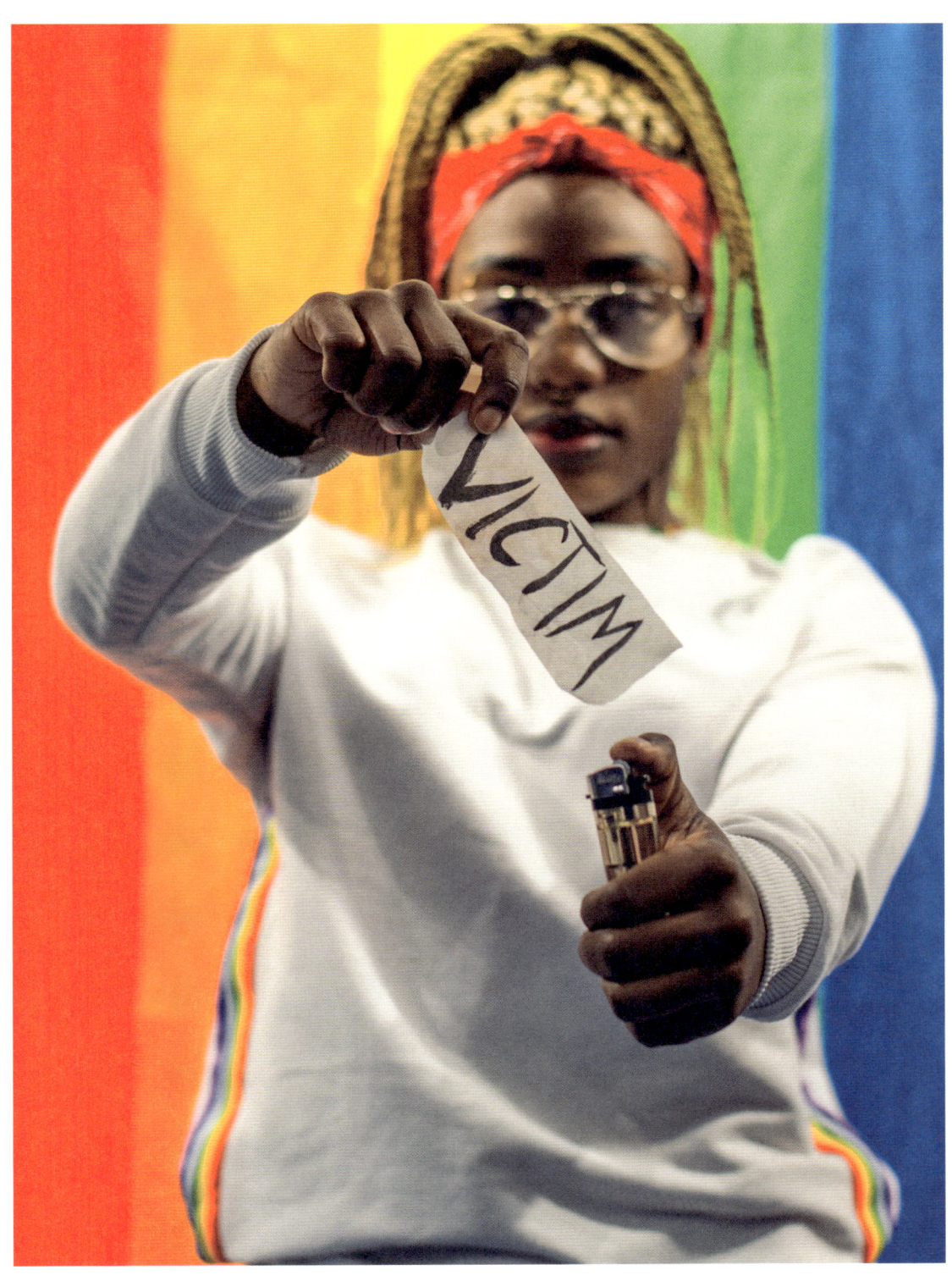

Sally Coker

MAKE IT MAKE SENSE (A POEM)

Set right, with my mind.
My mind will heal once I deal with the imagination
of the past, but it's happened, and I was present
it's reality but Emotional.

The storm feels so heavy and loud you can't
Hide.
Its how my heart feels.
This could make me or break me

Make it make sense

My long brown soft hands,
I paint my nails, looking like pink panther
I slick my hairs back, clip on a ponytail
looking like a goddess.

Old Street
              walking
                      drown
                                station
                                        seeing Letitia Wright
holding an award with a quote 'every winner has their journey'
I think, I can't wait for the journey, for me to shine.

MY HEAD

I feel like I haven't found myself. I hate this feeling. It makes me think about what I have been doing for 24 years in this world. I have been living on earth. Why did my life end up the way it did? I always seem to be alone no matter what I do or how I interact with people.

I seem to be walking on a long road that never finishes. This is the reflection of my thought. Sometimes I just imagine myself getting hit by a car or a bus just to end the pain that I feel. Sometimes.

Living at the hostel, my new home. I don't call it home but there are things that make me smile: they remember my name. I find it hard to remember anyone's name like it goes in then like a minute later I've forgotten who you are again, how strange. The universe has a way of putting people in place in my life. It's become a blessing or a lesson. I seem to have learnt my lesson rather than a blessing. Don't you get the feeling of wanting to fit in, that you are destined to stand out and you get up, make mistakes and start all over? I just start where I left off.

It's been a week or two since I was here, at the YMCA. I finally settled down, mostly in my room, pink pillow case and pink duvet with a desk, table. I like my room's good side. Don't have much in my room yet. Need to get myself a laptop, tv and mini fridge and make it look homely — rather than looking like a prison. I only really come out when it's breakfast but not dinner...

4:45pm on my way to the lift as I walk to the canteen, the canteen opens at 5pm but sometimes earlier. I really don't like waiting in a queue. So that's why I like to be extra early. The Lady asks me for my room number. 'Urm, 343' I reply with a quiet voice. '344 did u say?' I take a deep breath and reply again '3... 4... 3...' She writes it down and serves me spaghetti and garlic bread with tomato sauce. Can't lie, the food here is like Marmite — one day you hate it the next you want seconds. It could do with some seasoning. Trying not to give any eye contact to anyone as they whisper to themselves 'Who is that girl?' I never thought I would get noticed but everyone knows everyone who lives in the hostel. It reminds me of the time I went to university in New York City at Mercy College, living in a dorm full of drama every way I turned. For me to make it out of the hostel I need to keep to myself and be me.

Ever since I've been soft sleeping it's been hard to get on my feet, have a girls' night out. It's hard not having no money and when I do I end up buying lots of take away. I really love food — more than clothes. I haven't bought clothes in two years — just been borrowing clothes, stealing my stepmom's clothes when I go and see her. I like to use the word soft sleeping rather than the word 'homeless' because the word 'homeless' makes me feel very depressed. This is the worst thing that can happen to me or anyone, to have everything taken away from you to have to rebuild it again just so the universe can teach you a lesson. Or, maybe I just was not born with a silver spoon.

Sean Gonçalves-Berriero

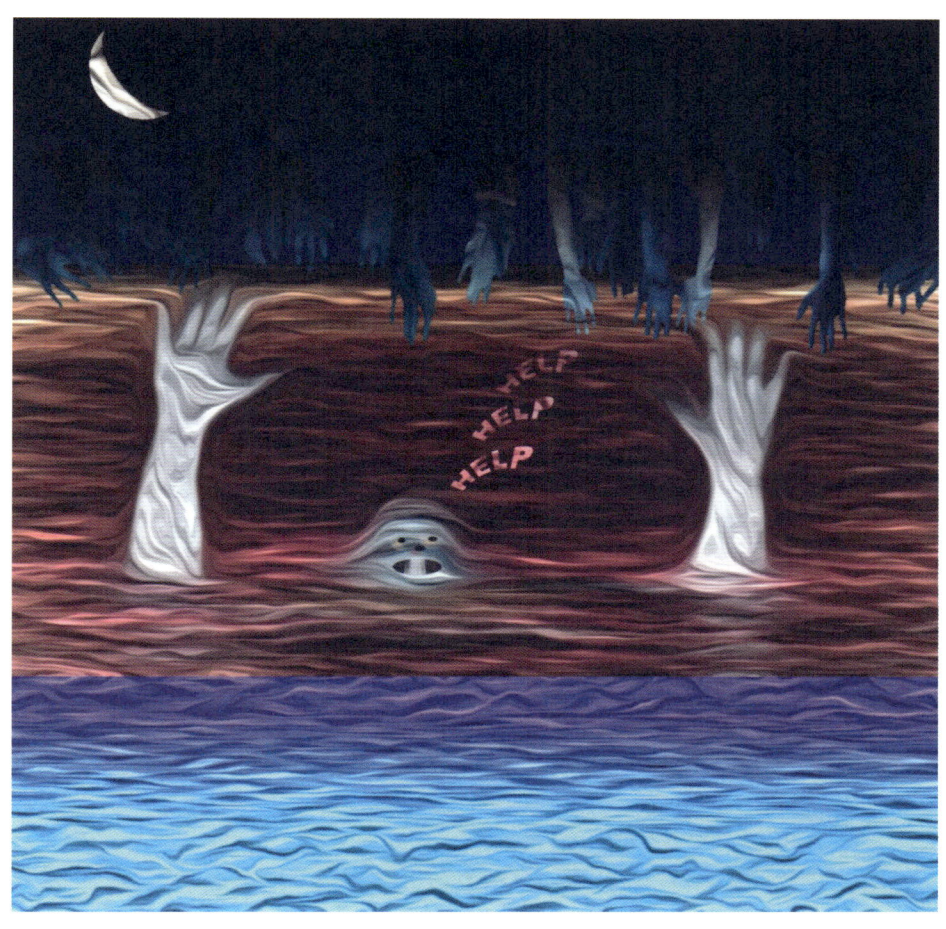

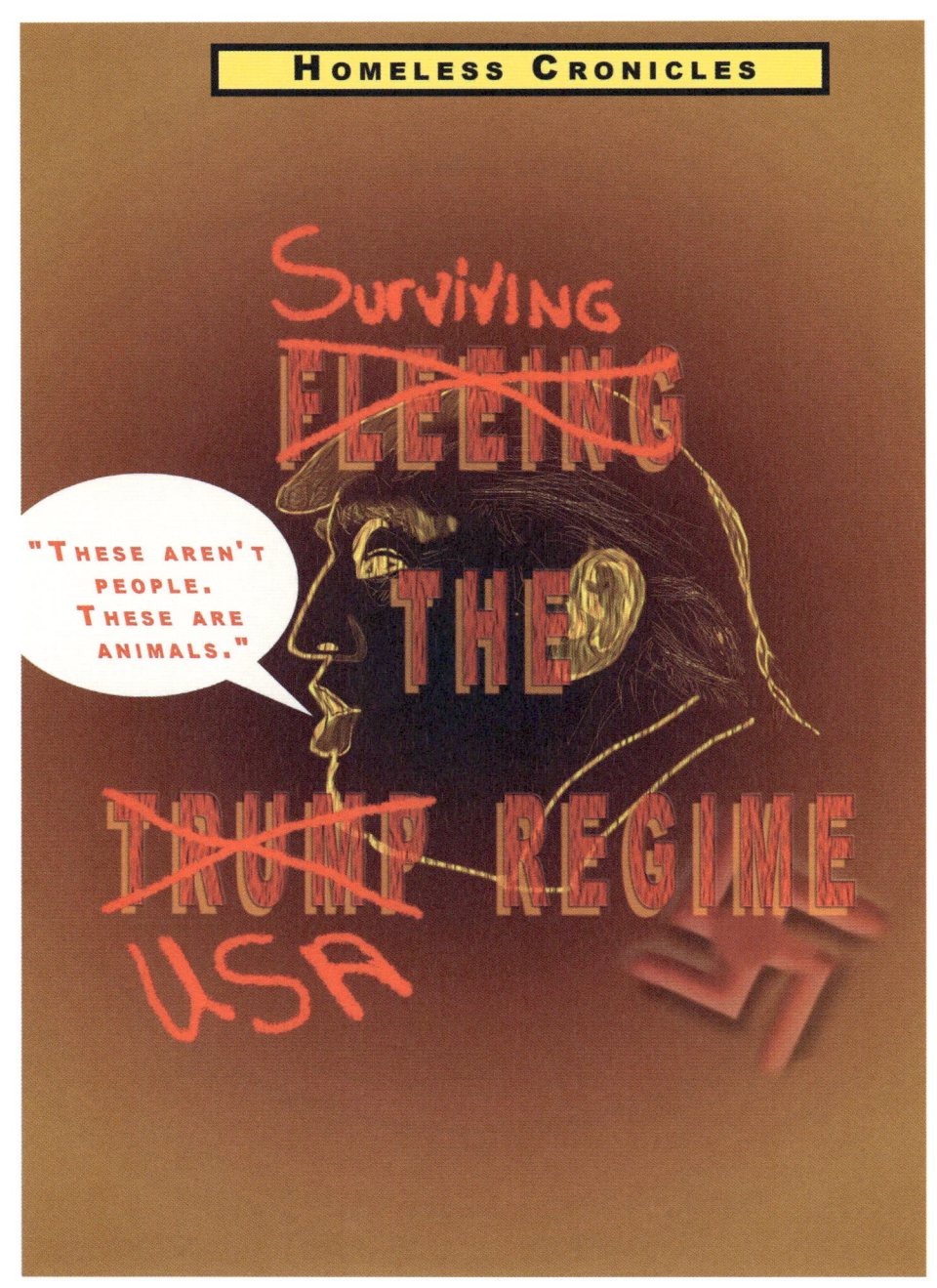

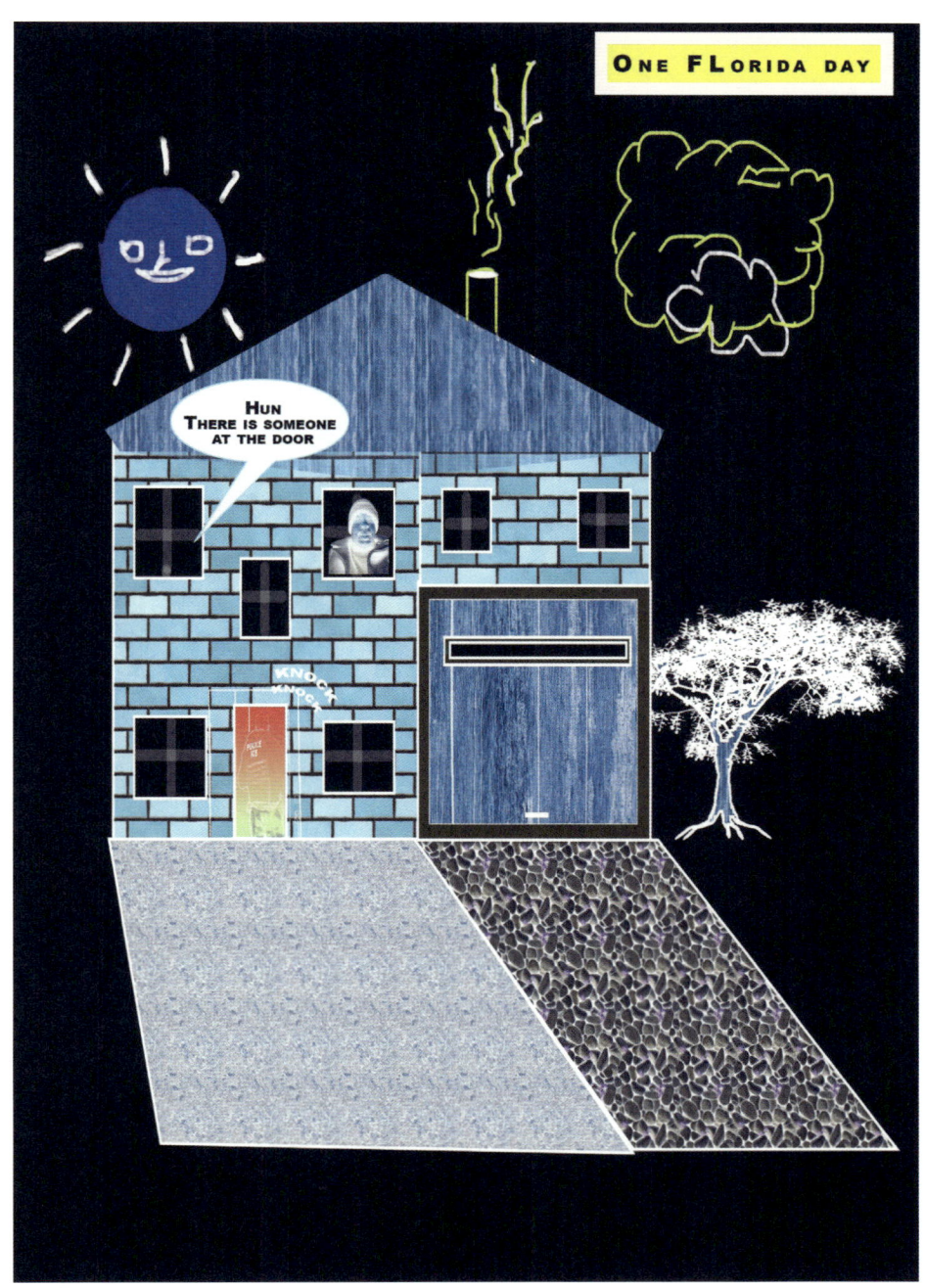

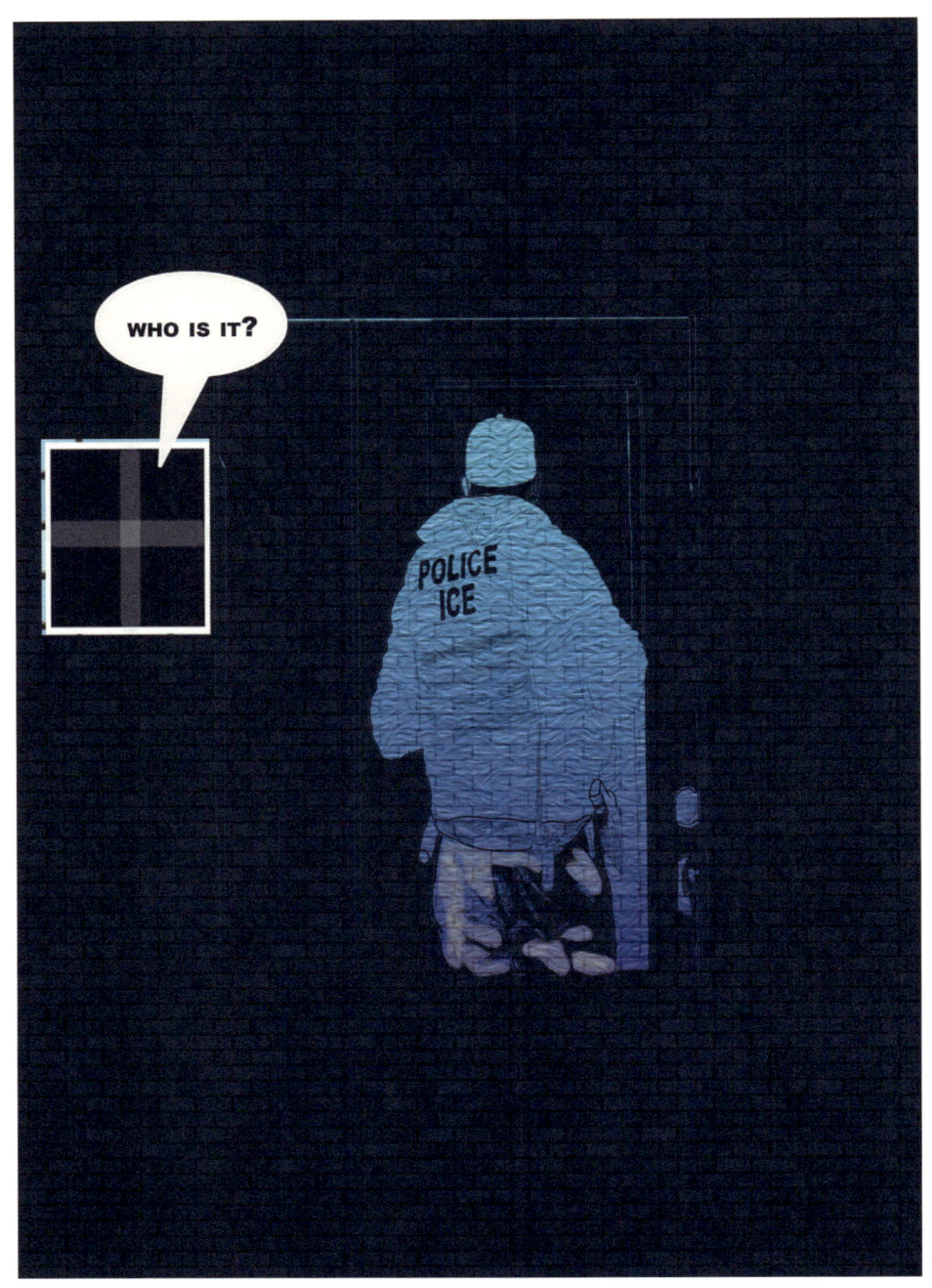

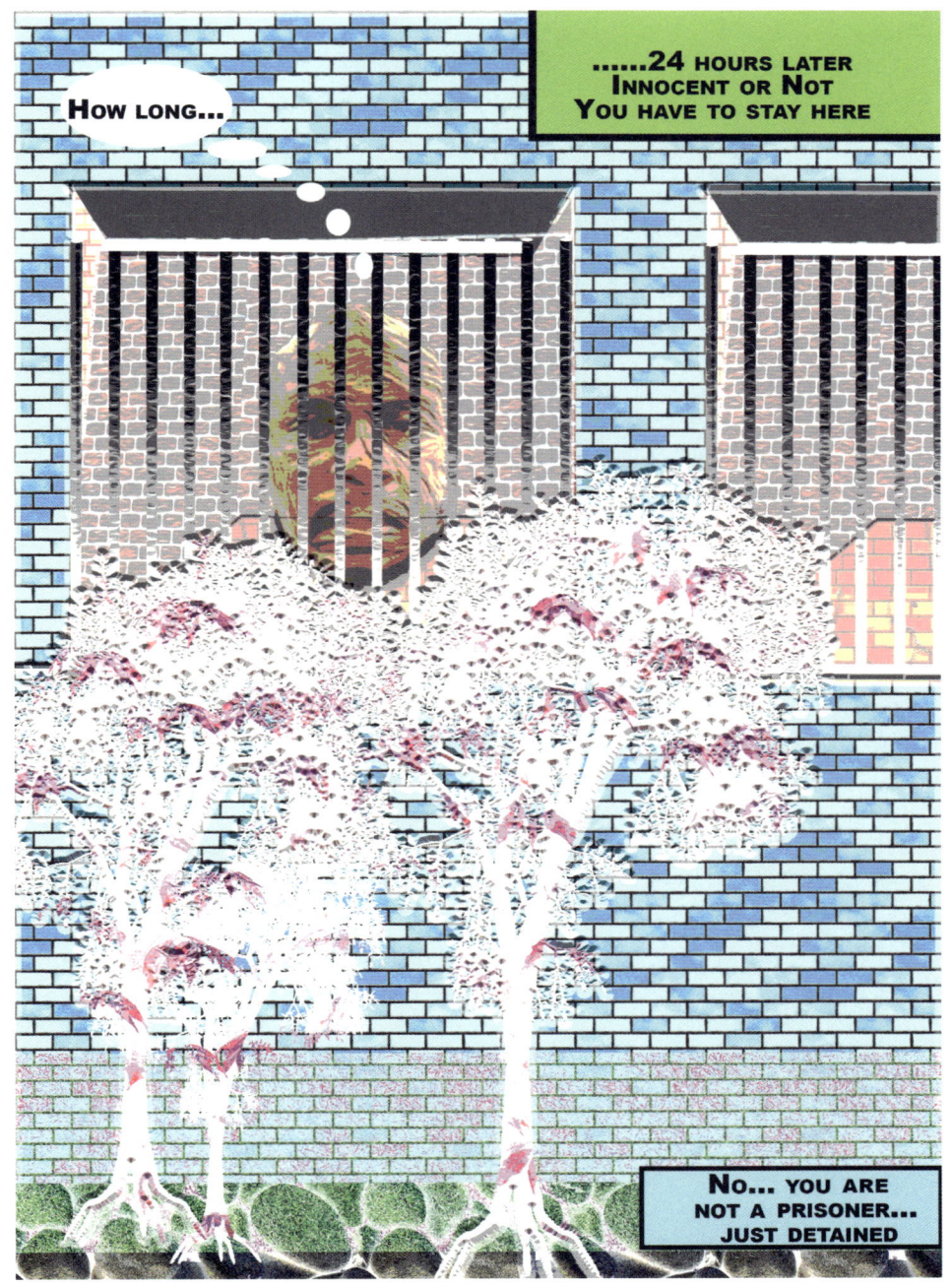

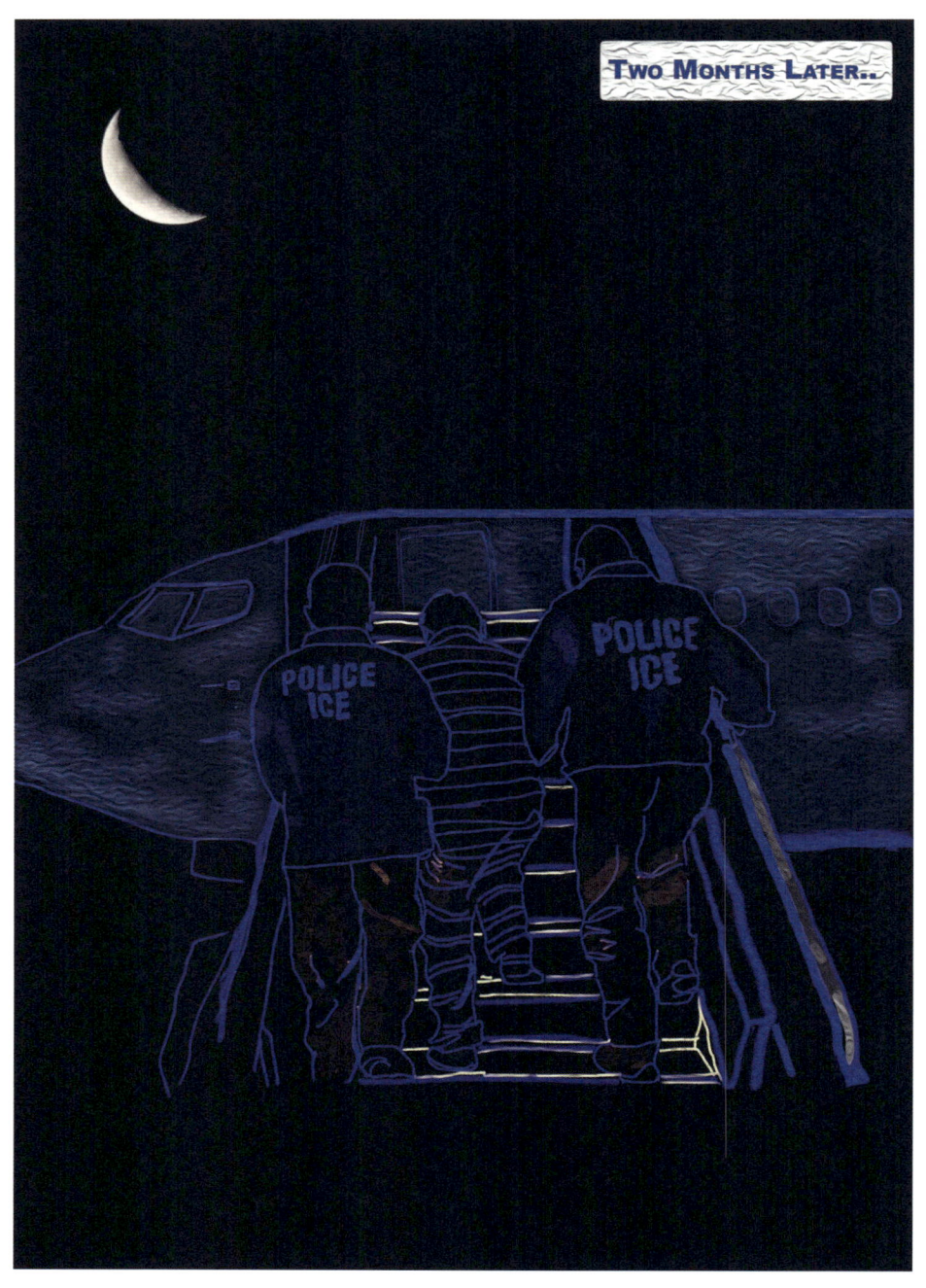

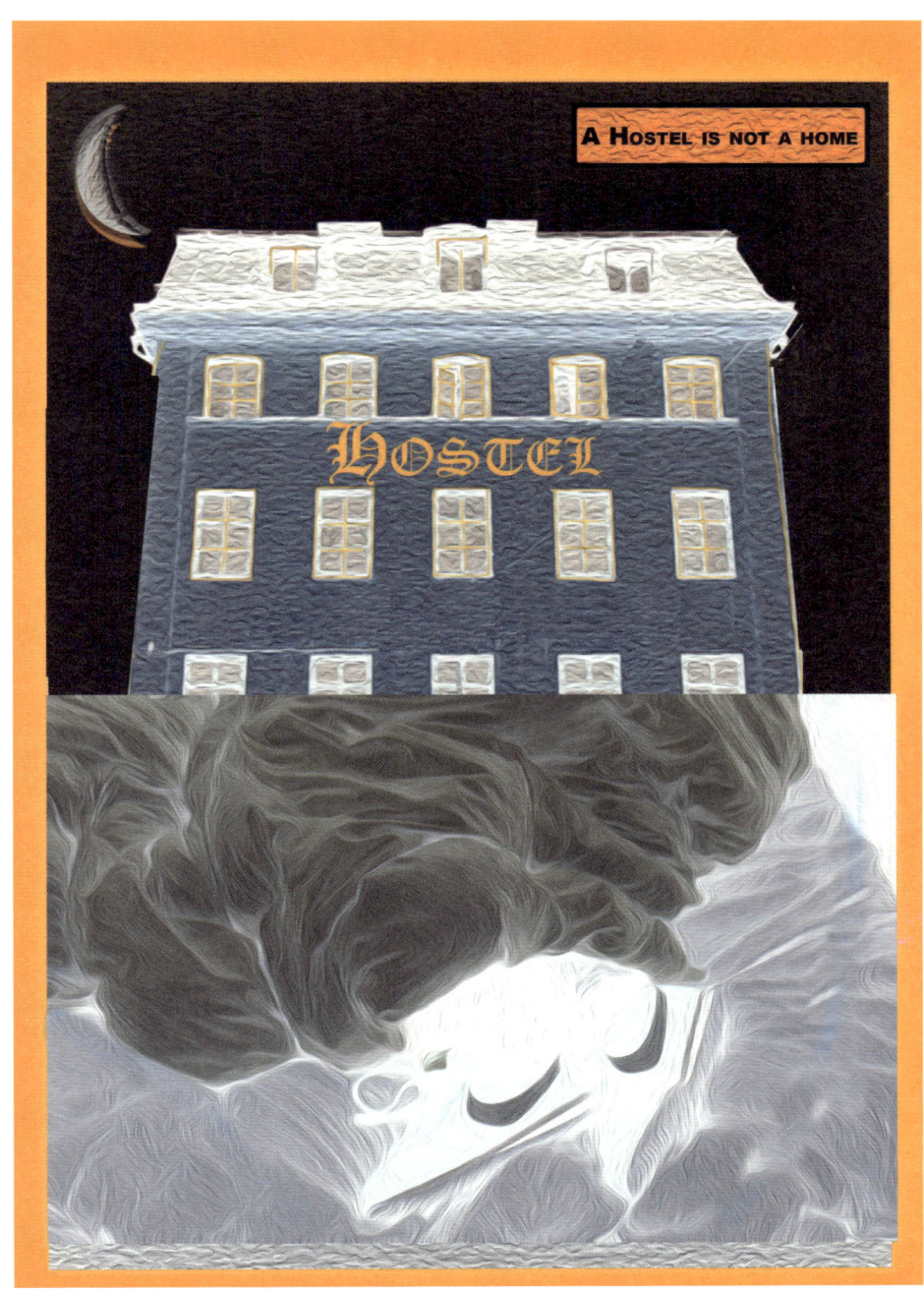

Shianne Wright

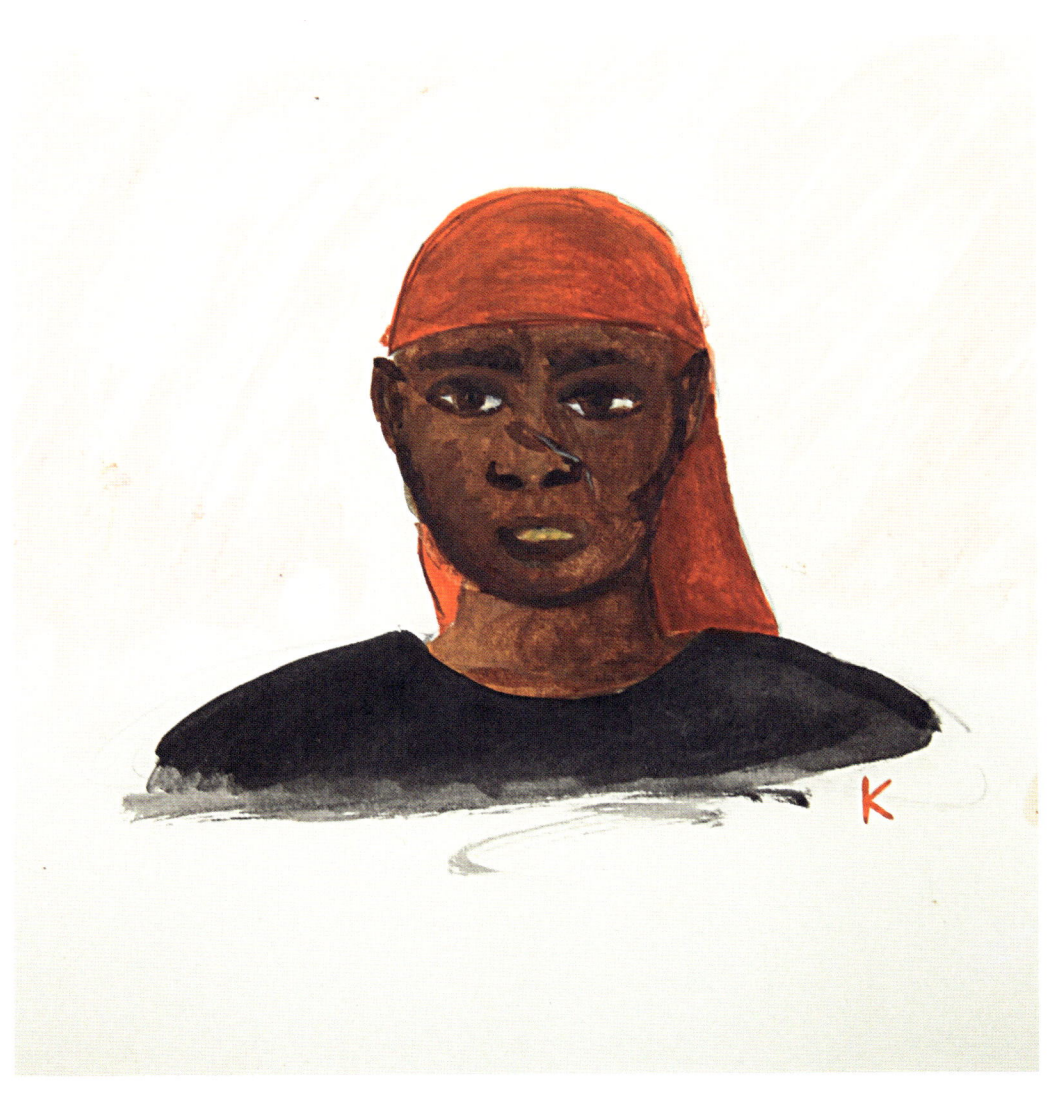

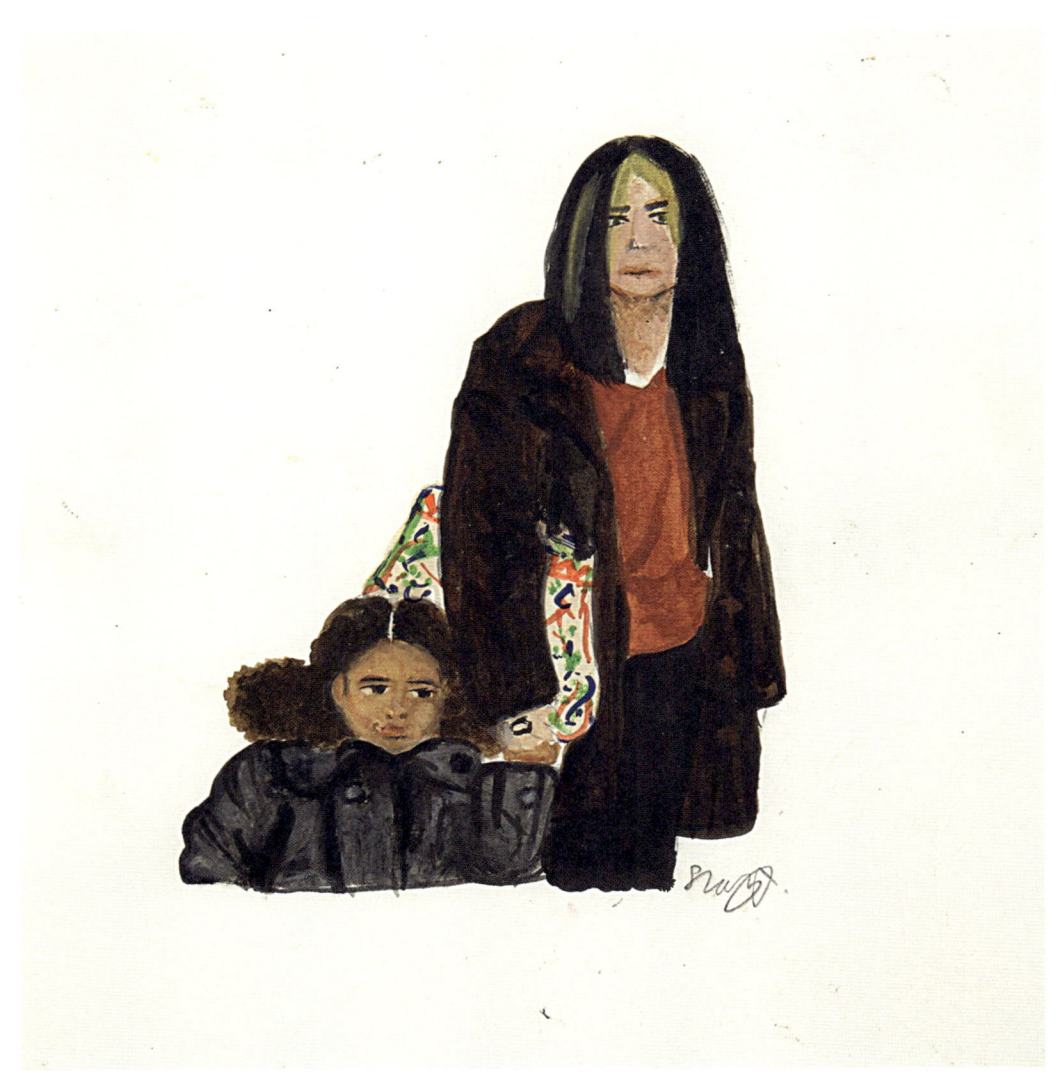

Ulika Valentim

MY STATE OF
DEPRESSION
LED ME
      TO MAKE
      THE WORST
      MISTAKE OF
      MY LIFE.

Because of my stress I could not sleep for a long time. I asked for help from my GP and they gave me anti-depressants, but they never really worked. I was awake every night. One day someone I knew asked me to help him with his nightwork in a fruit shop in the market during Ramadan. It was hard for him to work at night while he was fasting in the daytime. He looked pale and sick: I felt sorry for him, so I started working with him every night from midnight through to 5am. That helped me to get to sleep when I was finished.

I enjoyed working in the shop. It gave me a sense of purpose and I found it relaxing to work during the night, rather than trying to get to sleep with so much noise going on around me. I worked there for around three months, giving my time for free: I wasn't paid. I would tidy and sweep the place, replace old and rotten fruit with fresh fruit. One of my jobs was to cut fruit, watermelons, for example, with a large knife. I would keep the knife on my belt while I worked. One night my colleague sent me across the road to buy something from the 24/7 shop. Off I went.

There was a police station next to the shop and suddenly policemen — men I knew and had been friendly with — were walking towards me, walking around me, and suddenly they had my hands behind my back. I didn't know what was happening or why until I realised that I had completely forgotten to take the knife from my belt. I didn't put up any resistance, I was very calm, but I kept trying to explain why I had the knife on me.

When they asked me where I got the knife from I told them that this was a tool for cutting fruit at work, that it was not my property, it was just a tool my boss at work had asked me to cut fruit and boxes with: that I had no intention of hurting anyone with it. I had just come to buy a drink for the man I was working for. I said that if they just crossed the road with me to the shop my colleague could explain that too, but they just wanted to do their job and arrest me. They took me back to the police station and arrested me for possession of the knife. The policeman who interviewed me there in the morning could not believe what was happening. He knew me. I used to wave to him every day when we passed each other at the end of his shift.

I asked him to ask his colleagues to drop the case but he said no, that his colleague said that I must be charged. But he did give me his phone number and told me to tell my colleague in the fruit shop to come forward as a witness. I did ask my colleague, and I asked other people too, people I had helped out in the past, but nobody came forward on my behalf. I had no witnesses but I had a good solicitor, and I brought all the evidence I could about my medication to the court. My medication can make me confused and cause me to forget things. I had a sick note from my GP saying so. The judge was understanding under the circumstances. I was charged and sentenced to eight weeks in prison.

On reflection, I do regret any stress I caused for anyone, and for myself. At the time I was on medication, and was simply trying to focus on the work I had to do. I certainly wasn't thinking about criminal activity.

I was given an eight week prison sentence, of which I served four weeks. While there though, I was treated for my illness and managed to get more rest. But when I came out, I was evicted from my house and had to sleep rough for two or three months. I lost all my belongings, including my bed, and had a very hard time. I was surrounded by fake friends, the housing services wouldn't help me and I was on a year's probation.

I found help with the Kingston YMCA and I've engaged in a variety of projects. I have volunteered with Change the World and Farm of the Future. We remove rubbish and plant fresh plants in its place. I have also worked at the Change Please café where I trained as a barista. And of course I've been doing these creative projects with Accumulate to tell my story. Other organisations that really helped me were Kingston Church Action for Homeless, and Look Ahead and St Mungo's in Shepherd's Bush.

The combination of work and study works very well for me. Today I look back and I understand how good life can be when you come through your problems. I suffered from depression for a long time and had low vitamin D. Now I use my time wisely and can even give good advice to others. I feel healthier, more active. I go to the gym, I eat properly and I sleep on time. I socialise more and spend more time with my family. Sometimes I think about going back to Portugal, where I grew up.

Where you live can really make a difference to your life: changing cities can be hard. You have to choose your friends wisely.

Portraits of Accumulate Authors: Photographs by Tori Taiwo.

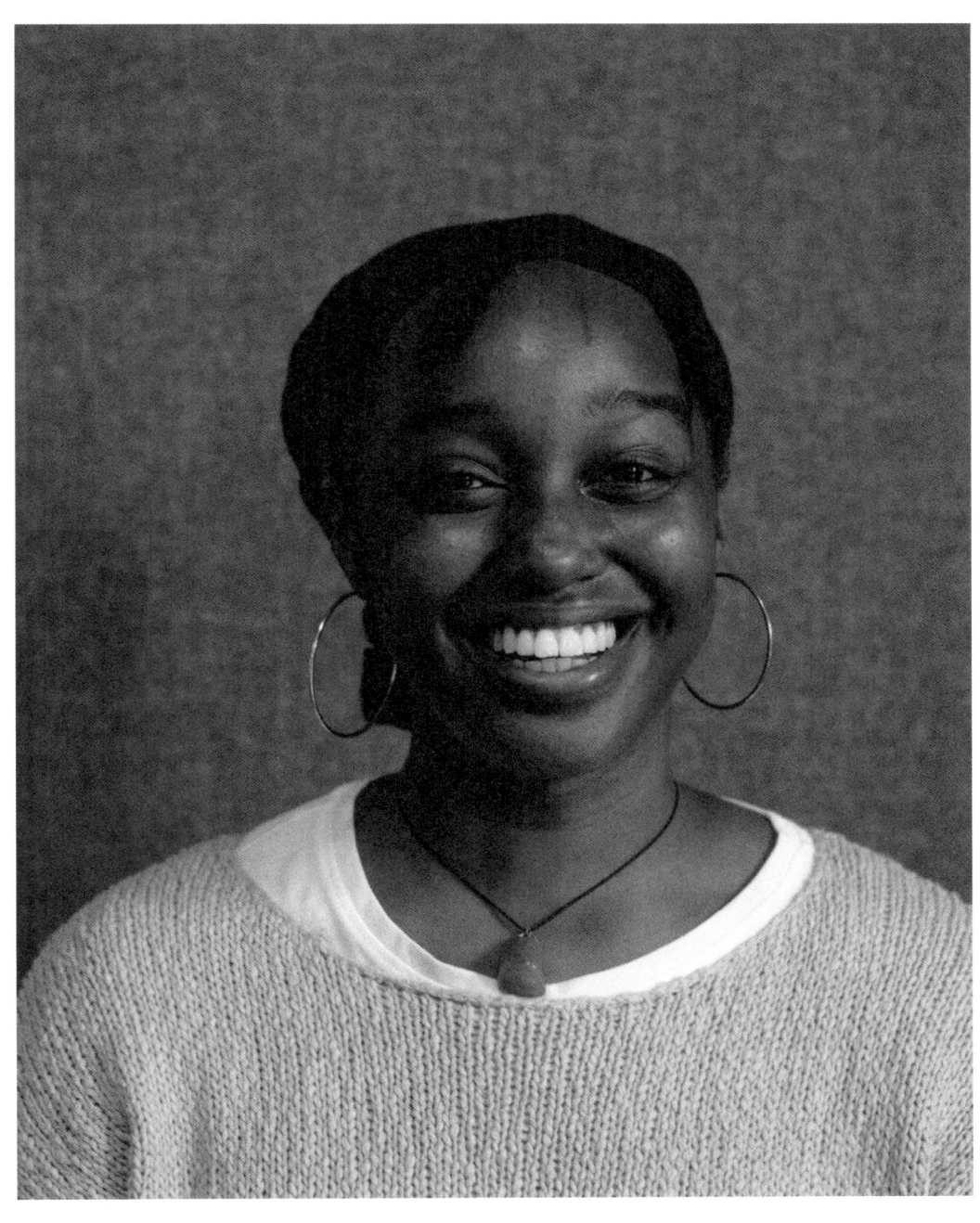

AMALIA WALROND

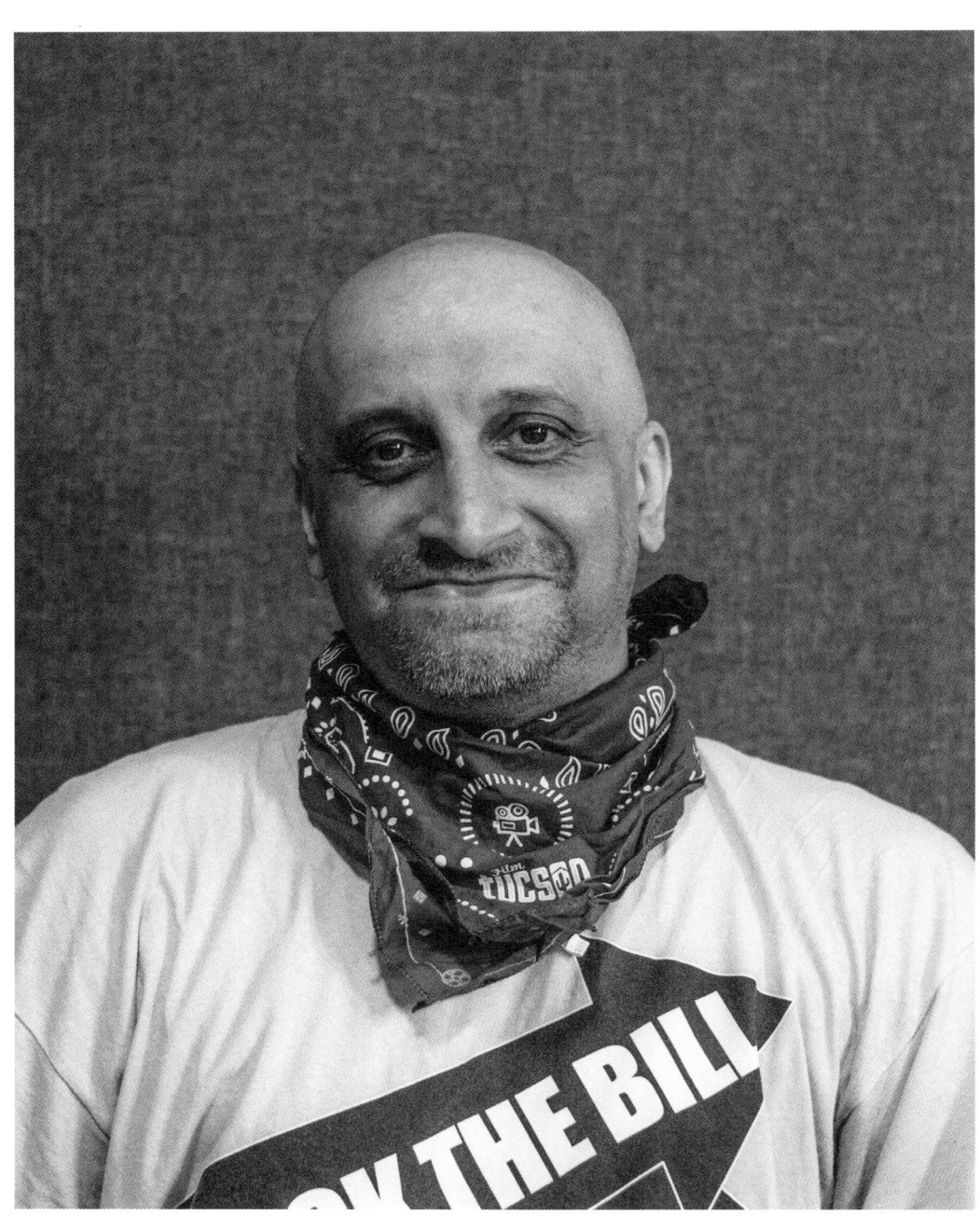

DAVE SOHANPAL

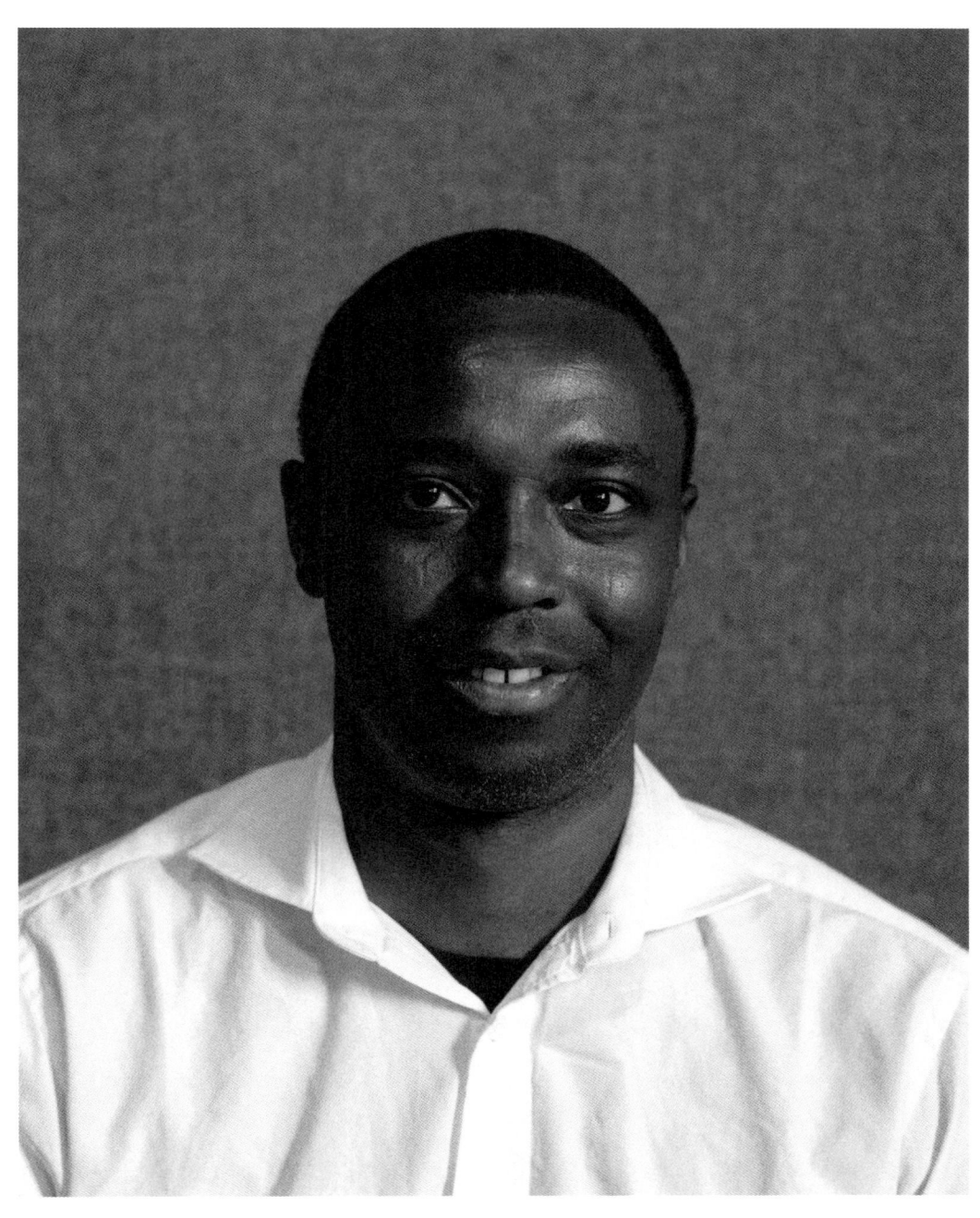

EYITAYO BABATOLA

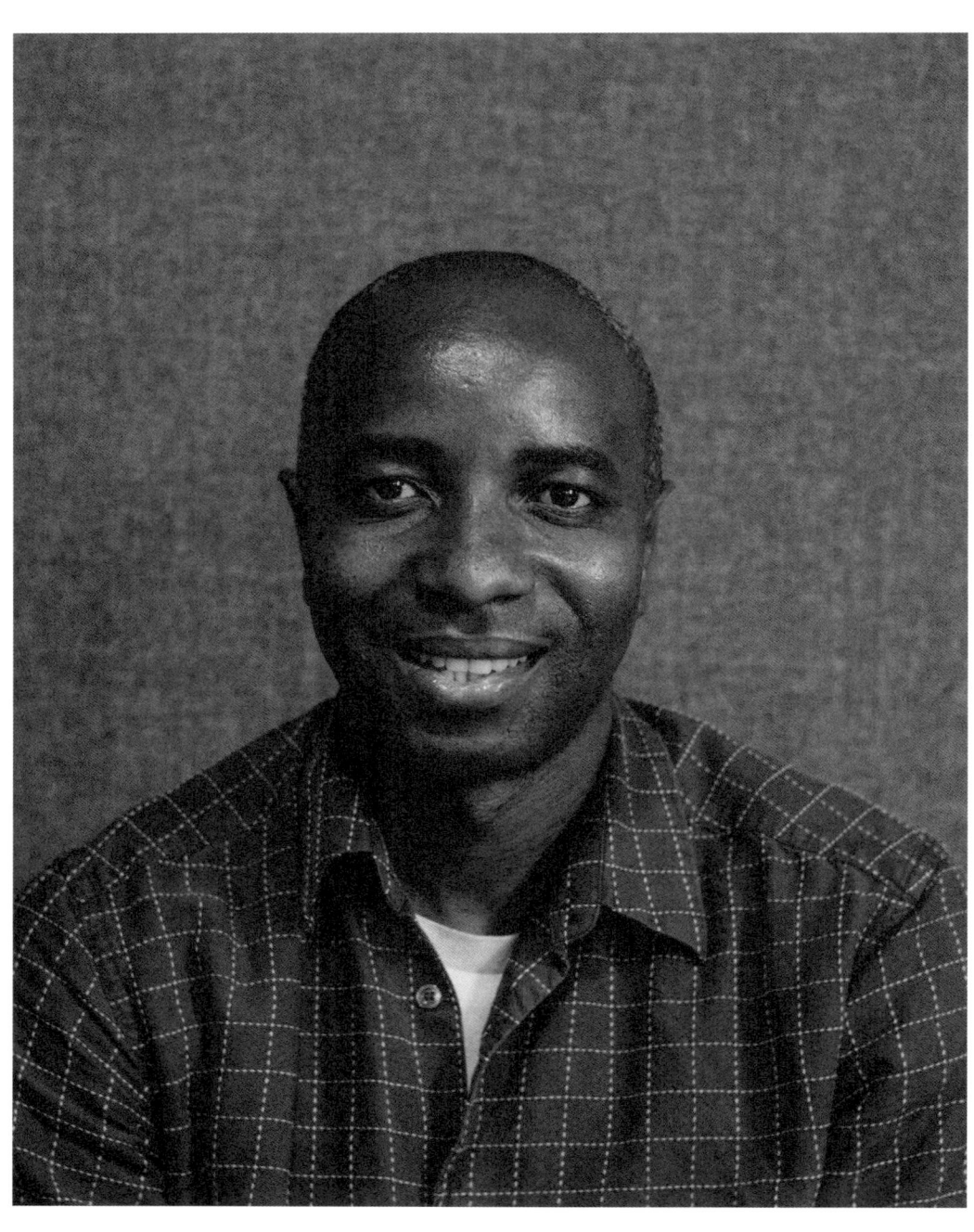

HAMAHOULLAH DIALLO

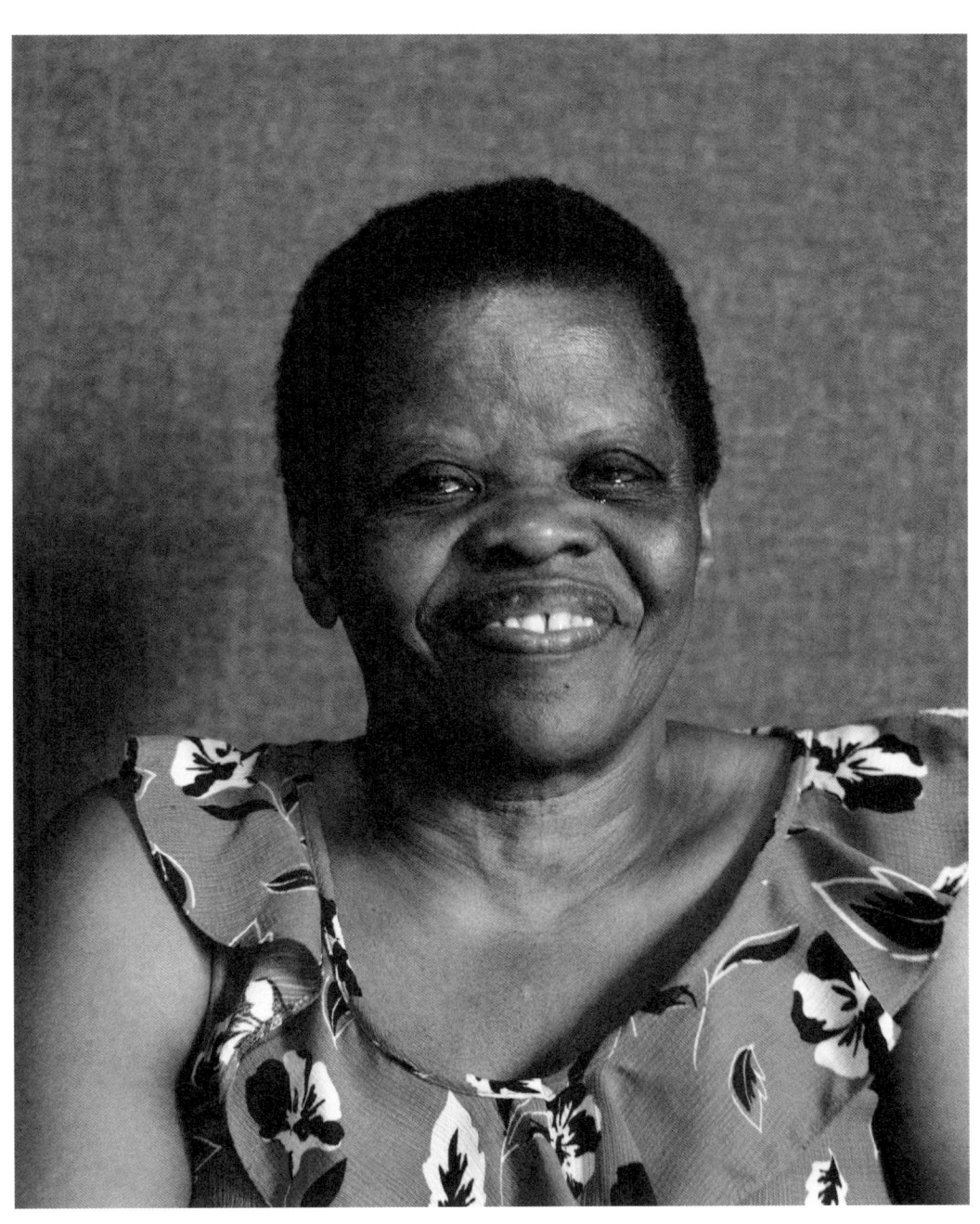

JADE AMOLI-JACKSON

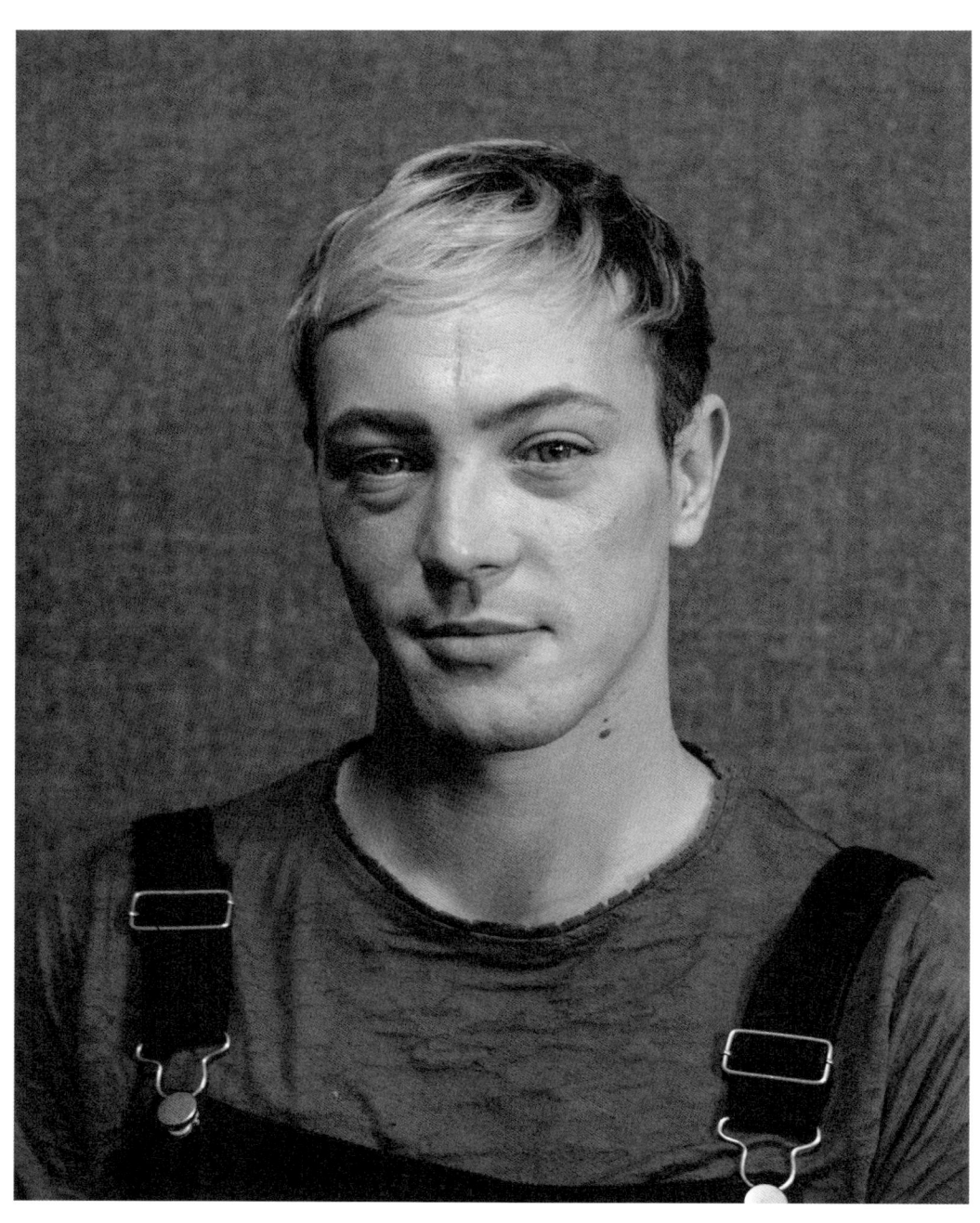

LUKE SMITH

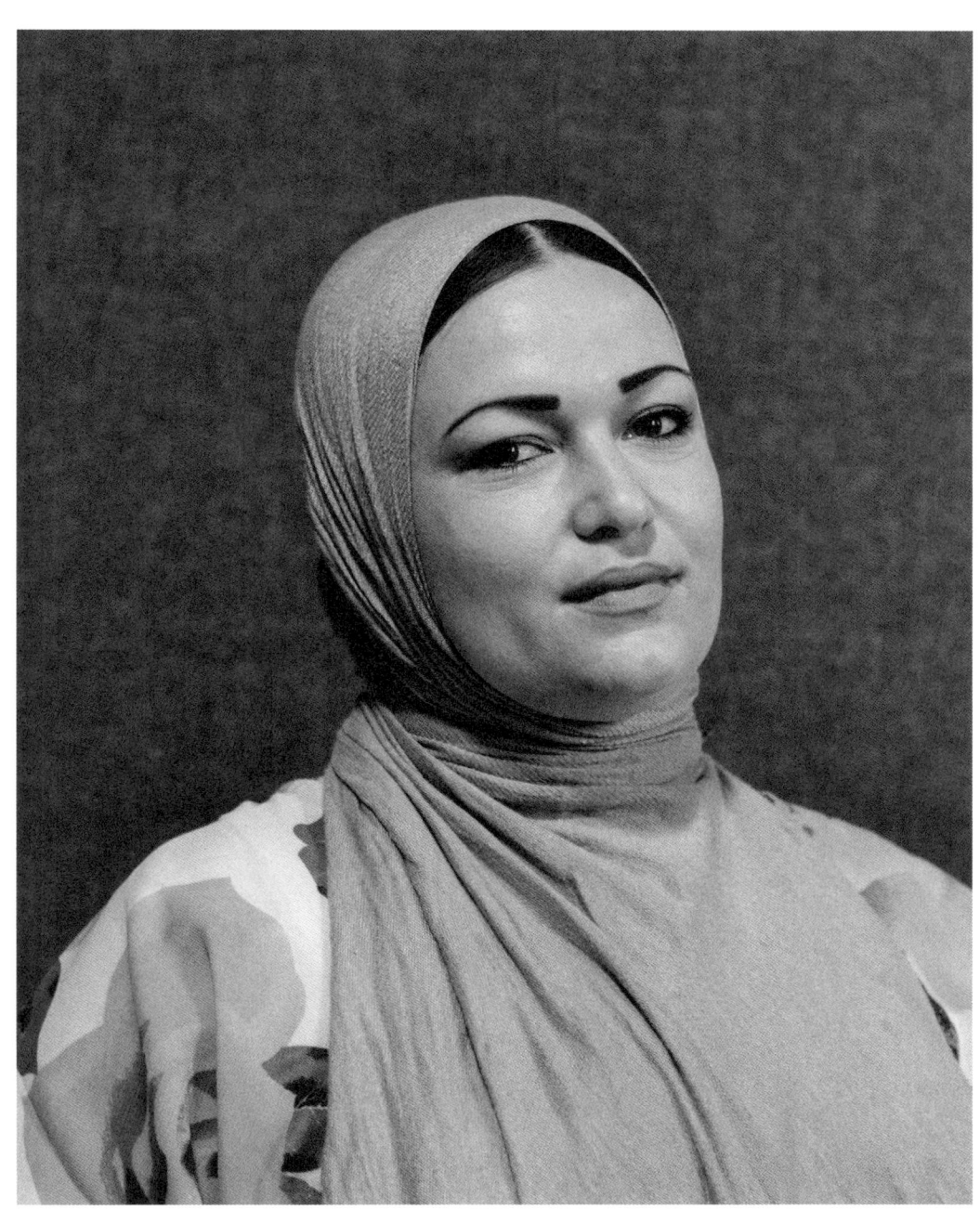

NIKOLETT ESZES

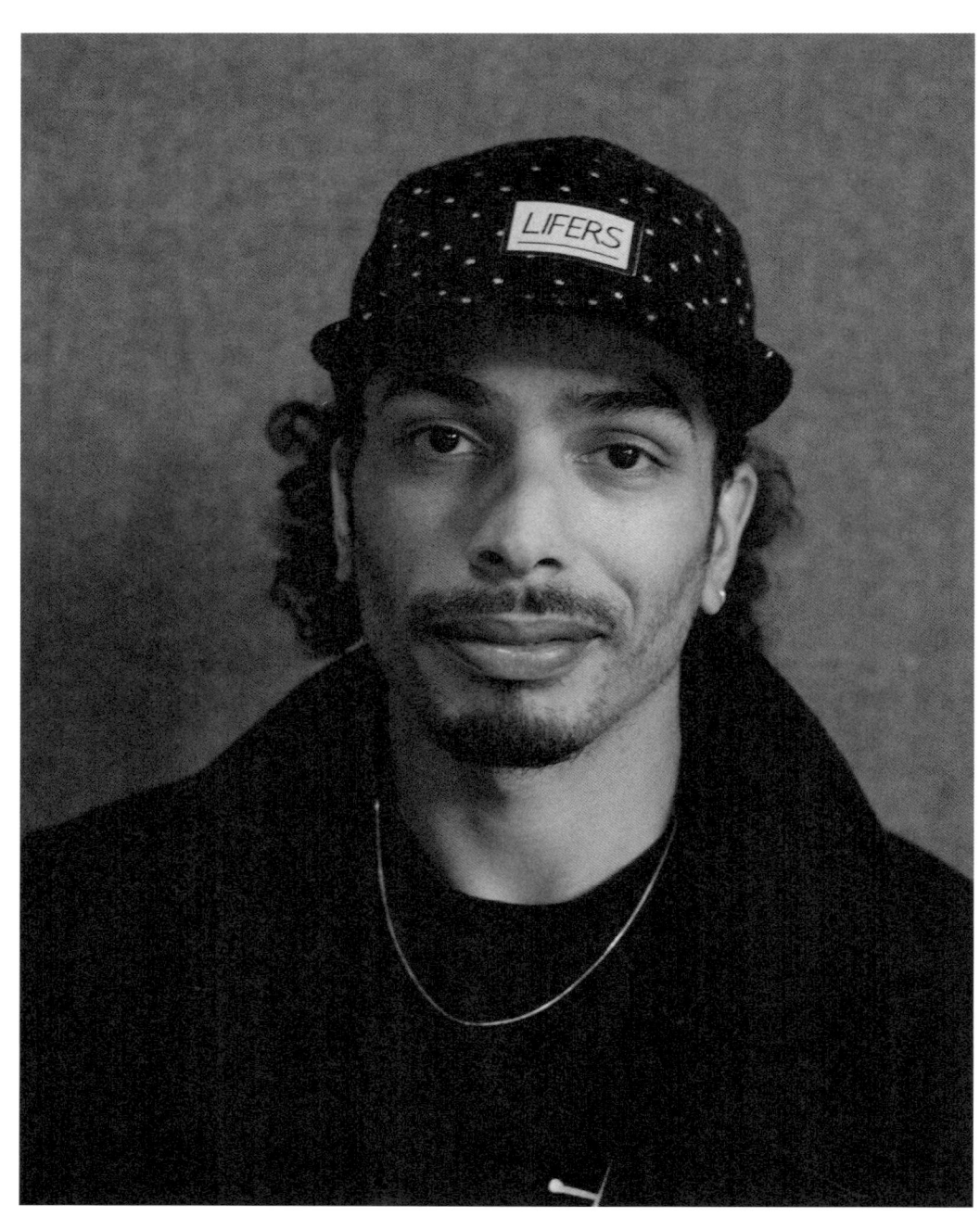

MITCHELL CENEY

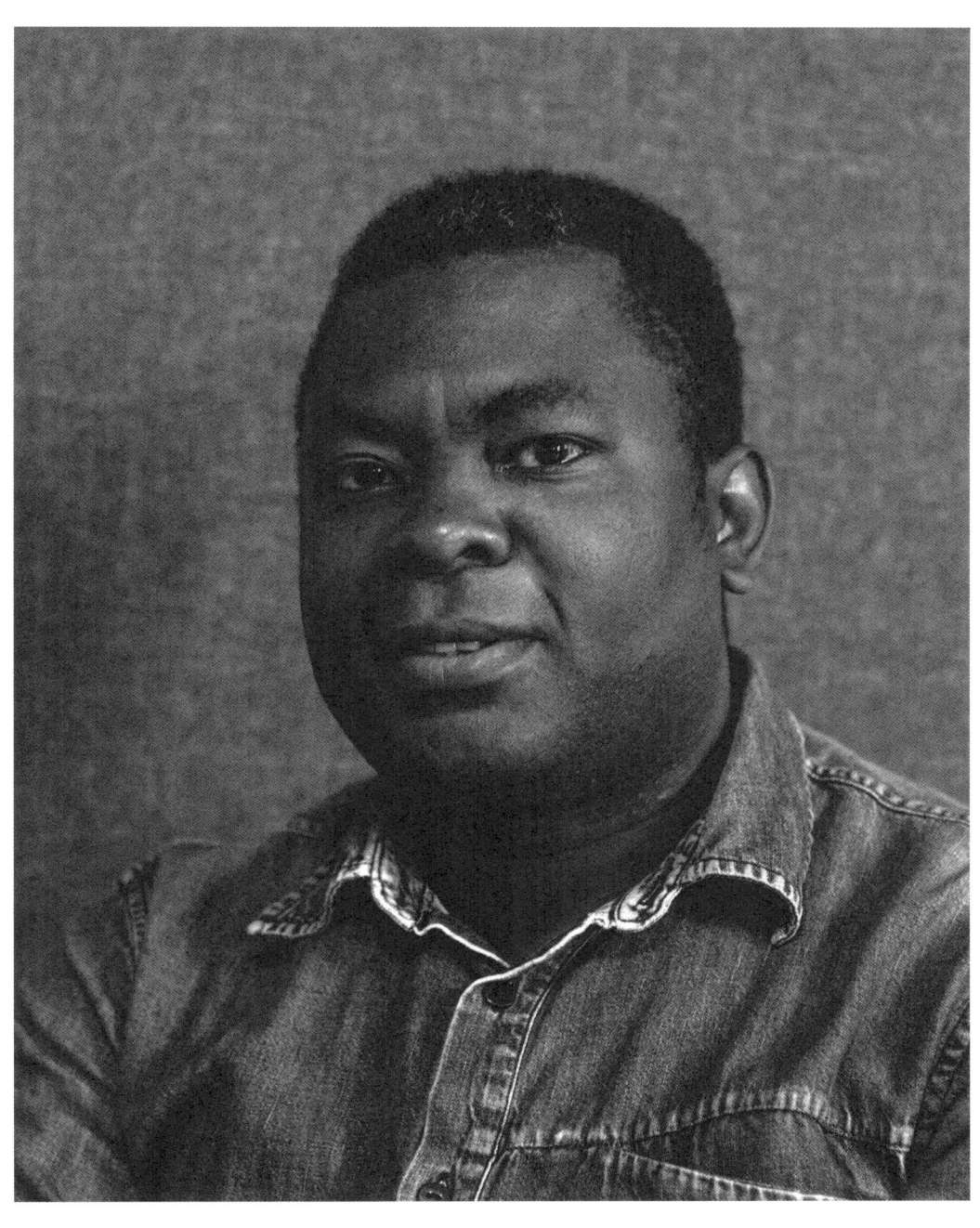

PROSPER KOUAYEP

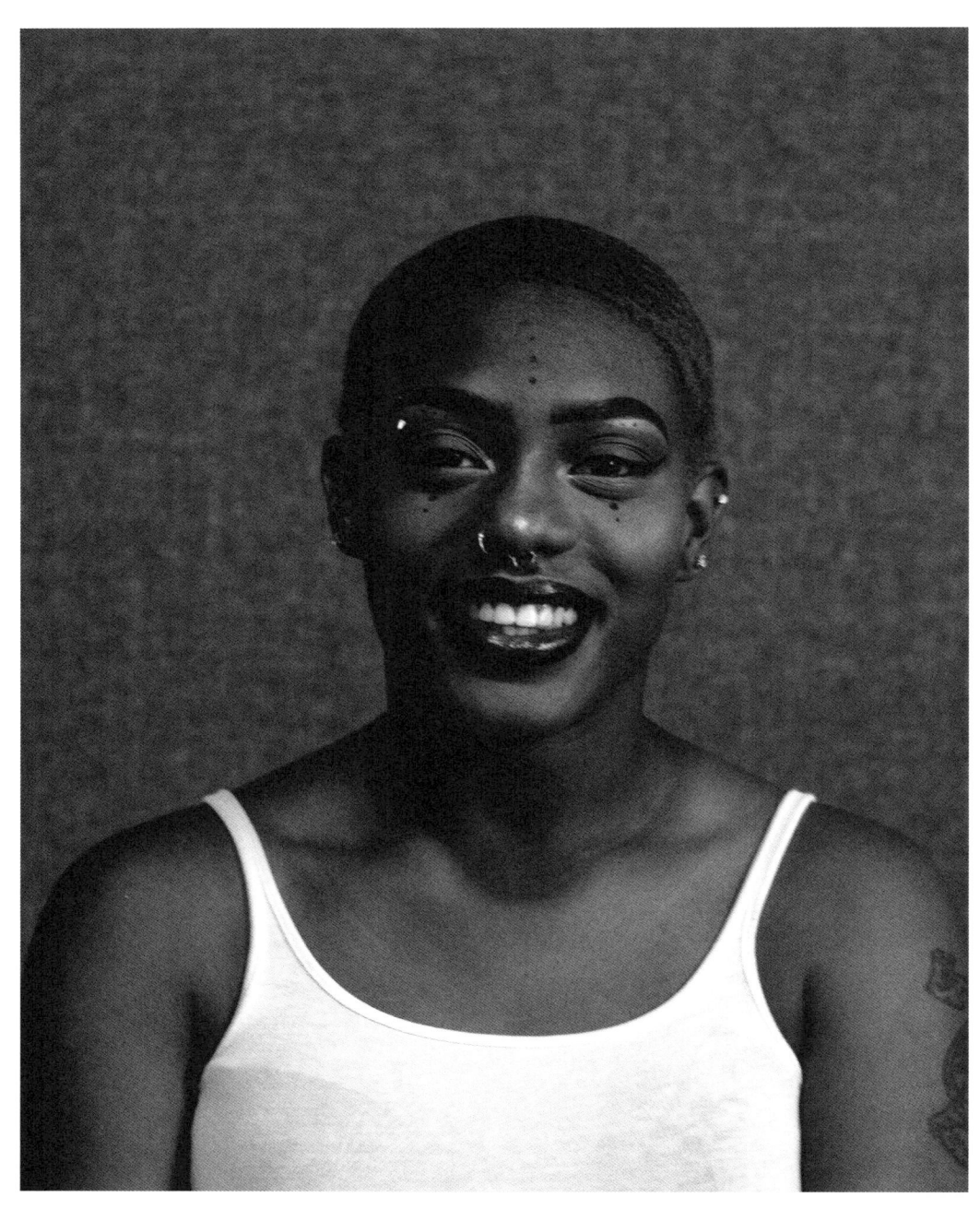

RIA WALLACE

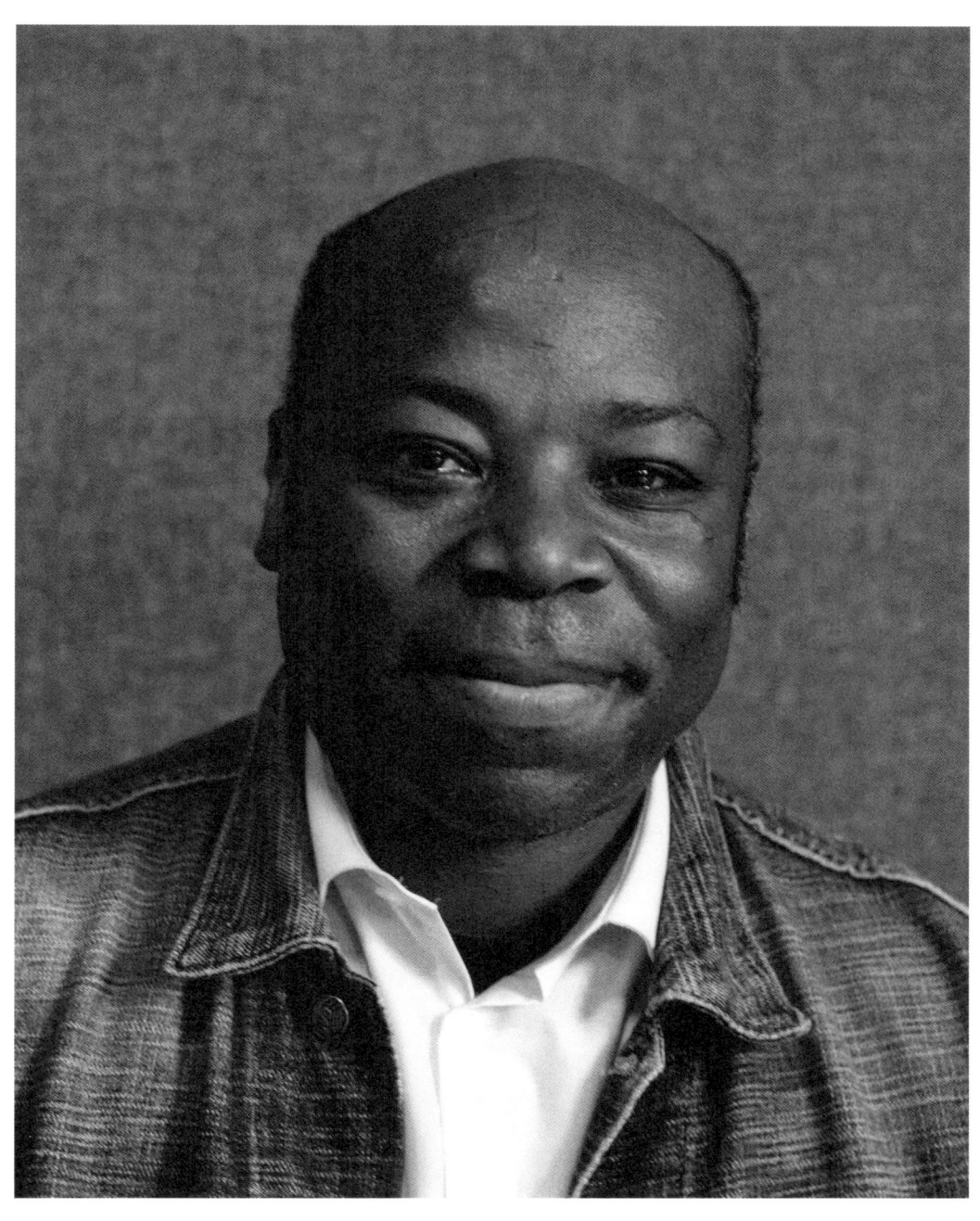

ULIKA VALENTIM

Brickworks is immensely proud to support Accumulate and the Book of Homelessness.

This innovative project has given young people affected by homelessness a chance to build self-confidence and well-being through creativity. At Brickworks, we believe that by channelling these young voices, we can make meaningful strides — not only for the young people involved, but for society as a whole.

Because we profit from property in the midst of a housing crisis in the UK, we feel an underlying political conflict. Working with Accumulate has given us the chance to grapple with this complex subject on a more personal level. By sharing stories and learning more about the participants' aspirations, we've come to realise how much easier the journey has been for our team—via access to art school and higher education in general — than for these young people.

The exploratory nature of expressing yourself through art and design is one that can be life changing, if not life saving. We've personally witnessed the positive change Accumulate inspires in young people through the artistic opportunities it brings.

That's why we've been delighted to contribute to the Book of Homelessness and are so excited to see how this remarkable work has come together.

It's been an honour to support Marice, Accumulate and everyone involved in this project.

Ellie, Rex and the Brickworks team
brickworkslondon.com

A project like The Book of Homelessness would not be possible without the many people who generously contributed their time, skills and expertise to nurture it and bring it to fruition. Thank you to the band of strong women, Henny Beaumont, Joanna Brown, Soofiya Chaudry and Tori Taiwo, for being exceptional Accumulate tutors and for giving so much energy, support, wisdom and creativity to the project. Thank you to David Tovey, Geraldine Crimmins, Sue Pickford Cheung, Claire Cheung, Hannah Wallwork, Sabela Peinado and Ben Peters for helping on the workshops and jumping in when there was loads to do. Thank you to Ali Eisa from Autograph for enabling us to use the gallery education space for this project and to make it our home. Thank you to Patrick Fry for expert art direction of the book and by going beyond this with so much support and wisdom. Thank you to Heather Mears and Emma Carboni, the constant Accumulate social media and PR women who are so valued and give so much support. Thank you to Bobby Joseph and Joseph Samuels for contributing their cartoon strip after I reached out to them on Instagram. Thank you to Samantha Morton and Sue Pickford Cheung for so brilliantly giving their honest stories to this book. Thank you to all the donors to The Book of Homelessness crowdfunder who had faith in this project and wanted to be a part of making it happen and especially to James Ward, Tom Campbell, Jack Brown, Elizabeth Rouse, Leila Cumber, Jason Scott-Taggart, Victoria Mahoney, Nicola O'Donnell, Natalie Greenwold, Timothy Lillicrap and Andrew Derrick. Thank you to Harry English for the translation work.

Thank you to Brickworks London Estate Agency for being The Book of Homelessness main sponsor and coming on board to support the project so generously, and deepest thank yous to our project partners, sponsors and funders: Autograph, Ravensbourne University London, Greenwich Digital Skills, Greenwich Council, AHMM, Say Property Consulting, Pret A Manger, Franco Manca, Agents Giving, The Worshipful Company of Art Scholars, Schroder Charitable Trust and Great Art.

A special thank you remains and that goes to Roland, Evie and Majenta who are the special people in my life and who make my life very special.

Thank you all for being part of all of this.

Marice Cumber
Accumulate Director and Founder
www.accumulate.org.uk
info@accumulate.org.uk
@accumulate_ldn

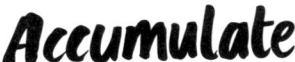

The Art School for The Homeless

All profits from The Book of Homelessness are shared between the authors, so that they can earn an income from their creativity, and Accumulate, so that it can continue to provide creative workshops for people that are homeless.

Edited by Marice Cumber
Copy Edited by Joanna Brown, Tom Campbell and Graham Hitchen
Designed by Patrick Fry
Printed by Gomer Press, Wales

THANK YOU TO THE WORKSHOP TUTORS

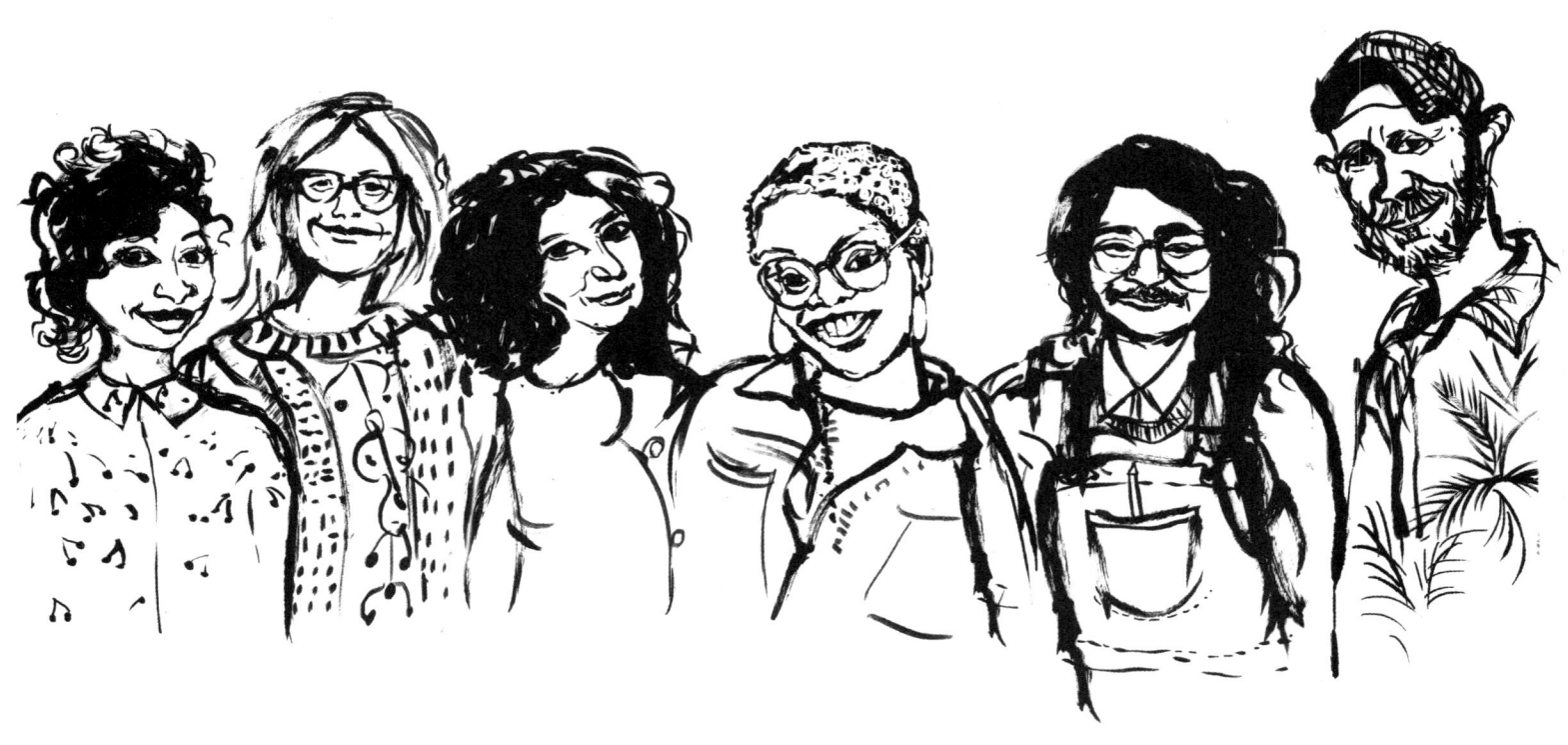

Joanna Brown
*Author and Accumulate
Creative Writing Tutor*

Marice Cumber
*Accumulate Founder
and Director*

Soofiya Chaudry
*Illustrator and
Accumulate
Illustration Tutor*

Henny Beaumont
*Graphic Novelist
and Accumulate
Illustration Tutor*

Tori Taiwo
*Previously Homeless,
Photographer and
Creative Director
and Accumulate
Creative Lead Tutor*

David Tovey
*Previously Homeless,
Artist and Campaigner
And Accumulate Visual
Arts Tutor*

*Illustration by
Henny Beaumont*